FROM "ABEND" TO "ZULU TIME"—
PLUS A SPECIAL SECTION ON NUMERICS—
ALL THE TERMS YOU NEED TO KNOW TO
MASTER THE NEW COMPUTERS

THE NEW AMERICAN COMPUTER DICTIONARY
is the one guide that takes the mystery out of "computerese" and helps you to become computer-literate.
Here is all the language you will need to bridge the technological communication gap, whether you want to:

- Buy and use your own computer
- Deal with scientists, programmers, and just plain "hackers"
- Work your way through a book on computer programming

With over 2000 terms arranged in alphabetical order, many with illustrations, you will be able to find the meaning of anything that puzzles you within seconds, explained in words that you can instantly understand. Clear, comprehensive, easy to use, this is the one book you need to plug into this exciting new age—the reference work you will find yourself turning to more and more as computers play a bigger and bigger part in your life.

All About Computers from SIGNET

THE
NEW AMERICAN
COMPUTER
DICTIONARY

by
Kent Porter

∅

A SIGNET BOOK
NEW AMERICAN LIBRARY
TIMES MIRROR

PUBLISHED BY
THE NEW AMERICAN LIBRARY
OF CANADA LIMITED

NAL BOOKS ARE AVAILABLE AT QUANTITY DISCOUNTS
WHEN USED TO PROMOTE PRODUCTS OR SERVICES.
FOR INFORMATION PLEASE WRITE TO PREMIUM MARKETING DIVISION,
THE NEW AMERICAN LIBRARY, INC., 1633 BROADWAY,
NEW YORK, NEW YORK 10019.

First Printing, October, 1983

2   3   4   5   6   7   8   9

SIGNET TRADEMARK REG. U.S. PAT. OFF. AND FOREIGN COUNTRIES
REGISTERED TRADEMARK · MARCA REGISTRADA
HECHO EN WINNIPEG, CANADA

SIGNET, SIGNET CLASSIC, MENTOR, PLUME, MERIDIAN
and NAL BOOKS are published in Canada by The New American
Library of Canada, Limited, Scarborough, Ontario

PRINTED IN CANADA
COVER PRINTED IN U.S.A.

Preface

Probably no other major technology arising from Man's "creative dissatisfaction" has spread so rapidly and affected its own time so profoundly as data processing. In the very brief period since computers thundered electronically over the horizon, an enormous specialized vocabulary has developed to describe this startling phenomenon. The only other profession with such a thorough (and thoroughly obscuring) jargon is medicine, and medicine has had centuries to work out the language by which it camouflages our condition from us and identifies insiders to each other. Data processing has had, at best, a couple or three decades.

That's not very long. This writer, who is just beginning to consider the possibility that some people might regard him as verging on middle age, clearly recalls a world without computers, when people actually did things by hand and didn't even feel inefficient about it. I saw my first computer when I was already a married man and our first child was in diapers, and computers were still a curiosity that they took you to see. The man who literally invented the first digital computer, the ENIAC, retired in 1982 at the normal age of 65. The computer, then, has happened entirely within a business career of ordinary duration, and mostly within the time it has taken that baby to become a college-age young man. With it have come a plethora of terms and new meanings that have inevitably found their way into the language as the phenomenon they describe has found its way into the lives of us all.

The computer invasion is definitely on, and for all its far-reaching impact it still seems only to be gathering momentum. The computer is in the 1980s as the television was when some of us were kids in the 1950s; everybody on the block either has one or is thinking of getting one, or else has made a conscious decision to resist the tide and be a little different in not having one. No doubt there are people who still don't have television sets, too.

A few years ago computers, like rulers, exercised their influence from majestic isolation, and only a privileged few had direct access to them. Today the workplace is filled with on-line terminals and personal workstations that let the folks who use the computer talk directly with it. When we go home in the evening we may balance the checkbook and file recipes and write letters and play video games on the computer on the dining room table.

With exposure to computers on a grand scale comes exposure to the language of computers, and with that comes linguistic change. Already words such as *input, output,* and *loop* have become common terms in contexts having nothing to do with computers. Not long ago in an article on human psychology I found the author referring to decisions as "conditional branches." The computer invasion is not limited to pieces of hardware that crop up in unexpected places.

That's what this dictionary is about. It's about the language of computers—including numerics, which are defined in their own section at the end of the book— explained in terms that non-computer people can understand. It is a somewhat informal dictionary, and I suppose purists, scholars, and others devoted to precision will differ with, or find omissions in, some of the definitions it contains. Therefore, I will define the intent of the definitions.

This dictionary is not specifically written for computer professionals (although certainly they, too, can benefit from it). It is likewise not a compendium of every term ever used in a computer room, or of every nuance and possible variation of every term that might conceivably be applied to data processing. (Such an effort would be doomed anyway, since the terminology expands as rapidly as the technology.) Instead, my intent is to give the feel and convey the underlying concepts of the more commonly used computer terms. I give the reader credit for being able to figure out that *validation* is an alternative form of *validate*, so only the one definition is included; there are many such instances to keep from cluttering up the book with the obvious. Similarly, I presume everyone knows what a *program* is and has at least a fairly clear notion of what a computer does, so some of these basic terms are not highlighted by the use of italics. On the other hand, some rather obvious terms that have a peculiar meaning in computerese are italicized to alert the reader to that fact—*file* and *record*, for example. Definitions of alien concepts such as *parity*, *Fibonacci numbers*, and *virtual storage*—that have no parallels in ordinary life—verge on the encyclopedic. Others are quite brief, but all seek to go a little beyond mere definition and explain terms in a way that a newcomer to computers (that is, most of the world) will understand what the term really means.

It is neither possible nor practical to name all of those to whom I owe some debt of gratitude in helping me compile the word list from which this dictionary was written. Most of them didn't realize they were doing it, anyway, as they went about their jobs in data processing, talking in meetings or over the lunch table, writing memos and articles and books, and in general using the language of computers in its natural setting.

On the other hand, I must acknowledge the essential part that Hugh Rawson took in initiating this project. Without him, it would never have happened, and for that I thank him. I also thank my family for putting up with my distractions, absences, and obsession with computers during the writing. In addition to their conscious support, they have unwittingly aided me in ''keeping it simple'' and in perspective by their almost total lack of interest in the technical trivia upon which data-processing terms rest.

A

Abend Contraction for abnormal end. An abend occurs when a program unexpectedly halts due to a *bug* or because it encounters data conditions it cannot handle, e.g., division by zero, or trying to add a number and a letter. Used as both a noun and a verb.

able A digit in the *hexadecimal* numbering system that is equivalent in value to 10. Written as X'A'.

abort To force a program to stop before it reaches its normal end. Similar to and sometimes interchangeable with *abend*. Also used in the sense of *cancel*, when a human intervenes to stop a running program.

absolute address The exact point in *memory* or on a *storage medium* where a specific item of information is located. The absolute address is expressed in a form immediately usable by the *CPU* without reference to other points and without further manipulation. Contrasts with *relative address*.

absolute value In mathematics, the value of a number without regard to its sign. The number -3 is relatively less than $+3$, but the absolute value of both numbers is the same.

acceptance test The final test of a new program to make sure it is ready to be used on a routine basis. Acceptance tests are usually run by the Computer Operations Department without the assistance of the programmer.

access method   A *utility program* that manages the storage and retrieval of data. Information is often organized and stored in a different format than that used in processing by a program. The access method relieves the programmer of the need to manage stored data and handle the reformatting.

access time   The amount of time it takes to read or write on a *storage medium*. For a *disk drive*, for example, access time is the sum of the various electronic and mechanical actions that occur during a read or write operation. See also *seek time*, *latency delay*, *rotational delay*.

accumulator   The primary *register* in a *CPU*, in which all operations can be performed. In large computers all the registers are accumulators; in smaller machines there might be only one.

ACK   Abbreviation for acknowledgement. In data transfer between devices, data are often blocked into units of a predetermined size. At the end of the block the transmitting device sends a *check character* that has been calculated from the content of the data in the block. The receiving device recalculates the check character and compares it to the one sent. If both check characters are the same, the received data are assumed to be without errors and the receiving device sends an ACK (one character of a standard value) to the transmitting unit to acknowledge receipt. The transmitting device then sends the next block. If the check characters differ, the receiver sends a *NAK* (negative acknowledgement) to indicate that the received data contain errors. The transmitting unit then resends the same block and the process is repeated.

acoustic coupler   An inexpensive device for receiving and transmitting data using an ordinary telephone handset. The handset is held against a microphone and a speaker in order to send and "hear" tones representing data. See also *modem*.

acoustic modem   See *acoustic coupler*.

acronym A word or abbreviation based upon the initials (and sometimes other letters) of the term it symbolizes. *DASD*, for example, is the acronym for Direct-Access Storage Device, and is used as a word (pronounced daz-dee). Acronyms abound in the data-processing field.

actuator A mechanical device that makes something happen. Most often used in connection with *disk drives*, where the actuator is a mechanism that moves the *read/write head* to the desired position over the disk surface.

ACU See *automatic calling unit*.

Ada A *programming language* developed by the U.S. Department of Defense as its standard language for computer *software*. Ada is a *structured language* similar to *Pascal*.

A/D convertor Analog-to-digital convertor. A type of device that periodically samples an *analog* signal, such as a temperature reading, and converts it into a *digital* (numeric) value suitable for processing by a computer.

adder An electronic circuit that adds two numbers and returns their sum.

Add-in Electronic components that can be placed on a *printed circuit board* already installed in a computer to increase capability. For example, suppose you buy a 32K *memory* board for a microcomputer, but you only purchase 16K of memory at a time. The board will arrive with empty sockets for 16K. If you later purchase the *chips* to expand to the full 32K, the new memory is an add-in because you can install it on the board you have. The term add-in is also sometimes used to mean an additional device installed inside the housing of a computer (rather than plugged into an external connection), such as an accessory printed circuit board.

add-on A new device added to a computer to expand capability or to add a feature. In the definition of *add-in* above, the 32K board when first purchased is an add-on. This term often refers to a product added to a computer that is made by someone other than the computer manufacturer.

address A numeric value indicating a location. The *memory* of a computer is divided into some number of "boxes," each of which contain one *byte* (character) of information. These boxes, or addresses, are numbered sequentially starting at Ø. The *CPU* writes to memory by specifying an address and sending information to it, and reads memory by specifying an address and requesting that its contents be sent. On *disks*, data are addressed by *track* and *sector* numbers, thus identifying their placement. *Peripherals*, such as *tape drives, disk drives, terminals* etc., are all identified to the computer system by addresses. The *CPU* then exchanges information with these devices by specifying their addresses and reading and writing to them, much as it does with memory. All movement of information within a computer system involves the addresses of the originating and receiving points.

addressability Referring to the capability to be *addressed*.

addressable cursor The *cursor* is a "blip" on a *display* that indicates where the next character will appear. An addressable cursor is one that can be moved at will, either by *software* or by controls on the keyboard, anywhere on the screen regardless of its current position. This is normally accomplished in software by expressing an address as coordinates that identify the desired row and column numbers on the screen.

addressable unit A computer-attached device that is capable of being *addressed*. An example of an addressable unit is a printer that, when addressed and written to (sent a character) by the *CPU*, prints that character on paper.

address bus The electrical conductors within a computer that carry *addresses* from the *CPU* to components under its control.

address space The amount of *memory* available to a computer program as work space under its control. The program itself, plus the data the program operates on, is contained within the address space. Normally, some portion of the program determines the boundaries of the address space and manages them so that no attempt is made to exceed the available memory.

ADP Automatic Data Processing.

affinity Refers to a specific relationship among data-processing elements where a choice might otherwise exist. Suppose a data-processing center has three computers called A, B, and C, and work is run on whichever machine happens to have available capacity at the moment. There is one particular program, however, which for some reason can only be run on B. This program has an affinity for the B system.

aggregate motion printer A type of printing mechanism in which the mechanism does not return to an "at rest" position between characters.

air-chilled Electronic equipment that is cooled by air. Contrasts with *water-chilled*.

ALGOL One of the oldest programming languages still in common use. An acronym for "*algorithmic* language."

algorithm A detailed, organized, step-by-step plan for performing an action or solving a problem. When a programmer is preparing to write a program, he or she normally writes algorithms for complex or unfamiliar operations, and these algorithms serve as specifications for the program. The term sometimes also refers directly to the main part of a complicated program.

alias A secondary name. In some systems, a device or a *file* can be referred to by two or more names. One is its primary ("real") name, the others aliases.

all-caps mode   Similar to the "shift lock" on a standard typewriter keyboard, except that only alphabetic letters are shifted to upper case (capitals). Found on most computer-attached keyboard devices.

allocation   The assignment of computing resources for some purpose. When a program is started, the *operating system* allocates an *address space* to it. If the program will be writing processed *results* to a *file*, it might allocate *disk* space for this purpose. It could also allocate a *tape drive* if it requires input from a tape file. Allocations are normally handled by the operating system based upon requests generated by the program. When a resource is no longer needed (e.g., the tape drive), the program notifies the operating system to *deallocate* it.

alphamerics   Letters and numbers. Contraction of alphabetics and numerics.

alphanumerics   Letters and numbers. Interchangeable with *alphamerics*.

alpha test   The initial stress test of a new product under laboratory conditions. In an Alpha test, the new product is subjected to every conceivable situation it might encounter in the real world, in order to ensure that it functions as designed.

alternate path   Another way of moving information and control signals between the computer and an attached device when the primary path is busy or out of order. Alternate paths are frequently used in large computer installations, where several programs run concurrently on the same machine. When a program requests data from a *disk drive*, it stops executing and another program runs while the first waits for the disk read to complete. During this time, the path (electrical connection) to the disk unit is busy servicing the first program's request. If the second program also requests a disk operation, the *operating system* "knows" that the path is busy, and it seeks an alternate path to handle the request. This is known as *overlapping I/O*.

alternating current Abbreviated AC. A form of electrical transmission used in electronics for sending information over long distances. AC begins at a reference voltage (normally Ø volts), passes through a positive phase, returns to the reference voltage, and then passes through a negative phase. When the voltage again reaches the reference point, one *cycle* has been completed.

Two characteristics of AC are of primary interest in information technology: *frequency* and *amplitude*. Frequency refers to the number of cycles occurring in one second, a measurement known as *hertz*. Amplitude measures the voltage of the signal strength by indicating how far the signal swings from the reference voltage during each cycle. Information may be *encoded* on an AC signal by *modulating* either the frequency (*FM*) or the amplitude (*AM*). These techniques are commonly used in radio communications, and also in long-haul data communications over telephone lines. See also *phase modulation*.

ALU Arithmetic/Logic Unit. (*Note:* the stress in *arithmetic* in this usage is often placed on the *met* syllable.) The component of the *CPU* where data processing actually occurs through the manipulation of information and the evaluation of results. The ALU consists chiefly of small memory devices called *registers* where information is held during processing, and of information-altering or information-evaluating circuits, such as *adders* and *comparators*, which manipulate data according to programmed instructions.

AM Amplitude Modulation. A means of superimposing information on a *carrier* signal by varying the strength of the signal's waves. See also *alternating current*.

ambiguous name An unspecified or partially specified name, usually of a *file*. Contrasts with *unambiguous name*, which is the name of a file exactly as it is known to the computer system. An ambiguous name is useful in searching, and often employs a *wild card* symbol such as * or &. Thus, for example, the ambiguous name PAYROLL*.* means "any file name beginning with the word PAYROLL." The command "DIR PAYROLL*.*" might produce the list PAYROLL1.DLY, PAYROLLX.ANN, etc., being a list of every file known to the computer that satisfies the ambiguous name.

American National Standards Institute   An organization that establishes standards for the data-processing industry. It is chiefly concerned with standardizing *programming languages.*

American Standard Code for Information Interchange   See *ASCII.*

ampersand   The symbol &.

amplitude   The strength in volts of an *alternating current.*

amplitude modulation   See *AM, alternating current.*

analog   A signal of continuously variable voltage used as a measurement of some infinitely variable quantity, such as temperature, water salinity, blood pressure, etc. The voltage of the signal is analogous to the quantity being measured, hence the term analog. As an example, a float measures the depth of fluid in a tank; as the fluid level drops, the output voltage level of the float's analog signal drops in direct porportion (this is the way a gas gauge works in a car). When fluid is added, the float rises and so does its analog signal. Because an analog signal is a continuous current, it is not compatible with most computers. A device called an *analog-to-digital (A/D) convertor* is used to sample the analog voltage level and turn it into a numeric value suitable for processing by a computer, much as the gas gauge needle gives a quantifiable reading of the float's analog signal.

The type of analog signal most often encountered in data

processing is the signal exchanged over communications facilities such as telephone lines. In this case, a special kind of A/D convertor called a *modem* is used to convert digital data to and from the analog (*AC*) tones required for transmission.

analog computer A special-purpose computer that accepts and processes *analog* signals without conversion to numeric values. Analog computers are extremely limited in their capabilities and are usually designed for one specific purpose, such as patient monitoring, onboard spacecraft control, and weather *telemetry*.

analog data Signals in an *analog* format.

analog device A device that generates, responds to, or acts upon *analog* data.

AND A *logic* operation in which two *bits* or electrical pulses are combined, producing one resulting bit according to the following rules:

$$\emptyset \text{ AND } \emptyset \longrightarrow \emptyset$$
$$\emptyset \text{ AND } 1 \longrightarrow \emptyset$$
$$1 \text{ AND } \emptyset \longrightarrow \emptyset$$
$$1 \text{ AND } 1 \longrightarrow 1$$

In electronic circuitry, an AND operation may involve three or more simultaneous inputs, in which all inputs must be in order to produce an output of 1; a ∅ on any input will inevitably force the output to ∅. In data processing, AND operations are performed in *registers* under program control, and only two *bytes* may be ANDed at a time. The AND operation is useful for testing to see whether a specific bit is set to 1, and also to turn certain bits on or off. As an example, the *ASCII* characters for digits all begin with the four bits ∅∅11. To convert any ASCII digit to the corresponding *binary* value, we AND the digit with the byte ∅∅∅∅1111 as follows:

        00110010   (ASCII 2)
        00001111   (AND *mask*)
        ———————
        00000010   (Result is binary 2)

AND gate   An electronic circuit that does *AND* operations.

ANSI   Acronym for American National Standards Institute.

answer back   The capability of a communicating device such as a computer or *terminal* to identify itself automatically when it is called by another communicating device.

antistatic mat   A floor mat placed in front of a device such as a tape drive that is sensitive to static, to prevent shocks that could cause loss of data during human handling of the device.

AP   See *attached processor*. Also written as A/P.

APL   A *programming language* intended chiefly for sophisticated mathematics. Stands for A Programming Language.

append   To add data to the end of an existing *file*.

application   In data processing, the use of a computer to solve a specific problem or perform a specific job. Also used interchangeably with the term *program*.

application-level timer   A computer-furnished *timer* that is set and used by an *application program* much like an alarm clock. The program sets the timer and goes about other tasks until the timer interrupts it, at which point the program takes some time-dependent action. Application-level timers usually have a lower priority than other machine-provided timers.

application-oriented language   A *programming language* developed for a particular kind of data-processing problem. The *APL* language, for example, is intended for high-level mathematics, while *COBOL* is oriented toward business uses. The thrust of an application-oriented language is to make it easy to express complex actions associated with the special problems the language deals with. Thus, a mathematical language will furnish simple symbols telling the computer to derive square roots, cosines, logarithms, etc., rather than require the programmer to code instructions for these functions.

application program   A computer program for a given user that solves a specific problem or performs a specific action, such as producing bills, printing a report, or entering new data into a *file*. Contrasts with *system control programs* and *utility programs*, which perform generalized tasks for the benefit of all users of the computer.

applications programmer   A person, usually a professional, who writes *application programs*.

applications software   A collective term for all *application programs* in general.

application system   A related group of *application programs*. For instance, a billing system might consist of a dozen different programs that are run at different times for various purposes, but collectively the programs all contribute to the billing process.

application trace   A report produced by the computer that shows each step the machine took in running a program. Invaluable in troubleshooting and *debugging* programs.

architecture   The way *hardware* and/or *software* is structured; the structure is usually based on grandiose design philosophies. Architecture deals with fundamental elements that affect the way a system operates, and thus defines both its maximum capabilities and its limitations.

archival   The act of placing computer-stored information in an *archive*.

archive   As a verb, to copy data and programs onto a low-cost *storage medium* such as *tape* for long-term retention. As a noun (archives), a collection of such storage media.

argument Approximately equivalent to an *operand* or a *parameter*, and bearing no similarity to the conventional meaning of "disagreement" when used in data processing. An argument defines the scope of an activity. In "print a list of accounts past due *over 60 days*," the portion in italics is the argument, since it defines the scope by excluding all accounts due 59 or fewer days.

arithmetic/logic unit See *ALU*.

arithmetic operation (*Note:* the stress is often placed on the *met* syllable in arithmetic.) A standard mathematical operation, such as addition, subtraction, division, etc.

ARQ Automatic Repeat reQuest. In data communications, a request sent by a receiving device to have the most recent block of data retransmitted. Similar to *NAK*.

array An organized collection of data arranged in rows and columns for ease in indexing. An individual item can be referenced (read or written) by specifying the name of the array and the row and column numbers of the item. Most *high-level programming languages* provide such a facility. Interchangeable with *matrix*.

array element An item within an *array*.

arrival rate The number of messages, characters, or other measurable entities arriving over a communications medium per unit of time.

artificial intelligence The simulation of human thought processes, reasoning, and experiential learning in computer technology.

ARU (Letters pronounced separately) Audio Response Unit: a *peripheral* device that connects with telephone lines, accepting tones from a phone dial as numeric data and responding with a computer-controlled human voice.

ASA control characters A standard group of nongraphic characters specified by the American Standards Association (different from *ANSI*) for the control of computer printers.

ascending sort A *sort* operation that arranges information in numeric or alphabetic order from lowest to highest, e.g. 0–9.

ASCII (Pronounced "askey") American Standard Code for Information Interchange. ASCII and *EBCDIC* are the most widely used *codes* for the representation of *alphameric* information. ASCII is an 8-*bit* code in which seven bits indicate the character represented and the eighth (*high-order*) is used for *parity*. ASCII could thus potentially represent 128 possible letters, numbers, punctuation marks, and other graphic symbols. In fact, the number is lower than that, since the first 32 ASCII bit patterns are reserved for various standard control characters, such as carriage return, horizontal tab, etc. ASCII, therefore, represents a total of 96 characters, the order of the major groupings being 0 through 9, A through Z, and lowercase a through z, with various symbols separating each grouping. This is different from EBCDIC, where the digits fall last in sequence instead of first. ASCII is most commonly used on *microcomputers* and large non-IBM *mainframe* computers.

aspect ratio The relationship of the height and width of a viewing area, usually in reference to a *video display* screen.

ASR Automatic Send and Receive. The capability of a machine to receive and send messages without human intervention.

assembler A program that translates *instructions* written in *assembly language* into *machine language*. An assembler is similar in concept to a *compiler*, but because assembly language is close to machine language, the assembler is considerably less sophisticated. Some assemblers produce a machine language program that can be run immediately; most, however, produce an output file (*object module*) that requires further processing by another utility called a *loader* (or *linkage editor*) to convert the program into executable form.

assembler directive   A *statement* placed in an *assembly language* program to give directions to the *assembler*. An assembler directive does not generate machine language; rather, the programmer uses directives to control the manner in which the assembler operates. For an example of using directives, see *conditional assembly*. An assembler directive is also called a *pseudo-op*.

assembly language   A *programming language* in which each action the *CPU* performs is represented by a symbolic instruction. Assembly language is thus a convenient way of expressing *machine language*. Writing programs in assembly language is extremely tedious and requires great skill and knowledge of the computer's inner workings, since every tiny step the machine takes must be spelled out. Consequently, assembly language is not generally considered suitable for *application programs*. On the other hand, assembly language programs run extremely fast, occupy relatively little space in *memory*, and provide absolute control over the computer. For these reasons assembly language is favored for writing *system control programs* and other programs where high performance is important. Because assembly language exactly parallels machine language, every *CPU* type has its own unique assembly language that is seldom compatible with other CPU types.

assembly listing   A printed report produced by an *assembler*. It lists the original *source program*, annotated to show what the assembler has done, and includes *addresses* assigned, error messages, and other information useful to the programmer.

assisted panel In an *interactive* system in which the computer and a person conduct a dialog using a *video display terminal* (VDT), an assisted panel is a screen that explains a question the computer has asked, the options available, the format expected, etc. Assisted panels are associated with *user-friendliness*.

asterisk The symbol *. Used as a multiplication sign instead of × in most *programming languages*. Also used as a *wild card* symbol and for other purposes.

asynchronous A data-communications term describing the method by which signals between machines are timed. Contrasts with *synchronous*. In asynchronous communications, data are sent a character at a time without any prior arrangement as to how many characters will be sent per unit time, as if one or both machines had keyboards and typists. While the number of characters per unit time is undefined, the rate at which a character's *bits* are sent is predetermined. Each character is preceded by a *start bit* to alert the receiving machine. Once the start bit is sent, the bits of the character itself (normally 8) immediately follow at a defined rate. This is followed by one or two *stop bits* (the number is prearranged) to give the receiving machine time to act on the character just received. Another character might follow immediately, or there might be an idle interval until the next. For this reason, asynchronous communications is sometimes called "start/stop." Asynchronous is a low-speed form of data communications, running in the range of 60 to 1200 bits per second. Because of the variable number of characters sent per second, the term "bits per second" defines the maximum rate of data transmission. Often abbreviated as "async."

asynchronous communications adaptor A device attached to a computer to enable it to effect *asynchronous* communications over a telephone line.

ATM Automated Teller Machine. A communicating device,

usually under computer control, that enables a customer to make bank deposits, cash withdrawals, and other financial transactions without human assistance.

attach (1) To connect a device electronically and sometimes physically to a computer in order to add capability. For an example, see *attached processor*.

(2) In *software*, the ability of a program to call upon and execute another independent program as though it were part of itself.

attached processor A secondary *CPU* electronically connected with and operating under the control of another (primary) CPU. An attached processor is a slave to the primary CPU for the purpose of increasing computing power, and it shares memory, *peripherals*, and other computing resources with the primary processor. It has no independent existence, depending on the primary CPU to give it direction (although the primary CPU can run without the attached processor). Abbreviated AP or A/P.

attenuation distortion A communications term describing an excessive loss of signal strength. Attenuation is the normal and expected weakening of a signal sent over a communications facility. Standards govern acceptable levels of attenuation, and communications facilities are designed to deliver signals within these tolerances. Attenuation distortion occurs when a signal is weaker than the standards permit, thus causing it to be unrecognizable at the receiving end.

attributes The characteristics of a *file*, such as *record format*, *logical record length*, *block size*, etc. In most computer systems, attributes are recorded along with the name of the file, since this information is useful and often necessary for file management. The term may also be used in a broader sense for the characteristics of any device in a computer system.

audible feedback A beeper or clicker that sounds whenever a key is depressed on a keyboard.

audio response unit See *ARU*.

audit total A sum or count of a known quantity, calculated for the purpose of verifying data. If a group of financial records is processed, audit totals might show how many records there are and the dollar total of all transactions. These totals can then be checked to make sure all the records are present.

audit trail Records created at various stages in processing an item of information so that the item can later be traced and a history of the process reconstructed. Useful for tracing lost payments and other such real transactions.

authorized library A collection of *authorized programs*.

authorized program A computer program capable of altering the fundamental operation or status of a computer system. Authorized programs are normally in the category of *systems software*. The concept of authorization is applicable chiefly to very large, sophisticated environments such as the IBM MVS *Operating System*, in which programs must be authorized to execute certain *machine instructions* and to gain access to certain *files*. Authorization is accomplished through elaborate procedures performed when the program is first placed in the computer system. Each time the program is run, it notifies the operating system that it is authorized so that *privileged* functions denied to unauthorized programs can be performed.

auto answer The capability of a communicating machine to answer an incoming call and establish communications without human assistance.

autocall Abbreviation for automatic calling. A feature on a *modem* enabling it to place a telephone call under the control of a machine such as a computer.

automated teller machine   See *ATM*.

automatic call origination   See *autocall*. Also refers to the ability of a computer to initiate a telephone call without direct human intervention.

automatic calling unit   An attachment to a *modem* that performs the function described under *autocall*.

automatic dialer   A telephone instrument that automatically places a call either when the handset is lifted (''one-number dialer'') or when one of several prerecorded numbers is selected by pressing an associated button.

automatic repeat request   See *ARQ*.

automatic shutdown   Refers to the ability of some *systems software* to stop a network or a computer system as a whole in an orderly fashion. Automatic shutdown occurs when the system's software determines that it has encountered unacceptable conditions (e.g., overload, excessive errors, *hardware* failures, etc.). The purpose of automatic shutdown is to stop work with as little loss of data and the least amount of other damage as possible.

automation   A very broad term meaning the general tendency to replace human labor with machines. Automation and *mechanization* are largely interchangeable terms.

aux channel   Short for auxiliary channel, a secondary path for communications using the same phone line as a higher speed stream of data. In most cases, a data-communications signal does not use the entire *bandwidth* (capacity) of the phone line. Some *modems* utilize the unused portion of the bandwidth to derive an aux channel, over which low-speed signals can be sent independently of the primary signal.

auxiliary storage   In general, any medium for the storage of data outside the main *memory* of the computer, such as *magnetic tape*, *punched cards*, *floppy disks*, etc.

availability ratio A percentage showing the amount of time a system was actually available for use as compared with the amount of time it should have been available. For instance, if a system is supposed to be "up" 20 hours a day and today it was "down" for 1 hour, the availability ratio is 19/20 = 95 percent.

B

B Abbreviation for *binary* as used in programming notation. In some *programming languages* the binary equivalent of the number 9, for example, is written as B'1001', and in other languages as 1001B.

backbone The central portion of a computer program, which serves as a concise list of tasks to be performed and controls the *execution* of those tasks. Not all programs have a backbone; it is merely one approach to the organization of complex activities. In a backbone structure, each instruction in the backbone points to the portion of the program to be done next. Normally, these steps represent logical units of thought, such as "open the file," "read the next record," "add the amount of money to a running subtotal," etc. When the step referred to has been completed, control returns to the following instruction in the backbone, which points to the next task to be done. A backbone is sometimes also called a program driver. See also *modular programming*.

backbone circuit In data communications, a single circuit running from a computer to one or more remote devices (such as *concentrators* or *multiplexers*) each of which has branch circuits. A backbone circuit is thus similar to a river with tributaries.

back-end processing A catchall term for additional processing of data after the main work has been done. In a business,

28

for instance, at different times during the day the computer system runs payroll, accounts receivable, accounts payable, etc. Back-end processing occurs when, at the end of the day, all these activities are summarized in a single report.

background Not under the direct control of, and/or not obvious to, a computer user. A user might enter a command to run a particular job. This program then goes to work for a period of time without further direction and without notifying the user of what it is doing. The user might meanwhile do other work on the system, checking back later to see whether the job is finished. Such a program is said to be "running in the background." Contrasts with *foreground*.

backing store A British term equivalent to *auxiliary storage*. Seldom used in the United States.

back out To remove. Most often applies to changes in programs. To say "we backed out the program change" means "we removed the change and put the program back as it was before." Back-out procedures are a written guide explaining how to remove a change.

backplane A *printed circuit board* into which other printed circuit boards plug at right angles. A backplane usually contains only electrical conductors that carry signals among the connectors for the boards that plug into it (such conductors are jointly often called a *bus*). A backplane and a *mother board* are the same thing.

backspace To move backward rather than forward, as on a typewriter or a printer. When used in connection with *magnetic tape*, it means to reverse the tape physically in order to reread a *block* of data that has already been passsed. To backspace a *file* is to move toward the start of the data rather than, as is customary, toward the end.

backup A redundant device or copy of information that is provided or made in case the primary becomes unusable. A backup *clock*, for example, takes over the timing of events in a computer if the main system clock is out of order; the backup copy of a *file* is used when the main copy is lost or found to be unreadable. Often used as a verb: to back up a file is to make an extra copy of it for safekeeping.

bad branch A program error in which *execution* jumps to the wrong place, causing unexpected results. Bad branches sometimes happen because of malfunctioning *hardware*, but most often they are the result of errors (*bugs*) in the writing of the program.

BAL Acronym for Basic *Assembly Language*, chiefly as used on IBM 360/370 computers.

balancing The distribution of work load among computing resources to achieve good performance. For example, in a computer system having several *disk drives*, balancing involves the careful placement of frequently used *files* among the drives so that one drive is not so busy that it degrades performance as a whole while other drives are underutilized.

balloon contract A financing plan occasionally used in data processing for large computer systems, in which monthly payments are kept low and the final payment is very high.

bandwidth The range of *frequencies* that a communications channel is capable of carrying. For example, a voice-grade telephone line carries frequencies between 300 and 3000 *hertz*, giving a bandwidth of 2700 Hz. Bandwidth is analogous to capacity for carrying information in much the same way that diameter of a pipe determines how much water it can carry.

bank select The capability to turn internal system components on and off with electronic control signals. As an example, many microcomputers have a *memory* limitation of 64K (65,536 *bytes*). Some, however, can have two or more such memories operating under the control of the same *CPU*. Only one memory can be active at a time, so activation is accomplished by bank selecting—electronically "waking up"—the desired memory via signals sent by the CPU.

bankswitching   Same as *bank select*.

bar code   A method of representing data so that they can be read by optical means. In bar code, values are represented by lines of differing widths. When bar code is passed across an optical sensor at a uniform speed, the sensor determines the rate of motion from a line of known breadth and then decodes values based on the relative widths of the other bars. Most supermarket items have bar code printed on them in about a 1-inch square.

bare board   A *printed circuit board* that has conductors on it but no electronic components. Often provided with electronic hobby kits, and also sold separately for engineers and fabricators who wish to build a design of their own.

bare drive   A *floppy disk drive* sold without electronic control circuitry.

barrier strip   A device for connecting two cables without the use of plugs. The bare wires from one cable are attached to lugs of screws on one side of the barrier strip, and the wires from another cable are fastened at corresponding points on the other side, providing a separate path for each conductor.

base   In mathematics, the number of unit values that comprise the basis for a numbering scheme. The familiar decimal numbering scheme in common use has a base of 10, since there are ten unit values represented by the digits Ø through 9.

base 2   See *binary*.

base 8   See *octal*.

base 10   See *base*.

base 16   See *hexadecimal*.

base address   A *memory address* that serves as a point of reference. All other points are located by offsetting (adding to or subtracting from) in relation to the base address. In an account *record*, for instance, the age of the customer might be the ninth character position. Thus, no matter where the record is placed in *memory*, as long as its base address (usually the starting point) is known, the age can be found by adding 9 to the base address. See also *base register*.

baseband   A data-communications term referring to the standard voice-grade transmission frequencies between 300 and 3000 *hertz*. A baseband *modem* works on an ordinary telephone line.

base register   A *register* in a *CPU* assigned to hold the *base address* of a program. In very large computer systems that run several programs concurrently, programs are randomly placed in *memory* wherever convenient. The starting point of a program, wherever it might be, thus becomes its base address, which is loaded into a base register at start-up time. The program itself contains many addresses that all assume a starting point of zero. Since the program never actually begins at address zero, but rather at some random address, all addresses within the program are recalculated during *execution* by adding the indicated address to the base register. This process is known as *dynamic address translation*.

BASIC   Acronym for Beginner's All-purpose Symbolic Instruction Code. A *programming language* that is probably more widely accepted than any other, it was originally developed as a tool for teaching computer programming. BASIC is similar to *FORTRAN* in many ways, but much easier to use. It relies on English-like *instructions*, thus accounting for its popularity and ease of learning.

batch processing   The processing of data that have been accumulated in advance and usually arranged into batches by kind, such that repetitive processes can be performed by working through the data in a sequential fashion. Batch processing is not interactive; that is, there is little or no communication between the program and the computer operator while the program is running.

batch terminal A communicating device capable of entering batches of data (e.g., punched cards) and getting back processed results (e.g., printed reports) even though it is not directly attached, but instead communicates with a computer over a phone line. Batch terminals are different from interactive terminals such as *CRT*'s in that they are oriented toward large amounts of data, and in that a keyboard is not mandatory for their operation. See also *RJE*.

batch terminal simulation A method for testing communications programs without having actual terminals in operation. In batch terminal simulation (BTS), a *batch* program generates messages and passes them to the communications program so that it is "tricked into believing" that it is actually interacting with a terminal. The BTS program also acts on messages returned by the communications program and responds as a human operator might. This furnishes an opportunity to test and perfect communications programs before they are placed in a real environment.

baud A measurement of signaling speed over a communications line. Also a signal element, as explained under *baud rate*.

baudot A *binary*-based code that represents *alphanumerics* and a limited number of symbols with 5-*bit* characters. The baudot code can only represent 64 values, and for that reason it is unsuited for data-communications and data-processing purposes. As a result, it is used only on old teleprinters and a limited number of modern devices.

baud rate The number of signal elements sent over a communications line in one second. In general, the baud rate of a line is slightly less than its *bandwidth* in *Hertz*. Thus, on a normal voice-grade phone line with a 2700-Hz bandwidth, the maximum baud rate is about 2400. There is considerable confusion of this term with the similar concept of *bits per second* (bps), and the two are often erroneously used interchangeably. The baud rate indicates how fast signals are being sent, whereas bits per second shows the rate at which information is being transferred. In lower speed data transmission (up to 2400 *bps*), the two are usually synonymous, i.e., there is one bit per baud. A baud as a signal element must be at least one cycle in length in order to carry information.

bay A rack or cabinet in which electronic gear is mounted.

BCC Block Check Character. When data are transferred in *blocks* of a fixed length between devices, an extra character is often added to the block, so that for 80-character blocks, 81 are actually sent. This additional character, the BCC, represents a sum of some form calculated from the contents of the data in the block. See also *ACK* and *block parity*.

BCD Binary Coded Decimal. A code for representing decimal digits in a *binary* format. Every digit value has a corresponding 4-*bit* BCD value, so that 0 is 0000, 1 is 0001, 2 is 0010 . . . 9 is 1001. Because computers almost universally deal with 8-bit *bytes*, two BCD digits are packed into each byte. This substantially reduces the space occupied by a large amount of numeric data, and arithmetic can be performed directly on BCD. The disadvantage of BCD is that it is cumbersome to represent the sign for a negative value. Consequently, a variation of BCD called *packed decimal* is more often used than pure BCD.

Bell-compatible A term used in connection with *modems* to indicate that they are capable of communicating with modems furnished by the Bell Telephone system, which are the de facto industry standard.

benchmark A standardized test used to compare the perfor-mance of various alternatives. For example, if a company is considering several competing computers, it might run ex-actly the same programs, processing exactly the same data on each machine in order to find out which computer performs best. Ideally, the benchmark represents the typical work load that will be run on the selected machine.

beta test The first test of a new product outside the laboratory. During a Beta test, the new product is exposed to the real world, and it is carefully monitored to make sure it performs as designed. This is usually the final step before the product is offered on the market.

bezel A bracket or frame used to hold a faceplate.

bidirectional printer A printer that prints the first line left to right, the second right to left, etc. This method increases the *effective speed* of the printer, since it reduces the amount of time that the print mechanism wastes traveling from line to line.

bifurcated Having two electrical contacts in parallel, both of which close at the same time. Many keyboards have bifurcated keys, which increase the reliability of the keyboard by minimizing the effect of mechanical failure; if one contact fails, the other still works.

big-bang implementation A daring way of implementing a major change, in which many changes are introduced at the same time instead of taking the more conservative phased approach. In a big-bang implementation a new computer, new *peripherals*, and new programs might all be put into service at the same moment. It seldom works very well. Big-bang implementations are usually the product of inexperi-ence and/or massive egos, liberally mixed with foolishness. Synonymous with *lightning cutover*.

binary In computers and related devices, the fundamental method of representing information with electrical pulses. At any given instant, the electricity in a conductor may be either on (represented by 1) or off (symbolized by Ø). Thus, a single conductor can convey one of two alternative pieces of information. If we add a second conductor, we can represent four possible states, as shown in the following table:

B	A	Value
Ø	Ø	Ø
Ø	1	1
1	Ø	2
1	1	3

A third conductor will increase the number of possible states to eight by extending the pattern of numbering: 1ØØ means 4, 1Ø1 means 5, etc. In computerese these pulses are called *bits*, and they can be sampled when sent side by side through conductors or stored as tiny charges of static electricity in *memory*. The pattern of a fixed number of bits—usually eight—is determined by, and thus conveys, their information content. A group of eight bits is called a *byte*, which can represent 256 possible values, the number of patterns that there are in 8 bits ($2^8 = 256$). These patterns are analogous to the visual shapes of printed characters, so that Ø1Ø1ØØ1Ø perhaps corresponds to the letter *R*, whereas Ø111ØØ1Ø conveys lowercase *r*. The formal establishment of agreements as to which bit patterns represent which characters is called a *code*. The two main binary codes in use among computers are *ASCII* and *EBCDIC*, both 8-bit codes.

Because there are two possible unit values, binary is a numbering scheme to the *base* 2. The familiar decimal numbering scheme is to the base 10, having ten possible unit values, Ø–9. Working from right to left, decimal numbers have place values of units, tens, hundreds, etc. In binary, working from right to left, the place values are 1, 2, 4, 8, 16, 32, 64, and 128 in an 8-bit code. Conversion from binary to decimal is done by adding the place values of every position in which a 1 bit is present. The binary number 00110001 has a value of 49, since 32 + 16 + 1 = 49.

binary coded decimal   See *BCD*.

binary synchronous transmission   See *synchronous*.

bipolar format   A method of arranging *binary* data in wnich 0 *bits* have zero voltage and each 1 bit has a *polarity* opposite to the preceding 1 bit, i.e., the first 1 bit is positive, the second is negative, the third is positive, and so on. This technique gives *digital data* the characteristics of *alternating current* and enables it to be sent over communications facilities without the use of *modems*.

bistable   Having two states, as in *binary* data.

bisync   Acronym for *binary synchronous*.

bit   The smallest unit of information. The term bit is an acronym for *binary* digit. A bit is represented electronically by a pulse or the absence of a pulse of electricity at an instant of time, or by the presence or absence, respectively, of a charge of static electricity in a *memory* device. In notation, the pulse is written 1; its absence as 0. See also *binary*.

bit bucket   The receptacle that catches the small pieces punched out of cards in card-punching equipment. The term has come to have a slangy connotation in data processing; when a program ignores part of the input data, or it does not output some of the information it creates, it is said that the program "drops it in the bit bucket."

bit density   The amount of information contained per measureable unit of space on a *storage medium*. See *bits per inch*.

bit-flipping   Same as *bit manipulation*. Also used as a slang term for *systems programming*.

bit manipulation   Turning *bits* on and off, usually to influence the way a program operates. See *status byte* and *logic operation*.

bits per inch   The number of characters recorded per linear inch on *magnetic tape*. All the *bits* of each character are written across the width of the tape, so bits per inch and characters per inch are synonymous. Abbreviated as bpi.

bits per second   The number of *bits* transmitted per second over a communications line. Normally in data communications the bits of each character are sent serially. Abbreviated as bps.

bit test   A check performed by *software* to determine whether a specific *bit* is on (1) or off (Ø).

black box   A general term describing any electronic component built for a special purpose, or which causes a system to operate in a nonstandard way.

blank   Usually refers to a space character, although it can also mean a *byte* in which all *bits* are set to Ø. This term is confusing and should be avoided

blink rate   The number of times per second that a *cursor* or text on a *video display* blinks. Ordinarily, blinking is used to call attention to something on a display.

block   A group of characters or *bytes* treated as a unit of information. Usually blocks consist of a fixed number of bytes; see *block length*. When there are not enough actual data to fill a complete block (e.g., it is the last block), the unused space is *padded* with meaningless characters, such as *binary* zeros. Data communications makes extensive use of blocks; see *ACK*. Also, data are normally blocked for storage on *media*, such as *disks*. A block is sometimes also called a physical record.

block check character   See *BCC*.

block length The number of characters or *bytes* contained within a *block* of data. Block length is usually fixed for a particular system or *application*. For instance, under the Digital Research CP/M® *operating system* for microcomputers, all data written on a *floppy disk* has a block length of 128 bytes; there is no alternative. In systems that permit a variable block length, the block length is recorded somewhere and usually is tagged onto the front of a block when it is transferred, so that the receiving device knows how many bytes to expect.

block multiplexer A device that receives *blocks* of data from various sources, combines them onto a single transmission path, and distributes them to various destinations. Block multiplexers are most often used as *channels* that connect a computer with its *peripherals*, and operate at speeds in the millions of *bits per second*.

block parity A method for determining whether a *block* of data as transferred from one device to another contains errors. A *parity bit* is a bit whose value (1 or Ø) is calculated from some number of other bits. For example, in *odd parity* the parity bit is Ø if the group of bits being checked contains an odd number of 1 bits; otherwise, the parity bit has a value of 1. In block parity, an entire extra *byte*, called a *block check character*, is constructed and added to the end of the block. The first bit of this byte is set by observing the first bits of every byte in the block and setting it according to the parity, the second by calculating parity for all the second bits, and so on. The receiving device calculates its own check character and compares that with the one received at the end of the block. If the two are different, the block is known to contain at least one error and the receiving device requests a retransmission. The type of block parity calculation described is called *longitudinal redundancy checking*. There is also another type called *cyclical redundancy checking*.

block search   To scan through data looking for a specific character or word.

block transfer   To move information from place to place in *blocks*.

blocking factor   The number of logical (data) *records* that are combined to form a *block*. For example, if logical records are 128 *bytes* each and the *block length* is 1280 bytes, the blocking factor is 10.

blow up   A verb used when a program unexpectedly ends because of bad data; "the program blew up." Same as *abend*.

BLP   Stands for Bypass Label Processing. Some systems write a label record at the start of a *magnetic tape* identifying the tape and the data it contains, and other systems do not. To bypass label processing means to disable the system feature that reads and writes the tape label.

BNPF format   A format sometimes used to record information on *punched paper tape*, in which each *byte* of data is represented by ten punched characters. The character B indicates the start of the byte, the character N signifies a Ø *bit*, the character P represents a 1 bit, and the character F signals the end of the byte. This is an extremely cumbersome and inefficient, but highly reliable, way to record information.

bomb   Same as *abend*.

Boolean value   Values generally referred to as TRUE and FALSE in computer programs, and which are treated as (and sometimes even called) switches because they control the way a program runs. In practice, a Boolean TRUE is usually a *byte* with all bits turned on (11111111) and a FALSE is all Øs. Features of a program can be turned on and off by setting a *status byte* as TRUE or FALSE. As the feature begins to run, it checks its status byte; if TRUE, it runs; if FALSE, it passes control to the next portion of the program. In this way, certain reports are only printed on selected days, special processing is done or not done, etc. Boolean values are used for many control functions.

boot To load the *operating system* into a computer after it has been turned on. Synonymous with *IPL*, but usually used in connection with small computers.

bootstrap A program that *boots* a computer. The term comes from the saying "to pull oneself up by the bootstraps." The bootstrap program is usually in a *ROM* (read-only memory) that gains control as soon as power is applied to the computer. This program loads the *operating system* from disk into *memory*, and then *bankswitches* the ROM off so that control of the system passes to the operating system. When the computer is running, the bootstrap program can again be activated by operating the machine's *RESET* or *IPL* switch.

bottleneck analysis A detailed and often voluminous study of the computer system's *configuration* to determine where bottlenecks occur, so that performance can be improved.

bottom The end of a *file*.

bpi See *bits per inch*.

bps See *bits per second*.

branch An *instruction* in a program that causes it to jump to a different part of the program. Normally instructions are executed in sequence. A branch interrupts the sequence by directing execution to an *address* other than the one following. The term is synonymous with *jump* and with *GOTO*.

branch and link An *instruction* in IBM *assembly language* that is used to call a *subroutine*. Before the branch is executed, the *address* of the next instruction is placed in a specified *register*, and then the branch occurs. At the end of the subroutine, another instruction causes a branch back to the address in that register, thereby resuming execution at the instruction following the branch and link.

branch on condition   See *conditional branch*.

breadboard   A *printed circuit board* specifically designed so that the buyer can use it to mount and wire whatever circuitry he or she wishes. The term also applies to custom-built, one-of-a-kind circuitry.

break key   A key on the keyboard of a communicating terminal which, when depressed, sends a stream of *binary* zeros to the device it is communicating with. This alerts the other device that it should break off transmission. The break key is used as an alarm button.

breakdown diode   See *zener diode*.

bridge   A device that connects several phone lines together to form a *multipoint* circuit.

bridged circuit   A phone line connected to a *bridge*.

broadband   A communications facility that furnishes a greater *bandwidth* than a normal voice-grade line. Broadband lines are used for extremely high-speed data communications. Contrasts with *baseband*; synonymous with *wideband*.

broadcast   A message distributed to several or all users of a system, e.g., ''The system will be shut down at 5:00 P.M.''

BTS   See *batch terminal simulation*.

bubble memory   A type of *memory* in which *bits* are recorded as ''bubbles'' of magnetism much as they are on *storage media* such as *disks*, except that in bubble memory they can be shifted about rather like the cars of a train in a switching yard. Bubble memory is cheaper, more reliable, faster, and consumes far less power than conventional *semiconductor* memory; it also retains its contents when power is turned off. It is a recent technology that promises to develop rapidly.

bucket A housing that usually also furnishes a power supply and other services to a small, self-contained electronic component, such as a *modem*.

buffer A *memory* in which information is temporarily stored during transfer from one device to another. A buffer is useful not only for holding data, but for adjusting for differences in speeds between the devices, or between the device and the communications facility.

buffered device A *peripheral* that has its own *buffer*. Many printers, for example, are buffered so that they can accept information more rapidly than they can print it. The buffer stores output from the computer at high speed as the printer runs at low speed. When the buffer fills up, the printer stops accepting information and the computer is then free to go about other tasks until the printer signals its readiness to accept information.

buffer pool An area in *memory* assigned as space for several *buffers*.

bug An error in a program that causes it to malfunction. Also applies to design flaws in *hardware*.

built-in function A capability that comes as a standard feature of *hardware* or *software*. Most *programming languages*, for example, have built-in functions to calculate square roots, logarithms, cosines, etc., so that the programmer does not have to write the *instructions* to do these things, but instead merely specifies that he or she wants the function to be performed.

built-in procedure Similar to a *built-in function*, except that built-in procedures are usually common tasks that appear in almost every program (e.g., reading and writing data on a *disk*) and are thus built in to save the programmer the job of rewriting the same instructions every time he or she writes a new program.

bundled   Refers to a "package deal" in which the *software* is included when you buy the *hardware*. Bundled software is sometimes not sold independently of the hardware.

burn-in   A testing period for a new piece of equipment, during which power is continually kept on, before the device is placed in production. The failure of most new electronic equipment occurs because of parts overheating, hence the term.

burst   (1) To take apart a computer printout, as in removing carbon paper, separating copies, and tearing into separate pages.

     (2) In data communications, a group of errors that occur together and cause data to arrive at the destination with a different content than sent.

burster   A mechanical machine that *bursts* printouts.

bus   A set of electrical conductors on a *backplane* that carry electronic signals to the various components of a computer. The conductors as a whole are called a bus. They are logically broken down into three subsets called a *data bus*, an *address bus*, and a *signal bus*.

bus cable   A cable that connects to a *bus* and extends it outside the computer housing, or to a different physical bus within the same computer.

bus extender   A *printed circuit board* that mates with a *bus* to extend its capacity. Buses have a limited number of *slots* for plugging in components; a bus extender adds more slots.

business computing   In general, the application of computers to solve business information needs. The term carries the connotation of performing relatively simple, repetitive operations on large masses of data. Contrasts with *scientific computing*.

business machine In data processing, a collective term encompassing computers and all types of *terminals* that are involved in data processing.

busy hour In communications, the hour of the day when traffic is at its peak. Communications systems are engineered to handle the work load normally encountered during the busy hour of the average day of the busiest month of the year.

bypass action An action taken to get around a problem and do as much work as possible until the problem is fixed. Bypass actions make the best of a bad situation, and they are always temporary solutions.

bypass label processing See *BLP*.

byte A group of some fixed number of *bits* that comprise a character, a *machine instruction*, or some other logical unit of information. The pattern of the bits determines the meaning of a byte, just as the shape of a printed character conveys meaning. In the vast majority of data-processing equipment, a byte consists of 8 bits.

byte multiplexer Similar to a *block multiplexer*, except that it handles data on a byte-by-byte basis rather than as entire *blocks*.

C

C   The name of a *programming language*. C was developed around the concept of *structured programming* and bears a strong resemblance to *Pascal*.

cabinetry   Housings that enclose large electronic components.

cable   A collection of electrical conductors enclosed within a sheath for connecting two devices together.

cable bridge   A rubber strip with a channel inside to enclose cables that run across a floor so that there is less chance of tripping over loose wires.

cable noise   Electrical disturbances, which can distort signals and cause errors, that are picked up by the wires in a cable.

cable trough   An enclosed channel, usually under a floor, through which cables are routed from one place to another.

cache memory   A small, extremely fast *memory* that services a *CPU*. The CPU can set aside subtotals and other such interim processing results in cache memory, where they are more quickly accessible than in main memory. Also, *instructions* that will soon be executed can be placed in cache memory shortly before they are needed, thus speeding up the CPU's processing. Also called scratchpad memory.

CAD   (Pronounced like the word "cad") Acronym for Computer-Aided Design. In CAD, specifications for items under design are entered into the computer, and the machine then uses *graphics* capabilities to draw three-dimensional pictures of the object for display. The engineer using CAD can "rotate" the object and make modifications as it is displayed, thus speeding up the process of design. CAD is closely related to computer-aided manufacturing (*CAM*), and the two are often referred to jointly as CAD/CAM.

CAI (The letters are pronounced separately) Computer-Aided Instruction. A method of drilling students and reinforcing lessons through question-and-answer dialogs with a computer.

calendar Most large-scale computer systems and many small ones have a system calendar that, when queried through a call to the *operating system*, returns the day's date. The calendar is kept up to date by the system clock, so that at midnight the date is automatically rolled over.

call An *instruction* that passes control to a different part of the program (a *subroutine*) or to another program, at the end of which control is returned to the calling point. A call is similar to a GOTO, except that it expects to regain control at the next instruction following the call. A call thus executes other programs or parts of programs as though they were written in at the point where the call occurs. Calls request services from the *operating system*. See also *subroutine*.

call setup time The period of time that elapses between lifting a handset to initiate a telephone call and the beginning of a conversation (or data transmission).

CAM (Pronounced as a word) Acronym for Computer-Aided Manufacturing. The application of computers to the manufacturing of products. Also called *process control*. CAM is closely associated with *CAD* (computer-aided design), such that it is possible for the results of CAD to be applied directly and immediately to manufacturing using CAM.

camp-on A feature of some telephone systems in which, if a line is busy when called, the caller can "camp on" (wait with the handset lifted) and will be connected when the line is free.

cancel To stop a program that is running without saving any results produced up to that point. The only way to restart a canceled job is to start it at the beginning again.

capacitance The characteristic of electrical conductors to build up a charge of static electricity. Capacitance can interfere with the flow of current, especially when it builds up between nearby conductors, and this must be anticipated in the design of electronic circuits. It is also a useful characteristic, as when it is necessary to "remember" if a pulse of electricity (a *bit*) has passed through a conductor; this is the basis of computer *memory* systems. The device that deliberately builds up capacitance is called a *capacitor*.

capacitor An electronic component that stores a charge of static electricity. As current passes across it, a capacitor "steals" a certain amount of the power and holds it. The static charge remains after the current in the conductor ends. The capacitor will release the static charge if properly stimulated. This is the way *bits* are written to and read from computer *memory*.

capacity planning An aspect of data-processing management: forecasting the growth of data-processing work load, translating that into requirements for additional equipment and the timing of those acquisitions, and usually preparing budgets and financial justifications for the expenditures.

caps mode See *all-caps mode*.

card (1) A punched card, on which data are encoded by punching holes that correspond to *bits*.
(2) A *printed circuit board*.

card cage A rack that holds several *printed circuit boards*.

card guide A U-shaped slot (viewed from the end) that holds the edge of a *printed circuit board* securely in a *card cage*.

card hopper A box or enclosure that holds *punched cards*. Card-handling equipment usually has two hoppers, one that feeds cards into the machine, another to catch them as they come out.

card-image file A collection of information stored on a *magnetic medium* (*tape* or *disk*, usually) in a format that enables the medium to be processed as though it were *punched cards*. Since most punched cards have 80 *columns*, the *records* in card-image files usually consist of 80 characters each.

cardkey access A system of physical security often found in computer rooms, and almost always under computer control, in which doors are unlocked by inserting a badge (''cardkey'') into a reader and punching on a keyboard the same code magnetically stored in the cardkey.

card punch A machine that records information by punching holes into *cards*. A hole represents a 1 *bit*, its absence a Ø. A card punch with a keyboard is usually called a *keypunch*; such machines, once a staple item in any data-processing installation, are now becoming scarce as more economical and efficient ways of capturing data are developed. Card punches may also be *peripherals* attached directly to a computer or a business machine, which punch cards under machine control.

card reader A machine that reads the holes in *punched cards* and passes the data to a computer as input.

card slot A position for a *printed circuit board* in a *card cage* or on a *backplane*.

card whalloper A machine that punches, reads, or otherwise handles *punched cards*.

carriage control character Information sent to a printer to control its operation, rather than to be printed on paper. Not all *bytes* have a corresponding graphic symbol (letter, number, etc.). Most printers are wired or programmed to respond to certain of these nongraphic characters, e.g., *vertically tabbing* to a specific line or skipping to the top of the next page.

carriage return A *carriage control character* that returns the printing mechanism to the left margin on a printer, and the *cursor* to the left margin on a display screen.

carrier A tone sent over a communications *medium* (radio or telephone line) that is acted upon in some way in order to convey information. For instance, the *frequency* of the carrier might be shifted up or down (see *FSK*), its *amplitude* might be varied (see *alternating current*), or some other characteristic might be used. To place information on a carrier is called *modulation*; to read the information from a carrier is *demodulation*. See also *modem*. The term *carrier* is abbreviated CXR.

carrier detect A signal sent from a *modem* to a *business machine* to indicate that it is receiving a *carrier*. The machine then knows it can begin sending and receiving signals.

carrier frequency The *frequency* of a *carrier* in *Hertz*. Carrier receiving and transmitting devices (e.g., *modems*) are set to narrow tolerances that don't permit the tone to vary by more than a few Hertz, thus reducing the possibility of picking up bad signals as a result of *crosstalk*. Also, the carrier frequency is ordinarily a prime number (one not divisible by any other number) to reduce the chances of interference by *harmonics* from other signals.

carry flag An indicator that is "turned on" in the *CPU* when a carry has resulted from adding two numbers. A carry occurs when the sum is too large to be held in a *register*. After doing addition, a program must check the carry flag and handle the carry if it is on. The carry flag is one *bit* of a *status byte* maintained within the CPU. In most CPUs it is normally set to Ø and only goes to 1 in case of a carry.

cartridge A small container of *magnetic tape* similar to but larger than an audio cassette, on which data are recorded. Because cartridges hold a large amount of data but are slow, they are most often used for *backup* copies of *files* held on faster *storage media*, such as *Winchester disks*, connected to microcomputers.

cartridge drive A device used to read and write *cartridges*.

cassette A closed container of *magnetic tape* with supply and take-up reels, normally used to record music and other audio signals. Cassettes are a popular *storage medium* for the low end of the home computer market because of their low cost. Because of their slowness and cumbersome operation they are unsatisfactory for most data-processing applications.

catalog (1) A *file* kept by a large computer system that serves as a comprehensive index to all files known to the system. It is analogous to the card catalog kept in a library, showing the name, location, and *attributes* of every file. Often referred to as the SYSCTLG (pronounced "sis-catalog"). The *operating system* usually provides *utility programs* to maintain the catalog.

(2) When used as a verb, to record a file in the catalog.

cataloged procedure A standardized set of *job control language* (JCL) statements that can be executed as a *subroutine* by other JCL, and which is recorded in the system *catalog*. Cataloged procedures are often (but not always) developed by the programmers at a data-processing installation to save the trouble of having to rewrite the statements for some recurring function. See *JCL*; also *procedure*.

catastrophic error Not as bad as it sounds. When *systems software* becomes overwhelmed with a heavy work load, it stops accepting new work and clears up some of what it already has. Also, when a *compiler* has detected so many errors in the program it is translating that further work would be pointless, it terminates with a catastrophic error.

CCITT Consultative Committee International Telegraph and Telephone. An organization established by the United Nations to develop worldwide standards for communications technology, as for example *protocols* to be used by devices exchanging data.

CCS Hundred call seconds. A term used in communications engineering to express the amount of traffic usage on a line or group of lines. One CCS means the line is in use 100 seconds during the hour. If there are eight calls with an average duration per call of 47 seconds ($8 \times 47 = 376$ seconds), there is 3.76 CCS of traffic during the hour. CCS, then, is total traffic in seconds divided by 100. Calculations leading to the design of communication systems use CCS extensively.

CCU Communications Control Unit. Usually a special-purpose small computer whose only job is to handle the flow of data-communications traffic to and from a larger main computer. Sometimes called a *front end processor*.

CCW Channel Command Word. A set of instructions passed from a *CPU* to a *channel* under its control that directs the activities of the channel in performing input/output operations. See also *channel program*.

CDU Coolant Distribution Unit. A device that pumps coolant into a water-chilled computer.

CE Customer Engineer.

cell A unit of *memory*, consisting of some fixed number of *bytes*, that is treated as a self-contained package of data. A cell is synonymous with a *word*, and its length is determined by the number of bytes that can be held in a *CPU register*.

central processing unit See *CPU*.

centralized configuration The structure of a data-communications system whose dominating feature is a central computer that is in one way or another involved in everything that happens in the system i.e., the remote devices have little or no ability to act on their own. Also called a *star network*.

century date A means of representing a calendar date with reference to January 1, 1900, i.e., the number of days that have elapsed in the century. June 25, 1981, for example, was century date 29761. A century date is simple to calculate and it eases the task of computing how many days separate two dates, since it is unaffected by differences in the lengths of months, leap years, and other quirks of the Gregorian (conventional) calendar. Nevertheless, century dating is less popular than *Julian* dates in computing systems.

certification Approval of a product by an organization that has legal jurisdiction or at least widespread recognition for the enforcement of established standards, such as Underwriters' Laboratories.

CFIA Component Failure Impact Analysis. A study that attempts to determine in advance the seriousness of potential failures of major system components. "If the *CPU* is down, this happens; if a *disk controller* breaks, that happens. . . ." A CFIA is used to prepare *contingency plans*.

chad The tiny pieces punched out of cards and paper tape.

chained list A collection of information in which no attempt is made to group items according to their relationship to each other; rather, relationships are indicated by the use of *chain pointers* that show where to find the next related item. For example, in a supply business where customers periodically and randomly place purchases on account, a chained list would be a *file* where such charges are recorded as they happen. Each time a new charge is added, the last item in the list pertaining to that customer is *updated* with a pointer to the new charge. In this way, the billing program can locate all charges for the month by following the chain through the list. This method of organizing data is also called a *linked list*. See also *data base*.

chaining   (1) Stringing together related items of information as discussed under *chained list*.

(2) In data communications, relating messages or *segments* of messages to each other with identification and serial numbers so that a complete transaction can be assembled by the receiving system.

(3) In programming, the execution of two or more separate but related programs in a certain sequence, such that when one program ends the next automatically begins; taken collectively the chained programs constitute a complete *job*.

(4) In sophisticated *programming languages*, the ability to write computer programs that are larger than available *memory* by using an *overlay* structure, wherein portions of the program are automatically brought into memory from *disk* when it is time to execute them.

chain pointer   The information that tells where to find the next item in a *chained list*.

chain printer   A kind of print mechanism in which the *slugs* are strung along a chain that moves across the width of the page. As a character to be printed arrives at the point where it is to appear, a hammer drives the slug forward to print the image.

channel   (1) The part of a computer that connects it with its *peripherals* and, in general, with the outside world. All communications between the *CPU* and devices outside the computer's housing pass through a channel, e.g., reading and writing on *tape* and *disk*, data communications via the *CCU*, sending message to the *system console*. Large computer systems have several channels called *byte* and *block multiplexers*;

small computers (minis and micros) have none, relying instead on specialized *ports* to communicate with the world. The channels of a computer are "intelligent" in having their own *microprocessors* to execute special *channel programs* under the direction of the CPU. Channels operate at speeds in the millions of *bits per second*.

(2) In communications, a telephone line or a radio connection that enables two or more devices to communicate.

channel-attached device A machine connected directly to a computer by means of a *channel*.

channel capacity The amount of information that can be handled by a computer *channel*. In general, it is not desirable to load a channel so that it is busy most or all of the time, because this will cause intolerable delays in running programs. Therefore, channel capacity is generally considered in terms of its optimum *throughput*: how much it can effectively handle without degrading system performance, rather than its maximum capacity.

channel command word   See *CCW*.

channel configuration The kinds and numbers of devices connnected to each *channel* on a computer. Also a diagram depicting the logical (rather than physical) layout of such devices, their *addresses*, etc. The design of channel configurations is an exacting pseudo-scientific art; it is the single most influential factor in the performance of a computer system.

channel director A special-purpose computer-within-a-computer that controls the activities of several *channels*. This is an *architectural* feature of extremely large computers, such as the IBM 308X series. A channel director frees the main *CPU* of the tasks of managing the system's channels.

channel program A program that operates a *channel* according to instructions contained in the *CCW*, which tells the channel what to do and where to do it.

channel skip   A *carriage control character* that tells a printer to do a *vertical tab* (skip down to a specified line on the page) or to skip to the top of the next page.

channel status word   Information by which a *channel program* reports back to the *CPU* (or *channel director*) on its condition or on the disposition of a *CCW* sent to it. Abbreviated CSW.

channel-to-channel adaptor   A device by which two independent but physically adjacent computers are connected to each other via a *channel* on each, for the purposes of communicating and resolving conflicts over shared devices, dividing the work load evenly, sharing data and programs, etc.

character   Specifically a letter, digit, or other graphic symbol. Generally, a *byte*.

character parity   See *vertical redundancy*.

character printer   A printer that prints as a typewriter does, by starting at the beginning of the line and printing each character in order to the end. Contrasts with *line printer*.

character set   All the letters, digits, and symbols that a printer is capable of producing.

chassis   The metal base upon which an electronic device is built, which gives it not only a mechanical foundation but also, usually, a common electrical reference. See *chassis ground*.

chassis ground   A common point of electrical reference for all electronic components mounted on a *chassis*. The negative side of a power supply is connected to the chassis. The positive side furnishes current to the circuitry in the machine. Wherever a circuit is completed, it connects to the chassis, thereby returning to a common *ground*.

Sometimes an *interface* between two devices contains a conductor called *chassis ground*. This lead connects the chassis of the two devices in order to equalize any differences and make the signals between the devices electrically compatible.

check character   See *BCC*; also *block parity*.

check digit   An extra digit added to a numeric value such as an account number for the purposes of verifying and preventing fraud. An account number might be known to the customer as an 8-digit number, whereas the computer regards it as a 7-digit number. The eighth number is calculated by a secret method and compared with the eighth digit as given by the customer. If the two are not the same, the customer has either entered the number incorrectly or is trying to perpetrate a fraud.

checkpoint   A *record* written periodically into a *file* that is collecting large amounts of data. The checkpoint is not true data but rather a *software*-generated note to itself. If the system *crashes*, the file becomes damaged, or some other problem arises that makes it necessary to restart the program, the last checkpoint tells where to resume without having to go all the way back to the very beginning.

checksum   See *audit total*.

child   A data *record* that can only be created based upon the contents of one or more other records (*parents*) already in existence.

chiller   A refrigeration unit that chills the coolant used in a water-cooled computer. Sometimes also applies to an air conditioning unit for an air-cooled machine.

chip   A small electronic component usually made of silicon that contains microscopic circuits. Also called an *integrated circuit*.

chunking along   A slang term referring to the operation of a long-running, dependable program. "It's been chunking merrily along for half an hour."

circuit (1) An electrical path that flows from a power source, passes through a resistance that performs work, and returns to the power source, sometimes also passing through various switches.

(2) In communications, a telephone line.

circuit capacity The amount of information that can be handled by a communications line.

circular polling *Polling* is the means by which traffic is moved in a network of many *nodes* (devices). A computer polls each node by sending out its address and a request for a response. If the node has traffic to send, it transmits it to the *host*; otherwise, it sends a "no-traffic" response. In circular polling the host computer passes through a list of all nodes and solicits a response from each station once during every pass. Contrasts with *priority polling*.

circumvention See *bypass action*.

clean and certify A "housekeeping" process in which a *magnetic tape* is run through a machine that physically cleans it, writes a data test pattern on it, and checks it for errors caused by surface flaws or other damage.

clear Generally, to wipe out the contents of *memory* (all or some selected portion) in a computer by writing *binary* Øs or a test pattern. In some *programming languages*, to release an area in memory that was previously reserved so that it can be reused.

clear to send A control signal from a *modem* to a transmitting device to indicate that the line and modems are ready.

CLIST (Pronounced "see-list") Acronym for Command List. A *file* containing a list of commands that would normally be typed one at a time on a keyboard. When the name of the CLIST file is entered, the system processes the commands in the file in the order they are given, as though each had been individually typed. A CLIST thus becomes a sort of program. The facility is useful for setting up complex, repetitive sequences and referring to them by a simple name.

clobber To write new data over the top of good data in a *file*, or otherwise to damage a file so that it becomes useless.

clock (1) The *system clock* in a computer, which tells the time of day in response to a *call* to the *operating system*.

(2) A timer within or adjacent to the *CPU* that sends out high-frequency "ticks" by which all internal events in the computer system are coordinated. A 4-MHz clock in a microcomputer, for example, emits four million "ticks" per second. This signal is sent to all components within the computer via the *bus*. Every single thing that happens is timed: so many ticks for this, so many for that.

clock frequency The number of "ticks" per second emitted by the internal *clock* of a computer. See (2) under *clock*.

clocking The timing of electronic events by a high-speed internal *clock*.

clock pulse A "tick" emitted by the computer's internal *clock* and sent on the *bus*.

clock speed Same as *clock frequency*.

close To make a *file* no longer available to a computer program after the program has had access to it. Analogous to closing the drawer of a filing cabinet.

closed shop A peculiar data-processing term of which probably no one knows the origin. Closed shop jobs are computer programs under development and being test-run on the system, and other programmer-related work, such as *compiles* and *links*.

clustered devices A group of *terminals* such as *CRTs* and printers that are all connected to a common *controller*. The controller (often called a *device cluster controller*) handles all communications with the computer and provides *local* services for the clustered devices, e.g., the ability to print a screen display on *hard copy*.

CMI Computer-Managed Instruction. Similar to *CAI*, except that the computer becomes the primary teacher and the student only needs human assistance in the form of tutoring and guidance.

CMOS (Pronounced "see-moss") Complementary Metal-Oxide Semiconductor. A method for making silicon *chips*.

CNOP (Pronounced "see-nop") Conditional Non-Operation. An *instruction* used in some *assembly languages* that causes the *assembler* to generate *NOP* ("do-nothing") machine instructions as a filler until the next *full-word boundary* is reached.

COAM (Pronounced "co-am") Acronym for Customer Owned And Maintained. Chiefly a Bell System term for communicating equipment not owned by the Bell System but attached to their facilities.

coax (Pronounced "co-ax") Short for *coaxial cable*.

coaxial cable A tubular cable in which one conductor is a sleeve that completely encircles the other, which is a wire. Coax (pronounced "co-ax") is electrically impervious to most external influences that disturb and distort signals, such as commercial power lines and *crosstalk*. It is therefore a good though rather expensive means of carrying high-speed data signals.

COBOL Acronym for COmmon Business Oriented Language. A *programming language* that is based on plain English, so that nonprogrammers can read and immediately understand programs, even if they know nothing about data processing. COBOL is the most widely used programming language for business *applications*.

CODASYL (Pronounced CODE-a-sil) Acronym for Conference On DAta SYstems Languages. A regularly meeting committee concerned with the development and standards of *programming languages*. CODASYL developed *COBOL*.

code (1) A means of electronically representing letters, digits, and other data symbols with *binary* numbers, e.g., *ASCII*.

(2) A numeric indicator sent to the computer operator by a program when it ends, showing whether or not the program completed successfully and if not, why not. Usually referred to as a *return code, completion code*, or *condition code*.

(3) Sometimes, loosely, a *programming language*: "According to the rules of COBOL code. . . ."

(4) *Statements* in a *source* program: "That program has a thousand lines of code."

(5) As a verb, to convert a program specification into a source program by actually writing statements in a programming language: "The specs are done, and now we're coding and testing."

code conversion Changing the way data are represented from one machine-readable *code* to another, e.g., from *ASCII* to *EBCDIC*.

code sensitivity Most *hardware* and *software* is code sensitive, i.e., it expects all data to be represented in one consistent *code*, such as *EBCDIC*. If presented with a code different than that for which it was designed, a code-sensitive system will produce bizarre results or fail to function altogether.

code translation (1) Same as *code conversion*.

(2) Occasionally, to *compile* a program.

code transparency The opposite of *code sensitivity*, i.e., not "caring" which *data representation code* is used. An example of a code-transparent device is a *modem*, which passes *bits* without regard for their meaning.

cold start   To start running a program from the very beginning as though it had never been run before. A cold start contrasts with a *warm start* in that a cold start does not attempt to pick up where it left off from a previous run. The term usually applies to *systems software* programs, not *applications*.

collate   To bring together information from two or more sources and put it into some kind of order. The term usually refers to the physical combining and sorting of *decks* of *punch cards*. When a similar process is performed on *files* (e.g., *disk* files) it is called *merging*.

collating sequence   The numeric sequence of *binary* values representing data, such that when sorted the data will be in a predictable *alphanumeric* order. In *ASCII*, the collating sequence is Ø–9, A–Z, a–z. In *EBCDIC*, the collating sequence is a–z, A–Z, Ø–9. Thus, when sorting EBCDIC characters into collating sequence, a lowercase *a* is the first (lowest) in order and a digit 9 is highest.

color graphics   The capability of a system to draw pictures, create graphs, highlight text, etc., using colors.

column   A character position within a line of print or a data *record*. Columns are numbered left to right starting at 1.

COM   (Pronounced like the last syllable of "intercom") Acronym for Computer Output Microfilm. A technology for photographically writing dozens to hundreds of pages of computer printout onto a *fiche* card, which is about the same size as a *punched card*. COM printers are often attached directly to a computer and *emulate* a normal page printer; others produce fiche by reading data from a *magnetic tape*.

come down gracefully   When a system is brought to a halt, either on command or during *automatic shutdown*, without losing data or otherwise wreaking havoc.

command An instruction that controls the activity of a computer system, normally entered through the operator's *console* and acted upon immediately. Examples are to *cancel* a program, *vary* a system device active, stop accepting new work, etc. Commands are acted upon by *systems software* and should not be confused with *instructions* in programs.

command language The set of *commands* that are valid for a particular system, or in other words what you can tell a system to do, and how to tell it.

command level Referring to the ability to control a system via *commands*. The users of an *on-line system*, for example, can use the services it offers, but they cannot tell the system to shut itself down; therefore, they do not have access at the command level. The command level is normally available only to computer operators.

command list See *CLIST*.

command processor The portion of a *software* system that receives, interprets, and acts upon *commands*.

comment A *statement* included in a *source program* for information only. Comments are (or ought to be) used extensively to explain what the program is doing, so that someone can later understand it without having to decipher the *instructions* themselves. Comments are ignored when the program is translated into *executable* form.

COMMON An area in *memory* shared by two or more programs for the purpose of passing information. With program *chaining*, for example, the first program might calculate some values and store them in COMMON, then stop. When the second program starts, it retrieves those values from COMMON and uses them as it runs.

common carrier A business firm such as the telephone company that sells communications services to the public.

common ground See *chassis ground*.

communications channel A medium for communications such as a telephone line.

communications control unit See *CCU*.

compaction The rearrangement of data on a *disk* to open up large areas of free space. As data are written and later erased from a disk, especially during heavy processing, they tend to get scattered all over the *pack* in small pieces (*extents*). This phenomenon, called *fragmentation*, significantly slows data storage and retrieval and thus the overall performance of the system. Compaction attempts to resolve this problem by reassembling fragmented extents and consolidating them. Compaction is also called *squishing*. It is done by a special *utility* program.

comparator An electronic *logic circuit* that compares two values and sets an indicator according to its findings. In general, every comparison of *x* to *y* has one of three possible outcomes; less than, equal to, or greater than. Comparator circuits furnish the *hardware* basis for *decisions* made in *software*.

compatibility The ability of *hardware* and/or *software* components to work together. Compatibility is a serious and never-ending issue in data processing, and the driving force behind a vast effort to develop standard *interfaces*, yet it has been only partially successful.

compiled program A computer program that has been, or can be, translated by a *compiler* into a *machine language*.

compiler A *utility* that translates programs from a human-oriented *programming language* into a machine-oriented form. Compilers are extremely sophisticated programs that must not only be able to translate complex *statements* into *machine instructions* but must also resolve symbols, develop *memory* management based upon the activities of the program being compiled, and diagnose and report errors in the program as written. A compiler is dedicated exclusively to a specific programming language; no single compiler, for example, translates both *COBOL* and *FORTRAN*. Likewise, a compiler only produces machine code for a specific *CPU* type; the output from a Honeywell compiler will not run on an IBM system. The input data for a compiler are a *source program* written in a human-oriented language. Its output is an *object module* consisting of machine instructions for the *target* CPU. Usually, final preparation of an object module is done by another utility called a *linkage editor*, whose output is called a *load module*. Compilers differ from the other major type of language translator, *interpreters*, in that a compiler processes the source program one time to place it in executable form, whereas an interpreter translates the source program each time the program runs.

compiler listing A report produced by a *compiler* containing an annotated listing of the *source* program along with other information useful to a programmer.

compiler toggle A *parameter* passed to a compiler that turns on some special feature or otherwise controls the manner in which it operates.

complement To flip every *bit* in a *byte* to its opposite setting; all 1s become Øs and vice versa. Thus, the complement of the byte 1111ØØØ1 is ØØØØ111Ø. When used as a noun, the term means "the opposite."

completion code See *condition code*.

component failure impact analysis See *CFIA*.

compound statement In a *programming language*, a single instruction that contains two or more instructions that could be used separately. The following is a compound statement in BASIC:

' IF X = Y THEN PRINT X ELSE GOTO 1000

This is compound because IF ... THEN ... is one instruction, PRINT is another, and GOTO is yet another, all three of which could stand alone.

compress (1) To condense data in some fashion so that they occupy less storage space, e.g., converting numerics to *BCD* or replacing space characters with a single *byte* that can later be exploded back into the original number of space characters.

(2) To reduce the size of a *file* by moving all *records* forward into the spaces formerly occupied by deleted records.

(3) Same as *compaction*.

computer A machine that processes information. More specifically, a machine that accepts information, applies procedures defined by a program of instructions furnished in advance, and supplies the results of those procedures.

computer-aided design See *CAD*.

computer-aided instruction See *CAI*.

computer-aided manufacturing See *CAM*.

computerization The application of a computer to an activity formerly done by other means. Synonymous with *mechanization*; also sometimes with *automation*.

computer literacy A buzz word that broadly encompasses an understanding of computers and how to apply them to the solution of problems.

computer-managed instruction See *CMI*.

computer output microfilm See *COM*.

concatenate To connect together two or more physical *files* so that they are treated as one logical file. For example, during billing the invoice files for each business day are concatenated so that they can be processed as one large collection of invoices.

concentrator See *multiplexer*.

concurrent execution The ability of a computer system to have two or more separate and unrelated programs running at the same time. The *CPU* works on a program for a time, then sets it aside and works on another, etc. Eventually, it returns to the first program and picks up where it left off. This is made possible by the fact that a CPU processes data much faster than its *peripherals* operate. Also called *multiprogramming*.

conditional assembly A means of controlling whether or not certain portions of an *assembly language* program are translated into *machine language* during the process of *assembly*. Used to install or skip features in *software* written in assembly language. At the start of the program, a *Boolean* value relating to an optional feature is specified as TRUE or FALSE. Within the program where the *instructions* for that feature occur, a *directive* tells the assembler to check the Boolean value. If it is not TRUE, the instructions for the feature are ignored.

conditional branch An *instruction* that causes execution to jump elsewhere in the program if a certain condition is encountered as a result of a comparison. As an example, in *BASIC*:

300 IF X = Y THEN GOTO 1000

is a conditional branch because execution jumps to line 1000 if two variables X and Y are equal; if they are not, the condition is not met and execution "falls through" to the line following 300. Often called *IF . . . THEN . . . constructs*, conditional branches form the basis for decision making in programs.

conditional no-op See *CNOP*.

condition code A numeric *code* furnished to the operator by a program as it ends, indicating the reason ("condition") that caused it to stop. A condition code Ø means the program completed normally; other codes indicate various error conditions. Generally, the higher the condition code, the more serious the error. Also called *return code*, or *completion code*.

configuration   The relationship of data-processing elements to each other. A *hardware* configuration describes the way various devices in a system are electronically connected.

connector   (1) In *hardware*, a plug or receptacle for electrically joining cables and/or devices.
   (2) On *flow charts*, a symbol indicating that the flow jumps elsewhere on the diagram.

connector block   Similar to a *barrier strip*, but larger.

connect time   The total period of time during a transmission when an open communications path exists between two points, whether it is actually in use or not. In a telephone call, the period from when the called telephone's handset is lifted until it is hung up again.

console   The "command position" at which an operator controls a computer system. Ordinarily consists of a keyboard, a *video display*, certain special switches or other controls, and sometimes a printer.

conspicuous computing   A disparaging term that plays on "conspicuous consumption." Refers to an organization (or an individual) that makes a point of showing off how technologically advanced it is, as in putting a fancy terminal on the receptionist's desk or a glass wall between the reception room and the computer room, to impress.

constant   A value in a computer program that does not change.

construct   (Accent on first syllable) A method of organizing the logic of a computer program. See *loop* and *IF . . . THEN . . . ELSE*; also *structured programming*.

contact closure   A method of signaling analogous to a light switch: power on or power off.

contamination   The placement of data in the wrong place in *memory*, thus resulting in the *overlaying* of valid information or program *code* and producing bizarre results from continued processing.

contention   Uncontrolled competition for a single resource by several independent devices or programs. For instance, in *multiprogramming* several programs might try to use the same *disk drive* concurrently with the result that they all run very slowly. These programs are said to be "in contention."

context editor   A program that lets a computer user view and change data stored in a *file*.

contiguous   Relating to the placement of data on a *disk*, wherein the entire *file* is physically written in consecutive *blocks*, without *fragmentation* into *extents*.

contingency plan   A plan of action developed in advance for dealing with a potential emergency. In data processing, a set of detailed procedures to be followed in case of power failure, a fire in the computer room, etc.

continuation line   A secondary instruction line in a program. In some *high-level programming languages*, if an instruction contains too many characters for one line of print it may overflow to the next (continuation) line.

continuity   The ability of a communications channel to carry a signal from one to the other. A continuity test checks a line to make sure it is not broken.

continuous carrier   A *carrier* signal sent at all times during a communications connection, whether or not actual data are being transmitted.

continuous form A preprinted business form that repeats on each page, with the bottom of one page attached to the top of the next (a *fanfold*) so that they can be fed through a printer.

control block A unit of information by which *software* keeps track of a resource under its control. When a program *opens* a *file*, for example, it creates a file control block in which are noted the name and *address* of the file, its *attributes*, and other information needed to process the data in the file. The control block is actually a means of communication between the program and the *operating system*, both of which are involved in file operations and both of which use and maintain the same control block in order to remain in synchronization concerning the status of that file.

control code Information sent to a device to cause an action, rather than as data. See *carriage control character*.

CONTROL key A button on a keyboard similar to a SHIFT key in that it has no effect unless held down while another key is operated. Instead of shifting the depressed key to upper case, however, the CONTROL key causes it to generate a nongraphic character recognized by a computer as a *control code*.

control lead A character or sequence of characters sent to a device to alert it that the information following is a *control code* and not data.

controller Same as *control unit*.

control section (1) The portion of a computer program that contains *instructions* to be executed. Abbreviated CSECT.

(2) The portion of the *CPU* that executes *machine language instructions*. See *CPU*.

control total A running subtotal which is often used to trigger some action, kept by a program as it executes. For example, after processing 100 *records*, write them to a *file*. Also used in the sense of *audit total*.

control unit A *peripheral* device that controls other peripherals, thus relieving the *CPU* of time-consuming routine tasks. For instance, a control unit might manage several *disk drives*, acting upon instructions from the CPU and coordinating the various activities required to read and write data. A control unit is usually a small, special-purpose computer.

conventions Agreed-upon standards and disciplines with regard to *software*; e.g., *file* naming conventions govern the method and structure of naming files used at a particular data-processing site, so that the first two characters indicate whether it is a test or a production file, the next two indicate the *application system* the file belongs to, etc.

conversational mode A method of operation in which a user and a computer conduct a "conversation" or "dialog" via questions and answers, programmers can enter and test programs at a keyboard device, etc., with the computer acting immediately on information coming from the keyboard. Also called *interactive mode*.

cookbook A step-by-step document describing how to install and use a *software* product or accomplish other complex tasks.

coolant distribution unit See *CDU*.

coordinate addressing The use of XY coordinates to specify a location, most often the row and column where a character is to appear on a *video display screen*.

coprocessor A special-purpose *processor chip* that works in conjunction with a primary *CPU* to speed up time-consuming operations. A math coprocessor, for example, contains *hardware* circuitry to do *floating-point arithmetic*, calculate logarithms, etc., without a lot of "number crunching" by the main processor.

copy   To transfer data from one *file* to another so that the second file is a duplicate of the first.

core   Another name for *memory*, based upon a now-obsolete technology that used magnetic rings ("cores") to store *bits*. The term "memory" can mean either internal memory or an external *storage medium*; "core" always means internal memory.

core dump   A printout of the contents of *memory* used by programmers to diagnose the cause of a *software* failure.

core image   A visual representation of *memory*.

correspondence printer   A printer that produces typewriterlike copy. Also called letter-quality or letter-perfect printer.

corrupt   To destroy or alter information so that its validity is dubious. When a program *calls* the *operating system*, for example, it must first save the contents of important *registers* because when control returns from the operating system, the registers will be corrupted, i.e., their contents may be different than before the call, leading to unpredictable results.

counter   A *memory* location set up and maintained by a program for the purpose of counting certain occurrences. For an example of a counter, see *loop*.

coupled systems   Two or more computer systems electronically attached to each other. See *loosely coupled* and *tightly coupled*.

courseware   Computer programs written for educational purposes, as in *Computer-Aided Instruction*. Usually *interactive*.

CP   See *channel program*.

CPE   Customer Premises Equipment.

CPI Characters per inch. Refers to the density of data stored on *magnetic tape*. See also *bpi*.

CP/M® Stands for Control Program/Microcomputers, the most prevalent microcomputer *operating system*. Versions are sold for most popular small computers, enabling *software* to be moved with little or no modification among greatly differing machines. (® Registered trademark of Digital Research, Inc.)

CPS Characters per second. The speed at which information is transmitted over a communications *medium*.

CPU Central Processing Unit. The "brain" and thus the focal point of a computer. A CPU consists of two functional areas, the *arithmetic/logic unit* (ALU) and the *control section* (CS), both of which are inextricably linked with internal *memory*. The control section fetches *machine language instructions* from memory, converting them into the appropriate electronic signals to bring about the actions implied by each instruction. It directly controls the ALU and, via the *bus* and other circuits, indirectly controls every function and device associated with the computer.

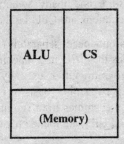

The ALU performs all manipulations of data according to signals furnished by the control section. The ALU consists of several small, high-speed memory devices called *registers*, in which data are temporarily held while being processed. A register holds from one to four *bytes*, depending upon the design of the CPU, the size of the register determining the *word length* of the computer. Under the direction of the control section, data are moved from memory into an ALU register where they are added to the contents of another register, compared with some value, modified, or otherwise manipulated according to the program's instructions. The results of the action are then moved, again under orders from the control unit, back to memory. The ALU also contains certain special-purpose registers used exclusively by the control section, e.g., the *Program Counter* ("PC register"), which tells the control section at which *address* to find the next instruction.

It is through the interaction of the CPU's two major components and the memory that all work within a computer is done.

CPU bound Refers to a program that does an enormous amount of calculation or internal shuffling of data, such that the limiting factor of system performance is the speed of the *CPU* and the *memory*. Normally, the CPU spends much of its time waiting for *disks* and other *peripherals* to complete actions; in a CPU-bound job the opposite is true. Business programs such as *sorts* and many scientific programs that compute complex equations are CPU bound.

CPUID (Letters pronounced separately) An identification number that identifies the *CPU* in a machine-readable format on demand by a program. Often used by *software* vendors who charge on a per-machine basis for the use of their software to prevent a customer from running the software on a different machine. CPUIDs are found only on large *mainframe* computers.

CR Carriage Return. A *control code* that repositions the print mechanism (or *cursor*) at the start of the line.

crash An abrupt and disorderly halt. In a system crash, the entire computer system stops working and all work in progress is lost.

CRC Cyclical Redundancy Check. A *block check character* calculated by adding the first *bit* of the first *byte* to the second bit of the second byte to the . . . eighth bit of the eighth byte to the first bit of the ninth, etc., "spiraling" through the block. A similar process occurs for each bit position, so that an entire check character is built. Used to determine whether a block of data contains errors. See *block check character*; also *ACK*.

crimp connection A method for joining a connector to a wire in which the connector is crimped around the wire to provide an electrical contact and mechanical strength.

cross assembler An *assembler* program run on one computer type to produce *machine language* for a different *CPU* type.

crossbar switch A highly complex electromechanical switching matrix used to connect any two out of perhaps thousands of devices. Frequently used as a telephone switching center. Each device is represented by a row and a column, with an electrical contact at each intersection. To connect two devices, the switch is closed at the appropriate intersection of one device's row and the other's column.

cross compiler Similar to *cross assembler*.

cross-connect To join two or more cables together at a *connecting block*.

crossfooting An accounting method used to check ledgers and other arrays of numeric information for addition errors. All the rows are added up and all the columns are added up. The row sums and the column sums are then totaled and compared. If there are no errors the sums will be the same. Often similarly used in financial programs run on computers.

cross-reference listing A report produced by a *compiler* or *assembler* showing the names of *symbolic variables* used in a program and the *memory addresses* assigned to them. Useful for *debugging* a program. Abbreviated XREF.

crosstalk   A phenomenon occurring in communications, wherein a portion of one signal interferes with another, i.e., you can hear someone else's conversation. An annoyance in voice communications and potentially disastrous in data communications.

CRT   (Letters pronounced separately) Cathode-Ray Tube. In the pure sense, a projection tube used to display a television picture or text and graphics from a computer by sweeping an electronic beam back and forth and bombarding a phosphorescent substance to make it glow (see *raster scan*). In vernacular, any *video display terminal* associated with a computer. Looks like a television set with a typewriter keyboard.

cryogenics   A technology involving superchilled substances at temperatures close to absolute zero. Applies to computer science because at extremely low temperatures conductors lose all resistance to the flow of electricity. This opens the way for the design of conductors the width of one electron that operate at the speed of light, i.e., the maximum limit of technology. At the moment, too exotic to be practical, but work progresses.

CS   Control Section of a *central processor*. See *CPU*.

CSECT   Control SECTion of a computer program, containing the instructions that constitute the program. Pronounced "see-sect."

CSW   See *channel status word*.

CTC   See *channel-to-channel adaptor*.

CU   See *control unit*.

current loop   See *contact closure*.

cursor A small mobile "blip" of light on a *CRT* screen indicating where the next character will appear. Corresponds to the print mechanism on a typewriter.

cursor arrows Arrows marked on the buttons on a *CRT* keyboard that control the movement of the *cursor*. The arrows indicate which way the buttons make the cursor move, hence the term.

custodian A term used in connection with *data security* to describe the person or organization responsible for the physical maintenance and safeguarding of data, e.g., *tape reels*. The custodian might or might not have access to the contents of these data.

customer engineer A repairer of computer equipment, usually employed by a vendor or by a repair service. Often called a CE, also an FE (for *Field Engineer*).

customer owned and maintained See *COAM*.

cutover As a verb, to place in active use. As a noun, the cutover is the point when testing ends and day-to-day usage commences.

cut-sheet printer A printer designed to produce output on individual (unjoined) pieces of paper rather than on the usual *fanfold* paper used in computer printers.

CXR Abbreviation for *carrier*.

cybernetics The quasi science of applying principles of human thought and brain processes to computers.

cycle One phase in the execution of an *instruction*, usually corresponding to a "tick" of the system *clock*. Every *machine instruction* takes several cycles to complete: request the next instruction from memory, bring it in to the *control section*, interpret it, send out electronic signals, etc. In the Intel 8080 microprocessor, for example, every instruction takes from four to fourteen cycles to execute, the average being about seven, meaning that the system clock "ticks" that many times to perform a given machine-level task. The expression "to eat cycles" or "to burn up cycles" means to use some portion of the computer's total capacity for processing, usually with the implication that the use is unproductive.

In a larger sense, a cycle is one *iteration* of any repetitive process performed by a computer.

cycle bound   Similar to *CPU bound*, except that it usually means the work load has exceeded the ability of the present computer to process it all.

cycle stealing   In a computer using *dynamic RAM*, the charges of electricity representing data stored in *memory* tend to decay. This makes it necessary periodically to read and re-write the data before the charges fade and the data are lost. In cycle stealing, the *CPU* is occasionally interrupted to perform this memory-servicing task, thereby "stealing *cycles*" that would otherwise be used in processing data.

cycle timing diagram   An engineering diagram showing, for a *machine language instruction*, the activity that occurs in each *cycle* of the *clock* during execution of the instruction.

cyclical parity   See *CRC*.

cyclical redundancy check   See *CRC*.

cylinder   A unit of storage space on a large *disk drive*. A cylinder might be all the *tracks* number 9 on the upper and lower surfaces of each *platter* in the *pack*, thus conceptually forming a cylinder-shaped unit of storage. See *disk storage*.

D

DAA (Letters pronounced separately) Data Access Arrangement. A device furnished by the telephone company to serve as a point of connection between the telephone network and a *COAM modem*.

D/A convertor Digital-to-Analog Convertor. A device that builds an *analog* signal from *digital* data. Very rare.

daisy chain A group of communicating devices connected in a closed loop so that each one receives and passes all messages to the next station in the chain until the message finally arrives at its destination.

daisywheel A type of print mechanism in which a wheel with character images spins in front of the paper, and when the character to be printed is in the proper position a hammer drives the *slug* against the paper. Used in high-quality *correspondence printers*, because it produces typewriter-quality copy.

damaged pack A *disk drive* that is rendered partially unusable by a scratch on the recording surface or by a serious *software* error that has caused control information on the disk to become unreadable.

DASD (Pronounced daz-dee) Acronym for Direct-Access Storage Device. A collective term for a group of *disk devices*, as in "How much DASD do you have?" or "We need to increase our DASD." In a purer sense, a DASD is any storage device that can immediately read or write anywhere on its recording surface. This contrasts with non-direct-access storage such as *tape*, in which a laborious and time-consuming process of physically positioning the recording *medium* precedes any read/write operation. In DASD every place on the surface is *addressable* and the read/write head can be electro-mechanically moved to an exact spot at high speed. Thus, the term DASD properly encompasses not only *disks*, but *drum storage* and *floppy disks* as well.

DAT   Acronym for Dynamic Address Translation. The ability of a computer to convert a *relative address* in a *machine instruction* into an *absolute address* in *memory* while a program is running. See *base register*.

data   In a pure sense, raw information presented to a computer for processing. In general usage, any information under the control of a computer system.

data-access arrangement   See *DAA*.

data administrator   A management person within a data-processing organization who has the responsibility of overseeing all aspects of data management, such as the development and enforcement of *standards*, the design of *data bases*, the proper usage and security of data, etc.

data base   A *file* containing information on a particular subject or subjects. For example, in a data base system, there are many such files, each one devoted to a particular kind of data element, so that one data base holds all the employee names, another all their addresses, another all their dates of birth, etc.

The relationships of elements among data bases are established by *pointers*, indicators showing where to find other elements related to the specific employee. Thus, for each name there is a pointer showing where to find that person's home address, and included with the address is another pointer indicating the location of the date of birth, etc. By following these *chained pointers*, it is possible very quickly to run down every item of information associated with a specific employee without having to search through records pertaining to other employees.

The pointer structure of data bases is usually more complex than simple chaining as described. For some data elements there are often several pointers that allow the search to skip unwanted items and go directly to the desired element. In the employee name data base, the first pointer associated with a name points to the home address, but a second pointer indicates where to find the home phone number. When the user asks the *software* to provide Joe Blow's phone number, the search uses the second pointer and goes directly to it, thus bypassing the chain. This dramatically reduces *overhead* by eliminating lengthy searches and makes all data elements almost instantly accessible.

Data bases are often shared by different *application systems*. In a bank, for instance, where a customer might have a checking account, a savings account, and a car loan, the data base structures for each of those applications would share the name and address data bases and perhaps others as well. This eliminates the duplication of information in computer files and makes it easier to ensure that all information is consistent (you only have to make a change in one place).

These efficiencies are accomplished at the expense of simplicity. Pointer structures are often horribly complicated, and if any one pointer is incorrect, the integrity of all data becomes questionable. For this reason, data bases are usually controlled, accessed, and updated by a special software system called a *data base management system* (DBMS).

data base administration The designing and setting up of *data bases* by a *data administration*.

data base management system Abbreviated DBMS. A comprehensive and usually very complex *software* system for controlling, reading, and updating *data bases*. A DBMS is a form of *access method*, the most important function of which is to deal with the *pointer* structures of data bases.

data bus A set of the electrical conductors that carry data from one internal part of a computer to another.

data capture A method of acquiring data for input to a computer. For example, electronic cash registers perform data capture by collecting the stock numbers of items sold so that at some point the inventory records can be updated.

data carrier detect See *carrier detect*.

data center A computer room and its support facilities.

data channel A phone line or other communications facility used for data transmission.

data check A message issued by a computer program when it detects that input data are "bad," e.g., in the wrong format, values are too high, or too low, etc. Often a data check causes the program to *abend* (stop unexpectedly).

data compression See *compression*.

data definition statement A *statement* in *job control language* that identifies and describes a *file* that will be used. Usually called a DD statement.

data dictionary A cross-reference *file* used in connection with a *data base management system*, which correlates data names with data bases. In the discussion of data bases above, if a programmer or user furnishes the name PHONE.NUMBER, the DBMS will look it up in the data dictionary to obtain the actual file name of the data base containing phone numbers.

data division One of the four required *divisions* of a *COBOL* program, in which all *variables* used in the program are named and described.

data entry   A function such as *keypunching* to capture data in a form suitable to be fed into a computer.

data entry system   Usually refers to a small computer that captures data, puts it into a predetermined format, and collects it in *batches* to be passed to a computer.

data patch panel   A plugboard arrangement by which lines and *modems* can be switched around by patching with double-ended cables, and/or a monitoring device such as a *data scope* that can be plugged into a circuit to analyze a signal.

data processing   The collection, arrangement, and refinement of data into a usable form, or to achieve a particular result, through the use of computers.

data reduction   (1) The process of picking through a large volume of data to extract and refine a subset of them for some particular purpose, usually a special study.
(2) The statistical summarization of data.

data representation code   A means of representing *alphanumerics* and other graphic symbols with *binary* numbers. See *code*.

data scope   A special *video display* device that monitors a communications channel and displays the content of the information being transmitted over it. Usually also includes a tape recorder that records and plays back signals.

data security   A broad term encompassing the safeguarding of data owned by an organization, both as to physical protection against theft, environmental damage, and loss, and controlling access to sensitive information by employees of the organization. As it becomes more widely understood that data are a vital corporate resource, data security becomes a more important aspect of data-processing management.

data set   (1) An IBM term synonymous with *file*, i.e., a set of data treated as a unit.

(2) A Bell System term synonymous with *modem*, i.e., a device for *modulating* and *demodulating* digital signals sent over a communications facility.

data set organization   A broad *attribute* describing the way a *file* is structured, e.g., *partitioned*, *sequential*, etc.

data set ready (Abbreviated DSR)   A control indicator sent from a *modem* to the machine attached to it, which turns on to signal the machine that the modem is ready to transmit and receive data.

data terminal ready   An indicator sent from a machine to a *modem* to signal that the machine is prepared to transmit and receive data.

data transfer rate   The speed at which information moves between devices, usually expressed in characters per second (cps) or in *bits* per second (bps).

dB   Abbreviation for decibel. A logarithmic ratio of audible signal strengths between two sounds or two levels of the same sound. In other words, it is the unit of measure used to express differences in loudness. For every 3 dB, the loudness changes by a factor of 2: -3 dB is half as loud, $+3$ dB is twice as loud. A 1-dB change in sound level is just detectable by the human ear.

DB25 connector   A standard connector for microcomputer printers that use the parallel ("Centronics") *interface*.

DBA   See *data base administration*.

DBMS   See *data base management system*.

dBRN   *Decibels* with Reference to Noise. A measurement in *dB* of the *signal-to-noise ratio* on a communications line.

DCC   Device Cluster Controller. See *clustered devices*.

DCE   Data Communications Equipment.

DDD Direct-Distance Dialing. The ability of a telephone subscriber to place a long-distance call without assistance.

DDP See *distributed data processing*.

DD statement See *data definition statement*.

dead letter box In data communications *software*, especially *message switching* systems, a *file* for capturing undeliverable messages.

deadlock A situation in which two *software* systems that exchange messages are both "hung up" waiting for a message from the other.

deadly embrace Same as *deadlock*.

dead man switch An electrical switch that activates some function if released.

deallocation The opposite of *allocation*: the release of a resource by a program when it no longer needs it. For example, if a program needs to write a *file* to *tape*, it allocates a *tape drive*; when the file has been written out, the program deallocates the drive by notifying the *operating system* that the drive is no longer needed. The operating system can then assign the tape drive to another program.

debouncing A delay built into *software* to prevent false input from a keyboard due to the bouncing of keys. On old or heavily used keyboards, the springs under keys get tired so that when a key pops back up after use, it bounces and sends extra signals. Debouncing disables the software's ability to accept a character for a few milliseconds after receiving one.

debug To research and fix *bugs* (errors) in a program.

debugger A program that aides in the *debugging* process. A debugger is *interactive* and lets a programmer at a *video display* view his or her program as it executes, stopping it and examining results as they are being produced, tracing events as they occur etc., to enable the programmer to find the errors.

decay The dissipation of static electricity representing *bits* in some types of *memory* which, if allowed to occur, would result in loss of the data. See *refresh*; also *cycle stealing*.

decibel See *dB*.

decimal The conventional *base* 10 numbering system used by people.

decipher To remove the effects of a secret *encryption* code or *scrambling* from data, restoring the code to an intelligible form.

decision In *software*, a comparison, the results of which affect the subsequent action of the program.

decision support system An interrelated system of computer programs and data specifically designed to assist managers in making informed decisions.

decision table A matrix symbolically showing all possible outcomes of a given problem. Used in designing computer programs.

deck A group of related *punched cards*; analogous to *file*.

declaration A *statement* at the start of a computer program that has a *global* effect on the program, e.g., declaring values associated with symbolically named constants, data *types* used in the program, the dimensions of *matrices*, and other fixed information that remains in effect for the entire program.

decode Same as *decipher*.

decollator (Emphasis on first syllable, pronounced ''deck'') A mechanical device that *bursts* multipart computer printouts.

decrement To subtract one from a value. Contrasts with *increment*.

decryption Same as *decipher*.

dedicated Assigned to one function or one system. When an entire *disk drive* is given to a particular *application system* for the storage of its data, it is said to be a dedicated drive; a "hot line" between two locations is a dedicated line.

default A value automatically assigned or an action automatically taken unless another is specified. In a communications system, for example, data might be automatically divided into *blocks* of 80 characters each unless the user tells the system to use a different block length; 80 characters is therefore the default block size.

deferred mount Ordinarily when a program that needs a *tape* starts to run, the tape is *mounted* (placed on the *drive*) right away, even though it might not be needed until later. A deferred mount postpones the tape mount until it is actually needed.

degausser A device that removes magnetically recorded data from a *storage medium* by applying a magnetic field.

degradation A decline in a computer system's performance.

degraded mode The condition of a system due to *degradation*. "The system is running in degraded mode because half the *disk drives* are down."

deinstall To remove a *hardware* or *software* feature from active service.

delay circuit An electronic circuit that deliberately delays the delivery of a signal for a preset interval. Used for timing and synchronizing.

delay distortion A communications term. The garbling of a signal's content because part of the signal moves more slowly through a line than other parts.

delete In *file* management, to remove all references to a file and thus make the space it occupies available for other uses. Same as *erase*.

delimiter A character that sets apart a unit of information. In "this, that, and the other thing," the commas are delimiters.

demarc Short for *demarcation*.

demarcation A physical point defining the boundary of responsibility. If you lease a line from the telephone company and plug it into your own *modem*, the demarcation is at the connector; the phone company's responsibility ends there.

demodulate To convert voicelike tones received from a phone line into digital *bits* for input to a machine. The opposite process is called *modulation*. Forms the basis for most data communications.

demount To remove a magnetic *storage medium* from a device that reads or writes on it, e.g., to demount a *tape* is to remove the reel of tape from the *drive*.

demountable pack A type of *disk drive* in which the *pack*, or physical *storage medium*, can be removed and replaced with another by a computer operator.

density The amount of information stored per physical unit of area or space on a magnetic *storage medium* such as *tape*.

dependency A sequence of program execution in which one *job* has to have completed before another can begin. If JOB1 collects and organizes data and JOB2 processes it, a dependency exists.

dequeue The selection of an item for a *queue* (a prioritized list of things to be done). Contrasts with *enqueue*.

descender The below-the-line tail of letters such as q and y.

descending sort An arrangement of information starting with the highest and going to the lowest, e.g., reverse alphabetic order.

desk check To read a computer program and check it for errors before entering it into the computer.

despooler *Software* that reads information waiting to be printed from the *spool file* and routes it to a printer.

device cluster A group of devices (usually *terminals*) that share a *controller*.

device end pending A *hardware* error in which a *peripheral* fails to respond when *addressed* by the *CPU*. Usually indicates that the device has become inoperative.

device-name assignment The use of a symbolic name rather than an *address* to refer to a *peripheral* device. For example, the *disk* holding the *operating system* is often called SYSRES (for SYStem RESidence). Device-name assignment permits this device to be called SYSRES when communicating with the system; *software* cross-references it to the actual address.

diagnostic message A brief explanation issued by a *compiler* or other software describing an error it has encountered.

diagnostics Usually *software* that performs tests and issues descriptions of any problems or errors it finds. Used to check *hardware, data*, or anything else that is subject to failure.

dial backup A dial telephone line to be activated in case a point-to-point line fails, so that data can still be transmitted.

dialect A version of a *programming language* that generally resembles other versions, but differs in some respects. An example is BASIC, which is essentially the same for all systems, except that *file* statements differ from one version to another.

dialog   A question-and-answer session between a human and a computer system, usually conducted via a *CRT*.

dial-up circuit   A dial telephone line used to transmit data.

digital   Refers to the representation of information using *binary* numbers to symbolize characters or values. The vast majority of computers are digital machines because they can only work with information in a binary format.

digital circuit   A communications channel that carries data in a *digital* (rather than an *analog*, or tone) format. Digital circuits do not have *modems*, but they do usually have some sort of device to convert the digital pulses into a *bipolar* format, since pure digital signals tend to deteriorate rapidly.

digital communications link   See *digital circuit*.

digital computer   A computer designed to process information in *digital* (numeric) form. Most computers are digital.

digital PABX   Digital Private Automatic Branch eXchange. A computer-operated telephone switching system that treats voice signals internally as digital data.

digital pipe   See *digital circuit*.

digital repeater   A device placed in a communications path to reconstruct *digital* pulses, which tend to deteriorate as they move through long conductors.

digitizer   A device that derives *digital* data from a nondigital source. See *digitizing pad*.

digitizing pad   A flat bed on which a piece of paper can be laid. A special pen is then used to trace lines or plot individual points on the paper, producing *digital* data that are input to a computer. These data indicate the *X-Y* coordinates of the pen's location, thus creating a digital representation of a drawing or other graphic information.

DIMENSION A *programming language declaration* that describes an *array*, so that the language translator can assign *memory* for it. The statement DIMENSION X(12,6) declares an array named X that has twelve rows of six columns each.

diode An electronic component that permits current to flow through it in one direction, but not the other.

DIP Acronym for Dual In-line Package. A socket soldered to a *printed circuit board*, into which a *chip* can be plugged. A DIP socket facilitates the replacement of defective chips, holding down repair costs. It is a boxlike structure that stands above the board with a row of holes along the top of each long side into which the pins of the chip are inserted.

DIP switch A unit that plugs into a *DIP* socket, containing several small rocker-type switches. Often used to set *strapping options* on a *printed circuit board*.

direct access A *file* organization in which individual *records* may be read or written directly, without having to go through all the preceding records to reach the desired one. Also called *random access*. Contrasts with *sequential access*.

direct-access storage device See *DASD*.

direct-distance dialing See *DDD*.

directive See *assembler directive*.

direct memory access An *architectural* feature of some computers in which information read from *disk* is written directly to a specified location in *memory* without interrupting the *CPU*, or read from memory to disk without assistance from the CPU. This enables the CPU to attend to other tasks while awaiting completion of the disk operation.

directory On a *floppy disk*, a system *file* indicating the names and locations of all files contained in the *diskette*. On large disks, the directory is called a *VTOC*.

disassemble The opposite of *assemble*; to translate a program from *machine language* into *assembly language* so that it is easier for a human to understand.

disassembler A program that *disassembles machine language*.

disaster recovery A plan for dealing with a catastrophe at a data-processing center (fire, flood, tornado, etc.) with the objective of restoring service as soon as possible at an alternate location.

disc An alternate spelling for *disk*, preferred in England but seldom used in the United States.

disclaimer A clause associated with most *software* products to the effect that the software might not work in all installations and that the vendor is not responsible for business losses in the event that the software does not function as advertised.

discrete components Pieces of electronic *hardware* that are individually soldered to *printed circuit boards*, such as transistors, resistors, and capacitors.

disk A high-speed data storage device operating as a *peripheral* under control of a computer. A disk is a circular platter that rotates rapidly; in large systems it usually consists of several such platters sharing a common axis (a *disk pack*). Data are recorded as magnetic spots representing *bits*, written in concentric circles called *tracks*. A *read/write head* moves toward or away from the center of the disk, positioning itself over the tracks as directed by the *CPU* or disk *controller*. Disk storage is an essential feature of virtually all modern computer systems and the mainstay of data processing. In large computer systems, with dozens to hundreds of disk units, disk storage typically holds between 100 million and 2 billion characters per unit, with any data being accessible within thousandths of a second. Smaller but comparatively powerful disk units are available for microcomputers. See *Winchester disk*.

disk drive The physical *hardware* supporting *disk* storage.

diskette A small version of *disk* storage. A diskette is a single, flexible magnetic disk enclosed within a sealed envelope that inserts into a diskette drive. It works on the same principle as larger disk units, but it holds considerably fewer data: typically between 80,000 and a million *bytes*, depending on the size and the technology used. Diskettes come in two standard sizes, 5¼" and 8" diameter; some bear data on one side and some on both surfaces, thus accounting for the wide variation in capacity. Diskettes compensate for lack of capacity by being easily portable and inexpensive. They are widely used with mini- and microcomputers. Also called *floppy disk* and *flexible disk*.

disk operating system A computer *operating system* oriented toward heavy utilization of *disk* storage.

disk pack A group of *disk* storage platters attached to a common axis so that they rotate together and form a unit of disk storage within a *disk drive*. Also called a *spindle*.

dispatch To place a *job* in execution. Used in connection with large computer systems, in which the operator places jobs to be run in a *queue* and the *operating system* selects jobs based on their relative priorities. Dispatching is the process of selecting the next job and getting it ready to start.

dispatching priority A numeric indicator that establishes the importance of a particular *job*, so that the *operating system* can select the most important job from the *queue*. See *dispatch*.

displacement The number of character positions or *memory addresses* away from some point of reference. If the point of reference is address 1000 and an item of the data is at address 1058, its displacement is .58. Also called an *offset*.

disposition   The status of a *file* after being *closed* by a program, e.g., if an existing file, keep it or *delete* it.

distortion   The altering of a signal by various electrical phenomena as it passes through a communications facility which causes the signal to be received in a different form than when sent. A certain amount of distortion is acceptable and tolerated, but excessive distortion causes loss of data.

distributed data processing   The simultaneous use of several geographically separated computers connected by communications facilities to work on a problem. An engineer connected with computer A asks to have a complex equation solved; the program for this equation is on computer B which, in running it, obtains data from computer C, and then returns the results to the engineer at computer A.

distribution   An organizational unit within a data-processing center, responsible for distributing printed reports and other forms of computer output to the appropriate users.

distribution cable   An electrical conductor that feeds several branch circuits to distribute power or signals.

distribution frame   A point where several cables converge and signals are redistributed among them. For example, office buildings always have a distribution frame where telephone cables coming in from outside are *cross-connected* with inside cables to deliver phone service to specific instruments.

division   In a *COBOL* program there are four required divisions, or parts, called *identification, environment, data, and procedure* divisions, with rules governing the contents of each.

DMA   See *direct memory access*.

documentation   Comprehensive written information about a program or *software* system, explaining what it does, how it works, how to operate it, the meaning of any *diagnostic messages* it issues, etc.

dog A digit in the hexadecimal numbering system that is equivalent in value to 13. Written as X'D'.

DO loop In *FORTRAN* and some other *programming languages*, a *loop* (a sequence of *instructions* repeated some number of times) begins with the statement 'DO.' The term DO loop has become a generic name for any loop whose *iterations* (repetitions) are counted.

dorfed up Damage to a *file* that renders its contents useless or at best questionable. "The file got dorfed up when the system *crashed* as data were being written to it."

DOS See *disk operating system*.

dot addressable The capability on a *video display screen* or a *dot-matrix printer* to specify (*address*) individual dots that form character images. This gives programs the ability to construct special characters and highly refined *graphics*.

dot graphics Pictures and other non-*alphanumeric* information formed from closely packed visual dots on a *CRT* screen or a *dot-matrix* printer.

dot-matrix character formation A technique for forming character images by the use of dots. The area a character can occupy is called a cell, and it consists of a matrix of some predetermined number of dots arranged in rows and columns. A 5×7 dot-matrix cell has five vertical columns and seven horizontal rows of dots. Fig. 1 is a blank space with all dots (represented by periods) turned off; Fig. 2 uses Xs to indicate dots that are turned on to form the digit 2. The number of dots in a character matrix affect the resolution, or quality, of the characters. That is, 7×9 is better than 5×7, which are the two most common resolutions. Dot-matrix character formation is most often used on *CRT* screens and on high-speed printers. See also *raster scan*.

DOT-MATRIX CHARACTER FORMATION

```
· · · · ·        . X X X .
· · · · ·        X . . . X
· · · · ·        . . X X .
· · · · ·        . X . . .
· · · · ·        X . . . .
· · · · ·        X X X X X
· · · · ·        . . . . .
   Fig. 1            Fig. 2
```

dot-matrix printer   A fast and relatively inexpensive type of printer that uses *dot-matrix character formation* to produce copy. The print mechanism consists of a vertical row of wires aimed at the paper. As the print head moves across the paper, high-speed solenoids drive the wires against an inked ribbon to make printed dots that form the character images. Speeds of 200 characters per second are not uncommon in printers costing well under $1000. Very popular as microcomputer printers.

double density   A technique for writing twice as many data per unit of storage space as the standard. Usually applied to *floppy disk* storage.

double-precision arithmetic   Computations performed within a computer that use twice as many *bits* as normal calculations. Ensures a greater degree of accuracy when dealing with very small or very large numbers, but dramatically slows execution.

double-sided media   *Storage media* that hold data on both surfaces. The term is usually applied to *floppy disks*.

doubleword   A unit of *memory* containing twice as many *bytes* of data as a *CPU register* can hold.

DO WHILE   A term used in *structured programming* to describe a *loop* that is repeated while some stated condition remains in effect. The following example is in *Pascal*:

```
COUNT := Ø;
LOOPS := 25;
WHILE COUNT < LOOPS DO
     BEGIN
          [Some operation occurs here];
          COUNT := COUNT + 1;
     END;
```

In this example, COUNT is initially set at Ø, and LOOPS specifies the number of times the loop will be repeated, or 25. The WHILE *statement* establishes the DO WHILE condition (while COUNT is less than LOOPS). The loop itself occurs between the BEGIN and END statements; at the end of the loop, COUNT is increased by one and, while it remains less than LOOPS, execution jumps back to the BEGIN statement and repeats. When COUNT equals LOOPS (i.e., reaches 25) the loop is not repeated, since the stated condition of DO WHILE is no longer true, and execution moves to the statement following END.

down Out of service. "The computer system is down."

down-line loading When a computer automatically updates a *file* on another computer using data communications.

download Same as *down-line loading*.

downtime The amount of time a system is *down*, especially during periods when it ought to be *up*. Data-processing centers set aside some periods for scheduled downtime, during which preventive maintenance is performed, but downtime in general is considered bad and is usually a measurement by which to judge the performance of the data center.

DPC See *data-processing center*.

driver A piece of *hardware* and/or *software* that controls other activities. A program driver is the same thing as a *backbone*. A video driver is the electronic circuitry that controls a *CRT* screen.

drum plotter   A computer-controlled device for drawing pictures, schematics, graphs, etc., on paper. So called because the paper is wrapped around a cylindrical drum. This drum then rotates back and forth at various speeds under a pen that slides to and fro, marking the paper.

drum printer   A type of high-speed *impact* printer often used in connection with large computer systems. So called because *slugs* for every graphic character are wrapped in a band around a large drum; there is one such band for every print position across the paper. The drum rotates rapidly behind the paper. As the character to be printed in a particular *column* passes behind the page, a hammer for that print position drives the paper and an inked ribbon back against the slug and prints its image. Characters are printed in no particular column order, but rather whenever the appropriate slug is in position. This is, therefore, a *line printer* because it prints a line at a time. Speeds of 3000 to 6000 lines per minute are common.

drum storage   A type of *direct-access storage device* that operates at extremely high speed. A cylinder spins past a group of fixed *read/write heads* that create tracks of data banding the drum. Each head is individually *addressable*, so that the only delay in gaining access to particular data is the rotational delay until the data pass under the head. At typical rotation speeds of 3600 rpm, this makes the drum the fastest type of mechanical storage device. Because of high cost, drum storage is found only in very large systems where it is used mainly for high-volume system control files.

DSDD   Double-Sided Double-Density.

DSECT   Dummy SECTion (or Data SECTion) of a program written in *assembly language*, in which the programmer specifies how the data workspace in *memory* is to be arranged.

DSR   See *data set ready*.

DSSD   Double-Sided Single-Density.

DTE   Data Terminal Equipment.

dual in-line package   See *DIP*.

dumb device   A device such as a communicating terminal that relies on the computer for all control functions and has no ability to do anything for itself. Most printers are dumb devices.

dummy file   A nonexistent *file* to which a program "thinks" it is writing output data. In fact, the data are simply being ignored, but signals indicating a successful file write are sent to the program each time the program outputs to the file. This is done to suppress the creation of files that are only needed on an occasional basis.

dummy parameter   A *parameter* that doesn't mean anything, but is included in a *command* or an *instruction* because the system expects it.

dummy record   Meaningless information; e.g., if a *block* consists of ten *records* and there are only nine to send, a dummy record of all *binary* zeros is included to fill the block length requirement.

dummy section   See *DSECT*.

dump   See *core dump*.

duplex   In communications, the ability to send and receive simultaneously over the same line. See also *half-duplex* and *full duplex*.

dyadic   In logic and mathematics, an *operator* that involves two values. An example of a dyadic operator is the plus sign (+), which implies the addition of two numbers.

dyadic processor   A type of exotic computer *architecture* in which two *CPUs* simultaneously run the same programs and work on the same data, comparing results. If different results occur, "tie-breaker" software attempts to determine which CPU is wrong and shuts down the one in error, or a third CPU intervenes. Likewise, if one CPU fails the other continues to process. A dyadic configuration slightly increases the reliability of processed results, moderately increases *uptime*, and vastly increases cost.

dynamic address translation See *DAT*.

dynamic allocation A programming technique in which, as the program runs, it calculates how much *memory, disk* space, etc., it needs under the circumstances, and handles the *allocation* of those resources itself. This saves the programmer the trouble of figuring out in advance how much to allocate, and it also makes more efficient use of system resources since people tend to overestimate resource requirements "just in case."

E

EAM Electrical Accounting Machine. An early term used to describe computers, and seldom heard anymore.

easy A digit in the hexadecimal numbering system that is equivalent in value to 14. Written as X'E'.

EBCDIC (pronounced "eb-si-dik" or sometimes "E-B-dik"). Abbreviation for Extended Binary Coded Decimal Interchange Code. An 8-*bit* code for representing *alphanumeric* information within a computer. EBCDIC is most widely used in large computer systems. See also *ASCII*.

echoplex A form of low-speed data transmission sometimes used between a keyboard device and a computer. When a key is struck on the keyboard, the character is sent over the line and echoed back to the sending device, where it is displayed on the screen or printed on paper.

echo suppressor A device built into telephone circuits that prevents echoes of transmitted signals from returning to the sending device and being interpreted as received data.

edit To check data for errors and (usually) to correct them.

editor A program that *edits* data. Interactive editors permit a terminal user to view stored information, alter it, and see the results. *Batch* editors process and check input data, weeding out detectable errors, as the first step of a batch *jobstream*.

EDP   Electronic Data Processing.

EFT   See *electronic funds transfer*.

egoless programming   A highly structured, disciplined, "formula"-oriented methodology for writing programs, the objective of which is to create standardized programs not subject to the individual whims of programmers. The underlying theory is that uniformity in programming makes it easier for others to *maintain* (modify and update) programs later.

EIA   Electronic Industries Association.

EIA interface   A standard physical and electronic connection between a communicating machine and a *modem*. The EIA standard has also been adapted for the connection of *peripherals* to microcomputers. Also called *RS-232*.

eject   To position the printing mechanism at the top of the next page, skipping the rest of the present page.

electronic funds transfer   The use of electronic means to move funds from one financial institution to another, or from one bank account to another, without paper documents.

electronic mail   The use of computerized *message switching* to send information from one person to another or from one organization to another.

electronics   The use of electricity to convey information.

elegant   An essentially meaningless buzz word popular chiefly with advocates of *structured programming*. It imbues more dignity than "slick" or "nifty," which is what it suggests.

element   (1) A piece or aspect of something, just as in common usage.

  (2) An item of information that is related to others, analogous to a *field* in a data *record*. See also *data base*.

ELSE   A catchall in a *conditional* (IF . . . THEN . . .)

statement in programming: IF X = Y THEN GOTO 1000 ELSE GOTO 2000. In this *BASIC* instruction, execution jumps to line 1000 if (and only if) X = Y, otherwise (ELSE) execution jumps to line 2000. Most *programming languages* have an ELSE statement.

empty shell   A fully prepared computer room awaiting the installation of data-processing equipment. Sometimes data-processing organizations build an empty shell in order to have a place ready in case the main data center becomes unusable because of fire, flood, or other disasters.

emulate   When one device behaves like another type of device, it is said to emulate it. Because of the vast proliferation of terminals and other system components in data processing, it is a common practice for new pieces of equipment to emulate certain more or less standard device types, even though there might be no resemblance between the emulator and the device it imitates. A minicomputer attached to a large *mainframe*, for example, might emulate an IBM 3270 *CRT* terminal. This is done so that special *software* does not have to be developed to support the device, since most *systems software* already includes the necessary support for a standard set of device types. Some emulating devices have options to emulate several other devices in order to widen the market appeal of the product.

emulation mode   When a device that has its own characteristics is instead set up to behave like a different device, it is said to be in emulation mode.

encipher   To scramble or otherwise alter data so that they are not readily usable unless the changes are first undone. This is done to protect data from disclosure, to send secret messages, etc.

encode   In general, to *encipher*. Also, occasionally, to convert printed information into a machine-readable format, as in *keypunching*.

encryption   The *enciphering* of information for purposes of security and secrecy.

encryption key   A group of *bytes* of data, themselves unintelligible, that hold the information required to *encipher* and *decipher* data according to some prearranged method.

endless loop   The endless repetition of a series of *instructions* due to a programming error, with no exit from the loop possible. The only way to stop an endless loop is to *cancel* the program or *reset* the computer system.

end-of-file mark   A character or *byte* that signifies the end of a *file* so that a program knows when it has read all the data.

end-of-record mark   A character that signifies the end of a *record* within a file, such as a *carriage return*.

end-of-tape mark   A reflective spot that marks the end of a reel of *magnetic tape*. As the end-of-reel is reached, light reflecting off the spot is detected by a photosensor and the *tape drive* stops advancing the tape.

end sentinel   A character whose only purpose is to signify the end of a message or of a *record*.

enhanced function   Both *hardware* and *software* are said to have enhanced function when they are improved to do more than an earlier version could do. The term "function," when used in the abstract, refers to a system's range of capabilities.

enhancement   An improvement in either *hardware* or *software*.

enqueue   To place in a *queue* (a prioritized list of things to do, *jobs* to run, etc.). Opposite of *dequeue*.

ENTER key A button on a keyboard corresponding to the RETURN key on a typewriter. The ENTER key usually acts as an *end sentinel* that signals the computer to act on the information just entered.

entry point The first *instruction* to be executed in a computer program or in a section of one.

environment The circumstances that influence the way a system is designed, operated, and used, or that surround some activity. An environment may be either physical or procedural in data-processing usage. A large computer, for example, needs a controlled environment in which temperature, humidity, dirt, and other physical matters are monitored. On the other hand, the "MVS environment" encompasses the general operational characteristics imposed by using IBM's OS/MVS *Operating System*.

environment division One of the four required sections of a *COBOL* program. In the environment division the programmer specifies the *hardware configuration* assumed in developing the program, other *software* required by the program (e.g., a *data base management system*), and any special needs or considerations.

EOF End Of *File*.

EOJ End Of *Job*. When a program "ran to EOJ," it completed normally and without apparent errors.

EOR End Of *Record*.

EOT mark See *end-of-tape mark*.

EPROM Erasable Programmable Read-Only Memory. A type of *memory chip* on which a program can be written electronically and which will not lose its contents even if power is removed. An EPROM can be erased by exposure to ultraviolet light, so that it becomes reusable by "burning" other information on it.

equipment bay   A cabinet into which electronic equipment is mounted.

erase   To remove all references to a *file* from *operating system* records (e.g., the *system catalog, diskette directories,* etc.) so that the system no longer knows of the file's existence. The storage space formerly used by the file can then be assigned to a new file.

Eratosthenes' sieve   A method for calculating all the prime numbers, i.e., numbers not divisible by any other numbers, within a given range. Although largely a pointless exercise in itself, Eratosthenes' sieve is a useful *benchmark* program in comparing the execution speeds of various computers or of different *programming languages.*

ergonomics   Human factors engineering as applied to the design of data-processing *hardware* and *software.* Similar in concept to *user-friendliness.*

Erlang measurements   A group of highly mathematical, statistically based measurements used to design communications systems. Erlang *algorithms* are predictive: given so much traffic and so many lines, what is the probability of a call getting through, what is the probability of delay, etc.

error burst   A burst of noise on a communications path, in which transmission errors tend to occur in groups.

error handling   The ability of *software* to deal automatically with errors in data.

error message   A message issued by *software* when it has encountered an abnormal situation or an error in data.

error recovery routine   A part of a computer program that attempts to deal with an error without halting the program.

ESC   Abbreviation for *ESCAPE.*

ESCAPE   An *ASCII* nongraphic character with the *decimal* value of 27. It is usually used to signify the start of a series of *control characters* so as to differentiate them from data; e.g., *cursor addressing* on a display screen. See *ESCAPE sequence*.

ESCAPE key The button on a keyboard that generates the *ESCAPE* character.

ESCAPE sequence A series of *control characters* beginning with *ESCAPE*. The next *byte* is usually a *code* that defines the function to be performed, followed by some number of *parameters* as required by that particular function. Often used for various display control operations such as *cursor addressing*, clearing the screen, etc.

esoteric name A symbolic name used to refer to a group of devices. For example, in a large computer system with 50 *disk drives*, perhaps 20 are available to be used as temporary workspace for programs. Rather than the programmer having to identify all these drives, they can be referred to by an esoteric name such as SYSWORK. The *operating system* can then *allocate* space for a program on whichever drive in that group is available at the time.

ETX A character signifying the end of text in a message.

even parity The setting of an extra (redundant) *bit* in order to have an even number of 1 bits. In the *ASCII code*, for example, a character consists of seven information bits and one *parity* bit, for a total of eight bits per *byte*; in even parity the eighth bit is set to 1 if there are an odd number of 1 bits in the character; otherwise, the parity bit is a Ø. Therefore, every character has an even number of 1 bits. At the receiving end of a transmission, if any character has an odd number of 1 bits, it is assumed to contain an error, and the receiving machine can then request a retransmission of those data. Even parity can also be used in *block* and *cyclical redundancy checking* (which see). The alternative is *odd parity*, which works similarly but forces an odd number of 1 bits.

even-word boundary   A *memory address* that is an even multiple of the *word length* of a computer. If a computer has a word length of four *bytes*, memory address 22 is not an even-word boundary since 22 is not evenly divisible by 4; 24, however, is.

event   A measurable occurrence within a computer system during processing, and which often involves one program calling upon another for service. The addition of two numbers is not an event because it is done internally by the executing program. The reading of data from *disk* is an event, since the executing program calls upon the *operating system* to do it and since the number of disk *I/Os* is measurable.

event-driven monitor   An event-driven monitor counts each task (*event*) performed by a computer system. (A *monitor* is, in this case, a program that gathers information for measuring the overall performance of a computer system.) The event-driven monitor therefore reports system activity more accurately than a statistical monitor, which collects information by periodically sampling all tasks awaiting completion (such as reads/writes to *disk*, lines of print waiting to be printed, programs in concurrent execution, etc.) and which, by assuming that these data are typical of any given moment, extrapolates them.

exception   An error in data or in the execution of a program that causes processing results to be incomplete.

exclusive OR   See *XOR*

executable module   A *file* containing a computer program in *machine language* form, i.e., a ready-to-run *compiled* or *assembled* program.

execute   (1) To run a program or a section of one. (2) To perform a single *machine language instruction*.

execute cycle   The period during the execution of one

machine language instruction when the *CPU* converts the instruction into electronic signals. Every instruction goes through two cycles: *fetch* and execute. In the fetch cycle the instruction is read from *memory* into the CPU *control section*. In the execute cycle it is acted upon. For further discussion, see *CPU*.

execution time   The time it takes for a program to run from start to finish.

expansion board   A printed circuit board that adds features or capabilities beyond those basic to a computer. For example, if a microcomputer comes with a standard *memory* of 32K and you buy more memory, that additional memory is an expansion board.

expansion slot   A place on a computer's *bus* for plugging in an *expansion board*.

explicit address   A *memory address* explicitly stated (rather than symbolically represented) in a computer program's *source* form. Explicit addresses are used to identify fixed places in memory beyond the control of the program, such as *entry points* to various services furnished by the *operating system*.

expression   A value or an equation that can be reduced to a value, used in a program *statement*. For example, in the *BASIC* statement PRINT (8/B) + 6, the portion (8/B) + 6 is an expression that the computer can readily reduce to a value so long as "B" is known; if B = 2, the computer will print 10.

extended binary coded decimal interchange code   See *EBCDIC*.

extensible language   A *programming language* that provides programmers with the capability to expand the basic *instruction set* with instructions they have developed themselves, so that these extensions become a part of the language as they use it. Suppose a programmer frequently has to compute the circumference of circles. With a nonextensible language, he or she would have to include instructions in every program to tell the computer how to do this. In an extensible language, the programmer simply writes a routine called CIRCUMFERENCE that would include statements (in the language itself) specifying how to calculate circumference, and then use that name as a program instruction without having to include the statements themselves. *LOGO* is one of the better known extensible languages.

extent   In writing a *file* onto a *disk,* it is often necessary to break the file up into two or more pieces. This is because as the file grows, it may come to an area already occupied by a different file and thus unavailable. Each such ''piece'' of a file is called an extent.

external clocking   Synchronization signals for one device are supplied by a different device, so that the two devices operate at the same rate of speed.

EXTERNAL declaration   A *declaration* in a *programming language* that identifies a symbolic name used in this program as being defined in a different program. The use of EXTERNAL requires that the two (or more) programs—the one defining the symbolic name and the other(s) declaring it as external—be combined into a single program using a *linkage editor*. EXTERNAL is a feature of sophisticated programming languages.

external interrupt   A signal that comes into a computer from an external device indicating that the *CPU* should interrupt its current activity to service the external device. For example, after a *disk drive* has been instructed to read a *block* of data, the computer goes about other tasks. When the disk drive is ready to pass the data into the computer, it sends an external interrupt. The CPU then lays aside whatever it is doing and tells the disk drive when it is ready to accept the data.

external label A *label* is another term for a symbolic (or in some programming languages, a variable) name. See *EXTERNAL*.

extract To pick selected pieces of information from a larger volume of data.

EXTRN Abbreviation for *EXTERNAL*.

F

facilities (1) In communications, the lines, amplifiers, switches, and other items required to carry signals. The term generally applies to services other than *modems* and instruments acquired from the telephone company.

(2) Physical plant, e.g., the premises of a data-processing center, including such services as power.

(3) Capabilities and *function* in *systems software*.

facsimile A technology for scanning visual documents and photographs, reducing images to digital form, transmitting them over a communications facility, and reconstructing identical images at the receiving end. Abbreviated fax.

fallback switch A mechanical switch which, if operated, throws a communications path from a primary device to a *standby* device of the same type. Conceptually, a fallback switch is located at the junction of a Y, and activates one or the other of the Y's upper branches. If the device on one upper branch fails, the "stem" is connected via operation of the fallback switch to an identical device on the other upper branch, thereby providing *backup* recovery.

fallout The failure of electronic components sometimes experienced during the *burn-in* of a new piece of equipment.

fall through To perform a program instruction without result. In a *conditional branch*, a comparison is performed, and if the specified condition is true, execution jumps elsewhere in the program. If the condition is not fulfilled, execution falls through to the next *instruction*.

FALSE   See *Boolean values*.

fanfold   Continuous paper perforated at page boundaries and folded in the manner of a fan to form a stack, i.e., folded back and forth on itself.

fatal error   An error during the execution of a program that causes execution to halt.

fax   See *facsimile*.

FCC   See *Federal Communications Commission*.

FDM   See *frequency division multiplexer*.

FDP   Field Developed Program. A program developed by computer vendor personnel who work outside the company's programming organization, which is marketed by that vendor to its customers. FDPs are normally not supported to the same extent as formal products.

FDX   See *full duplex*.

FE   Field Engineer.

feasibility study   In data-processing usage, a formal study to determine whether a business function should be automated, and if so, how and what costs and benefits would be incurred.

FEC   See *forward error correction*.

Federal Communications Commission   An organization of the U.S. government responsible for regulating interstate communications, the broadcast media, and communications *common carriers*.

feedback   (1) An audible beep or click heard when a key is depressed on a keyboard.

(2) A squeal or other disruptive noise, e.g., on a public

address system, when an amplifier picks up its own output and reamplifies it. Can also occur on phone lines and radio channels.

(3) Status messages or other information issued by a program to reassure the user that the program is running.

feeder cable   A main supply cable, such as the cable that delivers commercial power to a building.

female connector   A receptacle into which a connector with projecting electrical contacts (a *male*) plugs.

FEP   See *front-end processor*.

ferrite core   A tiny iron ring forming the basis for a now-obsolete type of computer *memory*. The core can be magnetized in either of two directions; when magnetized one way, it indicates a 1 *bit*; the other way, a Ø bit. Cores are strung at the intersections of a mesh of fine wires that serve both to magnetize and to sense their status, corresponding to write and read operations. Because of low *density* and high manufacturing costs, core memory has now been largely replaced by capacitive semiconductor memory.

fetch   To retrieve, as to fetch a *block* of data from a *storage device* into *memory* for processing.

fetch cycle   The period of time a *CPU* uses to read the next *machine instruction* prior to acting on it during program execution. See *execute cycle*.

FF   (1) Form Feed, a control character that makes a printer skip to the top of the next page.

(2) Flip-Flop, an electronic circuit that reverses its condition each time power is applied. Used in *memory* and also in electronic switching circuits.

fiber optics   A technology for transmitting information via light waves through a fine filament. Signals are *encoded* by varying some characteristic of the light waves generated by a low-power laser, whose output is sent through a light-conducting fiber to a receiving device that *decodes* the signals.

Fibonacci series A series of numbers in which each new value is calculated by adding the two most recent numbers: 1, 2, 3, 5, 8, 13, 21, 34 . . . etc. Useful for high-speed searches of extremely large *ordered lists*. The search skips forward in the list with the number of entries to skip being determined by the Fibonacci series. When the list entry is less than the *search argument*, the entry being sought has been passed, so the process reverses. The search jumps back to the previously checked entry and follows the Fibonacci series in decreasing order, jumping back and forth in ever-smaller skips (the direction depending on each comparison of the search argument with the current list entry) to narrow down the choices. The entry sought will either be found during comparisons, or when the series has been followed back to 1. While it sounds complex, this type of search typically finds one item out of a list of several thousand in about two dozen skips, which is much faster than scanning the same list entry by entry.

fiche a piece of high-resolution photographic material on which large volumes of printed output can be written by a laser. See *COM*.

field One item of information among several that comprise a *record*. For example, if a record contains name, address, and telephone number, each of those items is a field. Data within a computer are organized into the following hierarchy:

> Several bits form a character.
> Several characters form a field.
> Several fields form a record.
> Several records form a file.
> Several files form a library.

A field is therefore the smallest complete unit of data. Sometimes also called an *element*.

field designator A unique character, usually placed at the start of a *field*, which identifies the nature of the data contained within the field. Used when data are not rigidly formatted.

field developed program. See *FDP*.

field engineer A repairman of computer equipment, usually employed by the vendor or by a repair service. Often called an *FE*; also, a *CE*.

field upgrade The expansion of a *hardware* device such as a computer on the customer's premises, without replacing it with a new, larger device.

FIFO First-In, First-Out (Pronounced "fife-oh). A method of dealing with events, messages, etc., in the order of occurrence. Contrasts with *LIFO*.

FIFO buffering A method of handling communications messages in the order of arrival. Messages are stacked in a *buffer* in chronological order. The buffer is serviced periodically (cleared out and the messages processed), taking the oldest message first.

file A complete organized collection of information. A file is analogous to a folder in a filing cabinet in that it is an entity that can be retrieved, opened, processed, closed, moved, and placed back into storage as a unit. The documents within the file folder are comparable to *records* in a computer file in being related to each other and organized in some fashion. Every computer file has a unique name by which it is known and referred to both by humans and by the computer system. A file is a major element within the hierarchy of data organization described under the definition of *field*. A file may contain data, or it may be a computer program.

file-handling routine A portion of a computer program that reads data from, and/or writes data to, a *file*.

file organization The fundamental method by which a *file* is structured. There are four general file organizations, any one of which might or might not be available in a given computer system.

(1) Sequential: The data are written record after record within the file, suitable for repetitive (sequential) processing. An individual record can only be retrieved by reading all the preceding records.

(2) Direct (also called random): Records are written sequentially, but they are of a fixed length so that it is possible to calculate the exact position of any specific record within the file. This permits an individual record to be directly retrieved or written without having to pass through all the preceding data.

(3) Indexed sequential: Records are stored sequentially as in (1) above, but a separate area of the file contains an index showing the location of each record so that individual records can be directly accessed as in direct organization.

(4) Partitioned: The file is subdivided (''partitioned'') into sections called *members*, each of which is a complete file unto itself. Most often used for *program libraries*. See *partitioned file* for further discussion.

In IBM parlance, file organization is called *data set organization*, abbreviated DSORG (pronounced ''dis-org'').

file transfer The movement, under program control, of a *file* from one place to another, or from one *storage medium* to another (e.g., *tape* to *disk*). Most systems have a *utility* for this purpose.

fill To place meaningless information, such as SPACE characters or *binary* zeros, into the unused portions of a fixed-length *block* of data in order to comply with length requirements. Also called *padding*.

filter (1) In communications, a circuit that only lets certain tone frequencies pass. All unwanted frequencies on the communications path are filtered out.

(2) In software, an input-checking routine that catches "bad data" (values unacceptable to the program) and prevents them from causing a program failure.

firmware A program that has been permanently recorded in a *PROM* and is thus essentially a piece of *hardware* that does software functions. Also called *microcode*.

first-level interrupt handler See *FLIH*.

fix A modification to either *hardware* or *software* that corrects a problem.

fixed head On a rotating *storage device* (*disk* or *drum*), a read-write head permanently positioned over a single *track* to improve performance. When access to a track with a fixed head is desired, a movable head does not have to be positioned over it, thus substantially reducing the time required to read and write data. Because fixed heads are costly, they are installed sparingly and used only for special purposes where disk access time is critical to overall system performance.

fixed-head disk See *fixed head*.

fixed-length A format in which every data element (*record*, message, etc.) is exactly the same number of characters in length, the length being determined by information content. As an example, in an accounts receivable system it might take between 43 and 132 characters to describe an invoice; therefore, the *record* length for invoice *files* would be fixed at 132 characters. Records requiring fewer than 132 characters would be *padded* with fill characters to satisfy the fixed length.

fixed media Data *storage devices* that do not depend on mechanical movements to read and write data. A computer's internal *memory* is the most obvious example. Less common, but still fairly prevalent, is "fixed disk" (also called semiconductor disk), which is actually a large special-purpose memory that *emulates* (pretends to be) an extremely fast disk drive.

fixed-point arithmetic   The form of arithmetic performed in most computers, in which an implied decimal point is assumed to exist at a consistent position in every numeric value. Contrasts with *floating-point*.

flag   A *bit* or sometimes a character set to a value to indicate some condition. For instance, when addition is performed and the sum's value exceeds the capacity of the *register*, a bit in the *CPU*'s *status byte* is set to 1 to indicate that a carry has occurred that is not reflected in the sum; this bit is called the carry flag. Another example is the sign flag: if the result of subtraction is a negative number, the sign flag (another bit in the status byte) is set to 1; otherwise, it is Ø, indicating a positive number.

flexible disk   See *floppy disk*; also, *diskette*.

FLIH   (Pronounced "flea"). First-level interrupt handler. A *software* or *firmware* routine that "wakes up" each time an interrupt occurs, and decides the relative importance of the interrupt. An *interrupt* is a signal sent to the *CPU* by a device requesting attention. Some interrupts cause the present task in execution to stop. Others are put aside to be handled later ("later" being perhaps after a few thousandths of a second). Different devices have varying levels of importance; e.g., it is less significant that the printer is ready for more output to print than that a *disk drive* has completed a read and is ready to send data into *memory*.

flip-flop   See *FF*, definition 2.

floating-point arithmetic   A type of arithmetic performed in either *hardware* or *software* in which the position of the decimal point varies ("floats") from value to value. Floating-point arithmetic is extremely sophisticated from the standpoint of circuit design and requires special hardware in the *CPU*. It is therefore available only on very large or special-purpose scientific computers. Software that does floating-point arithmetic in fact converts numbers to a fixed-point format, processes them, and reconverts the results into floating-point. FORTRAN, COBOL, BASIC, PASCAL, and all other conventional *high-level programming languages* handle fractional ("real") numbers by software floating point.

floating-point register Special *hardware* in the *CPU* of a computer to handle *floating-point arithmetic*.

floppy disk A portable rotating *storage medium* frequently associated with small computers. A floppy disk is a flexible circle of magnetic material sealed inside an envelope. It has a hole in the center for engaging a hub that makes it rotate and a slot in the envelope in which a read/write head makes contact with the magnetic surface. Standard diameters are 5¼" and 8", and some are capable of holding data on both sides. Capacities range from 40,000 to 1.2 million characters per disk. Floppy disks can be easily inserted into and removed from a floppy disk drive, stored in paper files or binders, and carried from one machine to another (although compatibility of recording formats is often an issue). It is a low-cost, reliable means of storing data, with all the same benefits as large disk units for mainframe computers, and thus popular for small systems. Also called *diskette* and *flexible disk*.

flowchart A drawing that depicts reasoning and processes by means of lines and symbols. Flowcharts, though waning in popularity, are often used to work out and document the flow of a program, or at least of complex processes within a program. Lines with arrowheads indicate the direction of actions. They link geometric symbols which, by convention, have standard shapes to indicate different kinds of actions: a diamond for a *decision*, an oval for an entry or exit point, etc.

FM Frequency Modulation. A means of superimposing information on an *alternating current* by varying its *frequency*. FM is used in radio and in data communications. For an example of FM in data, see frequency shift keying.

footprint The amount and shape of floor space required for a machine or an *equipment bay*, including clearances for opening access doors.

foreground job A program that executes "in the foreground;" i.e., either interacting directly with a person at a terminal, or returning results to the terminal. The term is sometimes also applied to a high-priority *batch job* in a system that runs several programs concurrently.

format A broadly used term referring to the arrangement of information into some specified order.

form feed See *FF*, definition 1.

FORTH A *programming language* developed primarily for microcomputers.

FORTRAN FORmula TRANslator. One of the oldest *programming languages* still in frequent use. FORTRAN is primarily useful for mathematics.

forward error correction A somewhat exotic and not widely used method of dealing with transmission errors. By analyzing various *parity bits* and *check characters* embedded in data, a receiving machine locates and corrects errors occurring in data communications, rather than requesting a retransmission.

four-wire line A *full duplex* communications line on which data can be sent and received simultaneously.

fox A digit in a hexadecimal numbering system that is equivalent in value to 15. Written as X'F'.

fragmentation A phenomenon occurring on *disk storage*,

in which *files* tend to get broken up into many small *extents* scattered all over the disk. Fragmentation is especially prevalent and serious on heavily used disk units. See *compaction*.

framing   In complex data-communications systems messages are preceded and followed by control information indicating, among other things, the destination and origin of the message, the time sent, length of text, etc. This information is said to "frame" the message.

freeform text   A variable-lengh area within a *record,* or an entire record, in which plain unformatted English text is stored.

freeware   *Software* provided by a vendor at no charge.

frequency   The number of complete cycles (*Hertz*) of an *alternating current* or of a tone in one second. See *alternating current.*

frequency modulation   See *FM*.

frequency-shift keying   A form of *frequency modulation* performed by *modems* on low-speed data signals. In FSK, a *carrier* frequency of, say, 1420 *Hertz* (Hz), is sent from Point A to Point B. When the machine at Point A transmits a *byte* of data, the carrier frequency is shifted to 1320 Hz for a Ø bit and to 1520 Hz for a 1 bit. The receiving modem thus senses the absence of data (an idle state) by the presence of the unmodulated carrier frequency, and reconstructs 1 and Ø bits from the shifts plus and minus 100 Hz. FSK is used at speeds up to 300 bits per second (about 30 characters a second).

friction feed   The type of paper feed mechanism common in typewriters and some low-speed computer printers, in which the paper is held in place and advanced by mechanical pressure against the *platen* (roller).

front end   Any preprocessing of data before the main work of a program begins. An *edit* program that checks input data for acceptable ranges of values is an example of front-end processing. Also, see *front-end processor*.

front-end processor   A small special-purpose computer operating under the control of a larger *host* machine, for the purpose of controlling data-communications traffic to and from the host. Also called a communications control unit. Abbreviated as FE, F/E, or FEP.

FSK   See *frequency-shift keying*.

full duplex   A mode of data communications in which signals are sent and received simultaneously over the same line.

full-screen editor   An *interactive* computer program used in connection with a *video display terminal*. The terminal user can view data on the screen and change their content in *memory* by modifying the screen image. These changes can be made permanent by resaving the data in a *file*. A full-screen editor usually makes use of *cursor* controls so that the user can position the cursor at the point of change and type over the existing data. Though varying widely in capabilities, most full-screen editors include facilities for searching for specified character strings, doing replacements, rearranging blocks of text in a "cut and paste" mode, deleting and inserting characters, words, and lines, etc. Popular for *word processing* and program development.

fully populated   A printed circuit board is fully populated when all of its capabilities have been implemented and there is no room left for adding *function* by installing more *chips* or other electronic components.

function   (1) When used in the singular and without an article (*a* or *the*), refers to general capabilities. "A larger computer provides more function."

(2) A mechanical or electronic action. "One of the functions of this printer is that it prints underlines."

(3) In programming, a *subroutine* that returns a mathematical value (function), calculated using one or more input values (arguments), e.g., cosine, square root, logarithm, etc.

functional error recovery   Capabilities built into an *operating system* to intervene in certain common errors and attempt recovery action to prevent a *system crash* or a program failure. As an example, if a program attempts to divide by zero, an error occurs; functional error recovery issues an error message and replaces the 0 with a near-zero value such as .00001 so that execution can continue. Functional error recovery also handles *disk* failures, programmatic attempts to utilize devices, *files*, and *memory addresses* that don't exist, and other such foreseeable problems. If functional error recovery cannot handle the problem, it usually hands control to the *automatic shutdown* routine.

G

gain The change in audio signal level across an amplifier or other power-altering device. Positive gain is an increase, negative a decrease. Normally measured in *decibels*, a ratio of input signal strength to output.

gallium arsenide An exotic crystalline material used to make extremely high-grade *semiconductors*. Gallium arsenide is superior to silicon, but far more costly. It is one of the first products to be routinely manufactured in space aboard the Space Shuttle.

gap The physical unwritten space separating *blocks* of data on *magnetic tape*.

garbage Bad data, noise picked up from a communications line, incorrect *commands*, and any other undesirable or useless input to a computer.

garbage collection *Memory* management done automatically by some computer programs, in which the program consolidates memory work areas and frees space occupied by data no longer required.

gas panel A flat display screen filled with an inert gas that glows when current is applied. Character images are formed in a *dot matrix* fashion by applying power at the appropriate points to make "dots" of glowing gas.

gas tube Same as *gas panel*.

gate   An electronic switch whose output is determined by the states of two or more inputs. Usually called *logic gates*. See *AND, OR, XOR, NAND, NOR*.

gateway   A connection between two separate data-communications networks, enabling users on one network to exchange messages with users on the other. A gateway is usually a computer that has access to both networks and has the capability of passing traffic between them.

GDG   See *generation data group*.

gen   Short for *generate* or generation. To "gen a system" or "do a gen" means to set up an *operating system* or a *systems software* package for a particular computer *configuration*. This primarily entails building *tables* showing the *addresses* and characteristics of specific devices attached to the computer (an *IOGEN*), establishing *parameters* to govern system operation and performance, selecting options, and installing any special modifications and control programs (a *SYSGEN*).

gender   The "sex" of a connector (male or female).

gender changer   A small *passive device* placed between two connectors of the same *gender*, thereby enabling two male or two female connectors to mate.

general-purpose register   A small *memory* within the *CPU* of a computer, that can be used for a variety of purposes (mathematical and *logical* operations, *address* manipulation, etc.) A general-purpose register is under the direct control of a computer program.

generate   See *gen*.

generation data group   A "rolling" collection of like *files* having the same name, with each generation of the group relating to an execution of the program that creates that file. For instance, every day a business might post payments received and write them to a generation file; each day, then, a new file is created showing receipts for the day. Today's file becomes the Ø generation, yesterday's the − 1 generation, the day before yesterday's the − 2, etc. Tomorrow, the file created today will become the − 1. If payment records are retained for 45 days, there are 45 generations. Each time a new generation is added, the oldest generation "rolls off the end" or "drops off the bottom," meaning that the storage space occupied by those records is freed for other use. Usually called a GDG (letters pronounced separately).

generic device type A major component of data-processing equipment (terminal or *peripheral*) that other devices *emulate* for the purpose of simplifying installation. An example is the IBM 3270, a common *display* device; many devices not even remotely resembling a *CRT* emulate (copy the behavior of) the 3270 in communicating with a computer. This eliminates the need to write special programs to support the device, since most large computers' *systems software* includes 3270 support.

geometrical distortion A discrepancy between the vertical and horizontal dimensions of *picture elements* (pixels) on a display screen, such that five pixels high is a different distance than five pixels wide. In *graphics*, this causes circles to be drawn as ovals and other such visual distortions, unless corrected for in *software*.

GET In many *programming languages*, an *instruction* to read data from a *file*. It has become a generic term for file reading whether the language in use includes that specific instruction or not. Usually used as a noun: "At this point, the program does a GET." The opposite (a file write) is a *PUT*.

GETMAIN An *instruction* available in some *programming languages* working on large-scale computer systems to request *dynamic allocation* of additional *memory*. In a *multiprogramming* system, each program is given a certain amount of *address space* in which to work. When a program needs more, it issues a GETMAIN to signal this need to the *operating system*, which then suspends execution of the program until it can satisfy the request.

gibberish total   A total of all of a selected *field* in a group of *records*, accumulated for the purpose of ensuring that all the data are present without regard for whether the total itself has any significance. For example, in a group of 1000 records the gibberish total might be the sum of all customer account numbers, which is, of course, a nonsensical ("gibberish") number. If the data are written to a *storage device* with the gibberish total and later read into another program, that program can calculate a gibberish total and, by comparing with the one stored, determine whether all the records are present.

GIGO   Garbage In, Garbage Out. Given bad input data, a program will inevitably produce bad results.

glare   In telephone service, the situation that occurs when the handset is lifted to place a call before a currently incoming call to that phone has rung. When this happens in data communications using *autocall*, it can cause the line or even the entire computer to "lock up."

glare filter   A piece of transparent material placed over a *video display* screen to reduce the reflection of room light.

glitch   Usually a minor problem in a piece of equipment or in a program that causes an occasional malfunction.

global   In general, implying a great breadth of scope, as contrasted with *local*. In a computer room with several systems, global resource sharing means all the processors share such equipment resources as *disk* and *tape drives*, printers, etc. In a program, a global variable is the symbolic name of a *memory* location that is referred to repeatedly throughout the program. A global search scans an entire file and finds all occurrences of a specified word or group of characters.

GOOVOO (Pronounced like it looks) One *file* within a *generation data group* (GDG), so called because of the notation used (in IBM systems) for identifying the relative generation and volume numbers of the file: G005V001 is volume 1, generation −5 of a GDG.

GOTO (Pronounced "go to") An *instruction* in a *programming language* that causes execution to jump elsewhere in the program, rather than following the normal sequence of instructions.

GOTO-less programming An alternative term for *structured programming* that discourages the use of *GOTO* statements.

go to sleep A term used when a computer system halts or a program appears to be doing nothing because it is locked in an *endless loop*: "The system went to sleep."

graceful shutdown An *automatic shutdown* of a system accomplished without loss of data or other calamity.

grammar See *syntax*.

grandfather (1) A *file* two *generations* old, i.e., the current file contains information obtained partly from the *parent* file, which in turn contains information from the grandfather.

(2) When used as a verb, to discontinue offering new features or services associated with a product that has become obsolete. When a computer is grandfathered, for example, the vendor continues to repair it, but stops selling parts to expand it.

grandparent Same as *grandfather* in connection with *files*.

graphic character A printed character: a letter, number, symbol, punctuation mark, line, angle, etc., that produces a visual image on paper. Also, within a machine, the *byte* representing such a character.

graphic CRT   A *video display terminal* capable of producing pictures and drawings.

graphics   The production of lines, angles, curves, and other non*alphanumeric* information by a computer on a *video display*, a printer, or a *plotter*.

Gregorian calendar   The standard calendar in conventional use, which indicates days by month, date, and year.

ground   The common voltage reference point in a circuit or a group of circuits. In electronics, usually the positive pole of a power supply is used to develop various voltage levels as required for the components to be powered (e.g., +6 V, +9 V, and +12 V). These currents then flow through circuits. The negative pole of the power supply is connected with a metal plate or with a conductor that travels throughout the device. All currents, once having passed through their circuits, return to ''ground,'' i.e., the negative pole, to complete the circuit.

guest computer   A computer operating under the control of another (*host*) computer. The operator gives all *commands* to the host, and the host decides which ones ought to be passed on to the guest, what work it should run, etc.

H

half-adder An electronic circuit that adds two *bits* according to the following rules:

$$\emptyset + \emptyset = \emptyset$$
$$\emptyset + 1 = 1$$
$$1 + \emptyset = 1$$
$$1 + 1 = \emptyset \text{ with a carry}$$

This circuit is called a half-adder because it does not attempt to deal with the carry, but merely signals its existence. A group of half-adders working in a hierarchial arrangement form an *adder*, which adds (in some systems also subtracts) two *binary* numbers.

half carry A *flag* in the *CPU* of some computers that indicates that a carry occurred from the low-order four *bits* of a number to the high-order four bits. This flag is of no significance to the programmer, and most machines do not provide an *instruction* to read its status.

half duplex On a communications line, the ability to send and receive signals, but not simultaneously.

half-word A computer *word* is the number of *bytes* that can be held at one time in a *CPU register*; a half-word is therefore half that number. In a 32-*bit* machine where 8 bits constitute a byte, a word is $32/8 = 4$ bytes, so a half-word is 2 bytes.

halt   An *instruction* or a *command* that causes the *CPU* of a computer to suspend processing. In microcomputers the HALT instruction is used to "freeze" the system in some preestablished condition awaiting an *interrupt* that will unlock it and resume processing. In large computers a halt is often accomplished only by means of a hardware signal, such as a special button at the computer's console, to keep an adventurous programmer from "bringing the system to its knees."

hand-held computer   A very small, battery-powered computer that can literally be carried around in the hand or in a pocket. Some hand-held computers are quite powerful, but because of their limited keyboards and display capabilities they are useful mainly for doing computations too complex for a calculator.

handler   A communications program written to handle a specific type or class of message arriving and departing on a network connected with the computer. A handler interprets an incoming message, controls the processing of the message and the formulation of a response, and sends it back to the message originator.

handshake   The exchange of predetermined signals between two devices that have just established communications with each other.

handwriting recognition   The ability of a computer equipped with a visual scanning device to examine handwritten material, either to verify a signature or to determine information content.

hanger bar   A rack from which *magnetic tapes* can be hung for storage.

hard copy   Printed output (on paper).

hard disk   A small, high-capacity *disk* storage device for use with a microcomputer. See *Winchester disk*.

hard failure The failure of a piece of equipment, generally requiring repair before the device can be placed back in use.

hard patch A patch is a temporary *fix* to repair a *software* error. A hard patch is applied to the actual program *file* so that it becomes permanent, and if the program is reloaded into *memory*, the fix is still in effect.

hardware Physical equipment used in data processing. Hardware is anything that can be touched.

hardware configuration The arrangement and relationships of the various devices that comprise a computer system, including the physical and electrical paths that connect them. Generally, the term applies to a computer and all its directly connected *peripheral* devices (e.g., *disks, tape drives*, printers, etc.).

hardware division Electronic circuitry that performs division of one number by another as a result of one *machine instruction*. Found only on large computers.

hardware error A malfunction, usually in a computer program, caused by a failure of hardware and not by a *bug* in the program.

hardware floating point Sophisticated circuitry within a *CPU* that is able to do *floating-point arithmetic*.

hardware monitor A piece of test equipment that connects to a computer at numerous points for the purpose of making statistical measurements of the machine's activities based upon signals and voltages detected.

hardware multiplication Similar to *hardware division*.

hard-wired A term applying to the direct electrical connection of two devices to each other.

harness A group of separate conductors or cables that are bound together.

hash total   Same as *gibberish total*.

HDA   Head/Disk Assembly (letters pronounced separately). An airtight assembly consisting of a *disk pack* and read/write heads, used in a *Winchester disk*.

HDLC   Hierarchical Data Link Control. A sophisticated, highly structured set of standards governing the means by which unlike devices can communicate with each other on large data-communications networks.

HDX   Abbreviation for *half duplex*.

"he"   The *systems software* of a computer is often referred to as though it were a person: "When the *operating system* sees this *command*, he thinks it means. . . ." *Applications software* is not spoken of in the same way, usually being called simply *it*. This is perhaps due to the fact that applications programs are not as "smart" as systems software.

head   A unit on or very near to a magnetic recording surface that moves past the surface. The head senses tiny magnetic fields representing *bits*, and/or records such magnetic fields, these operations being "read" and "write," respectively.

head cleaning kit   A material containing a dirt solvent that is used to clean the read/write *head* of a *tape drive* or of a *floppy disk drive*.

head crash   A failure in a *disk drive*, when the read/write *head* becomes misaligned and cannot locate the *tracks* to which it is directed.

header record   A *record* written at the start of a *tape*, identifying the characteristics of data recorded on the tape, the name of the file it contains, and other control information.

head of string   The first *disk drive* in a group ("string"), which acts as a sort of group leader by performing certain control functions for the other drives.

head stepping rate   The speed at which a read/write *head* on a *disk drive* moves from *track* to track over the disk surface. One of the key factors in determining how fast a disk unit is.

heap A term occasionally used to describe the data work area in *memory* of a program, wherein the program "heaps up" its variables, control totals, counters, and other values used during processing.

heat sink A set of metal fins that dissipate the heat of a *chip* into the air.

HELLO A *sign-on* message entered by a terminal user on being connected with a dial-in *time-sharing* service. The system evaluates the *bit rate* of the HELLO message in order to set its own transmission speed in responding. This is made necessary because of the many different characteristics of subscribers' terminals.

HELP In many *interactive* computing systems, terminal users can type the *command* HELP when they are unsure about what to do next or how to perform some operations from the keyboard. The computer system then furnishes a *tutorial* (one or more screens of self-guiding information) about the function the user wants to perform. When the user exits from HELP, the system returns to the point where he or she left off.

help desk In a data-processing organization, a person or a group of people who are available to answer questions from computer users and to assist in diagnosing and fixing problems.

Hertz A measurement of the *frequency* of a tone or of an *alternating current*. Hertz corresponds to the term "cycles per second." Abbreviated Hz.

heuristic A sophisticated and somewhat experimental form of programming generally associated with *artificial intelligence*. In heuristic programming, a computer "learns" by its experience; e.g., in a chess game program, if the computer moves a bishop and the bishop is then captured by its human opponent's knight, the program "learns" not to place a bishop where it can be taken by a knight. Thereafter, it will not make that mistake again.

hex See *hexadecimal*.

hexadecimal A numbering system to the *base* 16, i.e., instead of the 10 unit values familiar in *decimal* numbers, hex has 16 unit values. It is the most commonly used numbering system within computers because it is, in effect, a shorthand notation for representing *binary* numbers of up to four *bits*. The hex values and their binary and decimal equivalents are as follows:

Hex	Binary	Decimal
0	0000	0
1	0001	1
2	0010	2
3	0011	3
4	0100	4
5	0101	5
6	0110	6
7	0111	7
8	1000	8
9	1001	9
A	1010	10
B	1011	11
C	1100	12
D	1101	13
E	1110	14
F	1111	15

In hex, as in decimal numbers, place values are significant; the equivalent of decimal 16 is 10 in hex; of 31, 1F in hex; of 32, 20 in hex; of 255, FF in hex; of 256, 100 in hex. To avoid confusion because of using symbols in common, hex notation is normally used so X'20' is taken to mean hex 20 and not decimal 20.

The 8-bit binary numbers that comprise a *byte* in most computers are ordinarily written as a two-digit hex number, that being easier for a person to read than strings of 1s and Øs. Thus, the byte Ø1Ø11101 is written X'5D', since the first four bits of the number equal X'5' and the second four equal X'D'.

Arithmetic is easier for a computer to perform in hex than in decimal, so most computer programs convert all numeric input data into hex before processing, and then convert the results back to decimal before output.

Hierarchical Data Link Control   See *HDLC*.

hierarchical network   A communications network with several levels of control. Terminals are at the lowest level. They communicate with small computers that also perform some control functions. These low-level computers communicate with larger systems that exercise a broader scope of control, and which in turn are subservient to yet higher level computers, and so on. Messages move through the network by passing up, down, and across levels of the hierarchy. See also *HDLC*.

hierarchical storage management   A time-and-usage sensitive method of managing large amounts of data, in which the selection of a *storage medium* for a particular *file* depends upon how soon and how frequently the file will be needed. Storage media are "graded" or prioritized, so that *DASD* is at the highest level, a *mass storage device* might be at the next-lower level, and *tape* at the lowest. When a file is new, it is placed on DASD (usually *disk*). After the file has not been used for some period of time, perhaps 24 hours, it is automatically downgraded to mass storage and removed from disk. After another interval, maybe a week, if the file has not been used it is *archived* to tape. Three months later, it might be purged altogether if it has not been accessed; on the other hand, if it has been utilized at any point in this process of retirement, it is restored to disk and the clock is reset. Hierarchical storage management is an automatic process under *software* control in most systems. It enables very large data-processing installations to make the most economical use of storage media.

high   See *logic high*.

high core   The upper *address* range of a computer, which in most machines is occupied by the *operating system*.

high-level index   The first part of a *file* name, which often indicates the category of data to which it belongs.

high-level programming language   A human-oriented language in which computer programs are written. In general, the higher the level of the language, the more closely it approximates human thought and natural forms of expression. Conversely, the lower the level, the closer it is to the *hardware* functions of the computer. Thus, *assembly language* is low-level because there is one instruction for each action at the machine level, and *COBOL* is high-level because it reads almost like everyday English.

highlight   On a *video display*, to call attention to an item by increasing the intensity of the characters, making them blink while others remain steady, or reversing the background and the character images (e.g., black characters on a white background, in contrast to the rest of the screen). Most video displays have *software* controls to accomplish this on a selective basis.

high-order   The most significant (first) digit or character in a group. In the number 952, 9 is the high-order digit.

high side   The side of a remote device that "faces" a computer. In a *device cluster controller*, the high side is the part of the controller that deals with communications to and from the computer; the *low side* is the part that has to do with the terminals it controls.

high-water mark In large systems in which work to be run is submitted to a *queue*, the high-water mark is the maximum number of *jobs* that were in the queue awaiting execution during some period of observation.

hi-res Short for high-resolution *graphics*.

histogram A horizontal bar chart that can easily be printed on any computer printer. The following is an example:

VALUE	Ø	1	2	3
2.5	************************			
3.2	********************************			
1.6	****************			

Histograms are often used to graph statistical information.

hold queue A *queue* in a large system where *jobs* that have been submitted for execution, but which should not be run yet, are held.

Hollerith code A *binary code* used only on *punched cards*. Hollerith is a 12-*bit* code offering 4096 possible combinations ("characters"), but because it is always translated to and from the 8-bit codes used in computers, only 256 combinations are used.

holography The construction of three-dimensional images using *graphics software* and, often, special devices capable of displaying such images so that the viewer can see them from any perspective.

home On a *video display*, the upper left corner. To "home the *cursor*" is to place it at the start of the first line.

home-grown software Computer programs written by the user of a computer system.

hood A protective covering on a *connector* to house and support the physical union of the cable with the connector's pins.

hook A modification to a program (usually *systems software*) to "hook" additional *instructions* into an existing part of the program. A hook is usually a *GOTO* that points to these added instructions, which are located elsewhere.

hopper A bin in which *punched cards* are stacked for processing by a machine.

horizontal pitch The number of characters per inch produced on a line by a printer or a display device.

horizontal tab A machine function that causes the printing mechanism or *cursor* to skip to a predetermined position.

hosed up Same as *dorfed up*.

host The computer that is in control of a communications network or of another computer.

hot I/O A *hardware* failure in a *peripheral device;* i.e., the device (e.g., a *disk drive*) signals the computer that it has completed an activity when in fact it has not been instructed to do anything.

hot spare An extra device such as a *modem* that is kept powered on but not active, to be used in case another similar device fails.

hot standby Same as *hot spare*.

house cable Wiring installed within a building for the purpose of carrying electronic and/or telephone signals.

housekeeping Various activities performed under program control in order to keep things in proper order. Housekeeping does not directly contribute to the processing of data, but rather contributes to the orderly functioning of the system. As an example, when a program ends, housekeeping routines make sure all the *files* it used have been *closed*.

housing A cabinet or other enclosure.

HT Horizontal Tab.

hub (1) In a communications network, the computer or the switching center that serves as the central focal point.

(2) On a *magnetic tape drive*, the mechanical capstan on which a reel is mounted.

hundred call seconds See *CCS*.

H/W Written abbreviation for *hardware*. Not used in speech.

hybrid coil A set of transformers connecting a two-wire local telephone line to a long-haul *four-wire* channel. *Modems* are often engineered for a two-wire line, but data circuits usually have separate paths for transmit and receive; the hybrid coil resolves this discrepancy by placing the transmit and receive sides of the channel on the same pair of wires for connection to the modem.

I

IC See *integrated Circuit.*

identification division The first of the four required divisions of a *COBOL* program. Lists the name of the program, its author, the data written, and other such information.

IEEE Institute of Electrical and Electronics Engineers.

IF . . . THEN . . . ELSE A type of logical decision-making *statement* used in computer programming. All *high-level programming languages* have this instruction or one that is functionally equivalent. In program *coding* the ellipses (". . .") are replaced by the appropriate statements to form a complete instruction: "IF (a certain condition is true) THEN (do thus-and-such) ELSE (do another thing)." Example in *BASIC*:

IF A = B THEN PRINT "EQUAL"

ELSE PRINT "NOT EQUAL"

The ELSE portion of the statement is usually optional and serves as a catchall. The example compares symbolic values called A and B and always tells us the result. If the ELSE portion had been left off (IF A = B THEN PRINT "EQUAL"), the program would only report when A and B are equal and nothing would be reported when A and B are not equal.

The IF . . . THEN . . . ELSE logic forms the basis for *conditional branches,* when execution is directed elsewhere in the program because of conditions encountered while processing.

IF A = B THEN GOTO 1000 ELSE GOTO 2000 causes execution to jump to line 1000 of the program when A and B are equal, and to line 2000 when they are not. The program has therefore made a decision based on the values of A and B.

illegal Unacceptable to *software* and therefore rejected. For instance, if a *programming language* contains the *instruction* 'READ,' it is illegal to use the 'READ' as a symbolic name for a data variable. A program attempting to do so will not run because the language software will reject the data name.

image The representation of information that is actually in a different form. If you display the contents of *memory* on a screen, you see an image of memory.

immediate address A *memory address* explicitly specified in an *instruction* so that it is not necessary to calculate it or look it up.

immediate data Data specified in an *instruction* exactly as it is to be processed. In X = A + 31, the '31' is immediate data.

impact printer A *line printer* that prints by striking the paper. See *chain printer*, also *drum printer*, *dot-matrix printer*, *daisywheel printer*.

impedance The opposition of an electrical circuit to the flow of electricity.

implementation (1) The process of installing a new piece of *hardware* or *software*.

(2) Details of the way a specific *programming language* or other software works in comparison with others of the same type. For example, some *PASCAL compilers* require that a keyboard/display unit be specifically defined as an input/output to the program, while others do not. This is a difference in the implementations of PASCAL.

impulse noise   Crackling and static on a communications line as a result of electrical disturbances.

increment   (1) To increase a numeric value, usually by 1, as in incrementing a counter.

(2) A uniform step value repeatedly applied, e.g., 100, 110, 120, 130 . . ., etc., is a series in increments of 10.

index   (1) A list of items and *pointers* that show where to find the items, comparable to the index of a book.

(2) The subscript of an *array* of data, showing the specific entry; e.g., in LIST(5), the '5' is an index indicating the fifth entry in an array named LIST.

(3) In general, any *displacement* value that is relative to a starting point. See *index register*.

indexed array   An *array* (i.e., a list of several items grouped for convenience) in which individual entries are accessible by specifying their position by the use of a subscript. See *index*, definition 2. Also called a *subscripted array*.

indexed list   Same as *indexed array*.

index register   A *general-purpose CPU register* that has been assigned to hold an *index*. The index is usually a *displacement* value that is added to a *base address* to derive the actual memory address of an item of data in a list. As an example, to access the fourth entry in a list of items each of which is 20 characters long, a program calculates $4 \times 20 = 80$ characters as the location of the entry in the list. This value is then loaded into a register, which is thereupon referred to as an index register. To find the actual memory location, the base address (or starting address) of the list is added to the index register; if the list begins at address 500, then the indexed (actual) address of the item is $500 + 80 = 580$.

information system   Any coordinated combination of computer *hardware*, *software*, and data that work together for a specific set of goals.

inhibit To stop something that would normally occur from happening. For example, if a program is designed to write certain output to a *file* but that information is not wanted during one run of the program, the file creation is inhibited by directing the output data to a *dummy file*.

initialize To set all variable information to its starting values. This is usually the first step in a computer program.

initial program load See *IPL*.

initiator A portion of the *operating system* of a large computer that runs several *jobs* concurrently. When a job is selected for execution, it is placed under the control of an initiator, which does all the required setup for the job, monitors the progress of the program, and performs any cleanup necessary after the job completes. Its full name is initiator/terminator, but this term is almost never used.

in-line (1) Anything that is part of a communications path, e.g., an amplifier is an in-line device.

(2) Within a sequential series of *instructions* in a computer program, or the sequential instructions themselves. In-line code is a long series of instructions done one after the other.

input (1) Data entered into a computer.

(2) A device that enters data into a computer.

instantiation To "fill in the missing blanks" in a set of information by deducing the omitted values from known values. The term is associated chiefly with *artificial intelligence*.

instruction In a *programming language,* a statement that causes the computer to do something. Instructions usually correspond to the imperative form of verbs: PRINT, READ, REWIND, GO TO, etc. Instructions may also be mathematical expressions: $X = A + B$. In this case, however, there is an implied verb LET or ASSIGN. In the IF . . . THEN . . . ELSE instruction there is also an implicit verb; (Do a comparison, and) IF . . ., etc. An instruction is always action causing, as contrasted with a *statement*, which can be any line of text in a program.

instruction set The set of all possible *instructions* for a particular type of computer, or within a specific *programming language*.

instrumentation That which is needed to measure some complex activity, such as the performance level of a computer system. Instrumentation is not necessarily gauges and dials on expensive boxes; it can also be *software* that captures and analyzes statistical data about the subject of measurement.

integer A whole number, i.e., a number without a fractional part or a decimal point. Contrasts with a *real number*.

integral modem A *modem* built directly into a communicating machine, as contrasted with an external modem.

integrated circuit A large number of related electrical conductors, transistors, and other electronic components densely and microscopically placed on a *semiconductor* substance. Abbreviated IC; often called a *chip*.

integration Combining diverse elements of *hardware* and *software*, often acquired from different vendors, into a unified system.

intelligence In reference to a machine, the ability to operate under the control of an internal program, and therefore able to modify behavior depending on circumstances.

intelligent device A machine whose internal functions are directed by a program. Intelligent devices are usually terminals or *peripherals* attached to a larger computer. They receive directions from the computer, but they do not rely on the computer to control their internal operations. Thus, once it is given a command by the computer, an intelligent device acts independently and notifies the computer when the command has been carried out. Intelligent terminals, in particular, are often able to operate wholly independently of a controlling computer, only calling on the larger machine on an as-needed basis. Also called a "smart device"; contrasts with "dumb."

intelligent mux A *multiplexer* operating under the control of an internally stored program.

interactive computing An operating *environment* in which a computer and a human at a keyboard terminal conduct a dialog. The human can enter programs and data, *edit*, execute programs, and otherwise direct the computer system, usually immediately seeing the results of computer activity.

interactive mode The state of *interactive computing*.

interactive panel A screen display sent to a *CRT* by a computer during a dialog that prompts the user for a response, explains some aspect of system operation, or reports the results of processing.

interblock gap The physical unwritten space on a *magnetic tape* separating data *blocks*.

interconnection The physical and electrical connection of equipment furnished by different vendors. This term most often applies to the connection of non-Bell *modems* or other non-Bell communications control equipment directly to lines provided by the Bell Telephone System.

interface The point where two distinct data-processing elements meet, e.g., the connector between a terminal and a *modem*. An interface may exist between pieces of *hardware*, between two *software* systems, or between a piece of hardware and a piece of software. Generally, an interface implies some form of mutual accommodation in which internal signals and operating characteristics are reorganized to put them into a format comprehensible to the other element. Some widespread interfaces are standardized, e.g., to modems (the *EIA* or *RS-232* interface); most, however, are not governed by industry standards and must be developed for a particular instance.

interleave To mix real data and control information in a stream of data on a communications path. An interleaved transmission *code,* for example, inserts *check characters* into data at predictable intervals to make it easier to find where an error has occurred. It is up to the receiving machine to pull the interleaved control information out of the data and interpret it.

intermediate language level Semi*compiled* program *code.* Some compilers convert a program into a form that does not resemble the original written program, but that also is not directly executable by the computer; this output is called intermediate language level. It is then *interpreted* by another program at run time so that it becomes executable. An example is *p-code* used on microcomputers.

internal clocking When synchronization of the electronic circuitry of a device is controlled by a timing *clock* within the device itself. Contrasts with *external clocking*.

internal hemorrhage When a program becomes confused but continues to run, producing dubious results and sometimes adversely affecting other programs or the performance of the system as a whole.

internal interrupt A signal for attention sent to the *CPU* by another component within the computer (not an attached device). The most common internal interrupt comes from a *timer* that is set to "go off" after an interval in order to trigger some time-driven action by the CPU.

internal reader *Software* within the *operating system* that *emulates* a *card reader* device. Instead of using *punch cards* to enter jobs and data into the system, this information can be stored *on-line* and sent to the internal reader, where it is read and treated as though it had come from the card reader. This greatly speeds up computer operation.

internals Detailed information about how *systems software* works. When someone "knows system internals," he or she has highly specialized skills as a *systems programmer*.

internetting Connections and communications paths that enable messages to be passed among separate data-communications networks.

interpose To place a device furnished by one vendor between two devices from another vendor that would normally be connected directly.

interpreter (1) A *utility* program that translates other programs. An interpreter reads the *source program*, translates its *instructions*, and executes them immediately. The fundamental difference between a *compiler* and an interpreter is that the compiler translates the program into executable form once, whereas the interpreter translates it every time it is run. Interpreters are especially popular for the *BASIC programming language*; usually the interpreter program is started by the command RUN.

(2) A machine that reads *punched cards* and prints the data punched in them onto the cards. The printing may be placed anywhere on the card, irrespective of where it is punched. Interpreters are used, among other things, to print payee and dollar amount on checks issued as punched cards, the amount due on phone bills, and other such familiar card documents.

interpretive language A *programming language* requiring the support of an *interpreter* during execution.

interrecord gap The physical unwritten space on a *magnetic tape* separating data *records*.

interrupt A signal sent to the *CPU* of a computer by a

device that requires attention. So called because the CPU must eventually interrupt what it is doing in order to respond. An interrupt is a *hardware* signal (a pulse carried on a conductor), to which the CPU replies using *software* called an *interrupt handler*. It saves the contents of the CPU *registers*, takes action to satisfy the interrupting device, and then restores the register contents and resumes processing; this is called "servicing an interrupt." For example, when a program issues instructions to read data from a disk, the CPU sends the appropriate commands and then, while awaiting completion of the disk read operation, it goes about other processing. When the read is finished, the disk controller sends an interrupt. The CPU stops what it is doing, saves the data from the disk in *memory*, and then resumes the interrupted task. At some point it again takes up the program that requested the data from disk. This sounds complex and time-consuming, but typically it might take a few hundredths of a second. During that period, however, the CPU can accomplish a great deal of work. The use of interrupts increases the efficiency of a computer system by utilizing CPU time that would otherwise be lost. Computer systems that are *interrupt-driven* usually have a system of evaluating the relative importance of interrupts. This is called *prioritized interrupts*, in which some merit immediate action and others can be deferred.

interrupt-driven   A computer system that makes extensive use of *interrupts*.

interrupt handler   A section of a program or of the *operating system* that gains control when an *interrupt* occurs, and performs the necessary operations to service the interrupt.

interrupt vector   A list showing the locations of various *interrupt handlers*. In systems using *prioritized interrupts*, the CPU translates an interrupt signal into a *memory address* that corresponds to an entry in the interrupt vector. This entry, in turn, contains an address pointing to the interrupt handler for the priority given by the device. The CPU is thus able to find the necessary instructions for servicing the interrupt.

I/O (Pronounced "eye oh") Input/Output. A general term that encompasses the input/output activity, the devices that accomplish it, and the data involved. Inasmuch as a computer is useless unless we can communicate instructions and information to it, and it can communicate the results of its activity back to us, I/O is one of the most important and time-consuming things it does.

I/O bound When a computer is excessively slowed down by input/output activity, to the extent that no improvement can be made in performance except by adding more or faster *hardware*, it is said to be "I/O bound."

IOGEN (Pronounced "eye-oh gen") Input/Output Generation. An activity required to install the *operating system* on a large computer, in which the *addresses* and *attributes* of all *peripheral* devices under control of the computer are described in a manner understandable to the operating system.

I/O path architecture The fundamental design of a system's input/output *hardware* (and to a lesser extent *software*) that governs the manner in which it handles *I/O*.

IPL (Letters pronounced separately) Initial Program Load. The start-up of a computer system. An IPL brings the *operating system* into *memory*, usually from *disk*, and places the computer into a state of readiness. An IPL is a significant event which, in large systems, can take half an hour; in small systems it is more often called a *boot* and takes only a few seconds to perhaps a minute. IPL is both a noun and a verb: "We have to IPL." An IPL is usually the only way to recover from a system *crash*, in which case it is called a "re-IPL."

IRG (Letters pronounced separately) InterRecord Gap.

irrational number   A number that exists in theory only, such as the square root of -1. The representation of such numbers in computer programs, which always deal in absolute real values, is a difficult challenge.

ISAM   (Pronounced "eye-sam") Indexed Sequential Access Method. See *file organization*.

ISO   International Standards Organization.

isochronous   A method of synchronizing all elements of a data-communications network, in which the timing signals are provided by the network itself. All devices connected with the network pick up the timing signal from communications lines and coordinate their transmissions according to it.

isolation coil   A set of transformers and other circuits on a phone line that prevent the data terminal equipment from sending harmful voltages and signals.

iteration   One pass through a set of *instructions* in a computer program. Several such passes (e.g., a *loop*) are called reiterations.

iterative process   Any process requiring several repetitions of the same activities. In programming, a *loop* is an iterative process.

J

JCL (Letters pronounced separately) See *Job Control Language*.

JES (Pronounced "jez") Job Entry System. In large-scale computer systems, the *systems software* that accepts and *schedules jobs* for execution and controls printing of output. JES is a portion of the *operating system*.

job One or more programs executed in sequence and handled as a single unit of work by the computer system. A job has a name by which it is identified. It is often broken down into *job steps*, with each step corresponding to the execution of one of the programs constituting the overall job.

job class A designation given to each *job* in a *multiprocessing* system, by which the *operating system* evaluates the relative priorities of several jobs awaiting or in execution. The higher the job class, the more preference it is given.

Job Control Language A special *programming language* used to give instructions to the *operating system* of a large computer. Job Control Language (JCL) is a series of *statements* telling the operating system how to run a specific *job*: the name of the job, the sequence of programs to execute, the *files* each program needs, what to do with those files before and after processing, special steps to take in the event of a program failure, etc. When a job is submitted to the system for execution, its JCL is read into the *Job Entry System*. The

JCL statements constitute input data that are processed by the operating system; it interprets the statements and uses them to control the way the job is run.

Job Entry System   See *JES*.

job queue   In large computer systems, a prioritized list of *jobs* waiting to be run. When a job is submitted and the system is busy, the *Job Entry System* places the new job into a queue (*schedules* it), where it awaits its turn to be executed.

job scheduling   The placement of a new entry into the *job queue* of a large system. Scheduling does not actually entail setting a time to start the *job*. Rather, the new job is evaluated with respect to the others already in the queue, chiefly on the basis of *job class*, and inserted at the appropriate point; normally, this is behind other jobs of the same class and ahead of jobs of lower classes. Thus, scheduling is actually a matter of prioritizing the order in which jobs are executed.

job step   One phase in the execution of a *job*. A job step corresponds to the running of one program. If a job consists of six programs run in sequence, it has six steps.

jobstream   A collective term for all the *jobs* of a certain type. The "production jobstream," for example, includes all the routine jobs in daily use and excludes test work and one-of-a-kind programs.

job swapping   Temporarily suspending work on a running *job* so that a higher priority can be given to another. When a job is swapped out, its *memory* workspace and various control information are written to a *file*, thus removing the job from the active status altogether. Later it is swapped back in and execution resumes where it left off. The *operating system* normally does job swapping automatically based upon the mix of jobs in execution and their relative priorities. It is usually the lowest priority job that gets swapped out when several high-priority jobs are running concurrently.

job turnaround The elapsed time from when a *job* is given to the computer system until its printed output reaches the person who submitted the job. The term applies to *batch* work only.

Josephson junction An extremely high-speed *semiconductor* switching technology utilized in experimental computers immersed in a bath of superchilled liquid gas. See *cryogenics*.

joystick A manual control most often seen in connection with computer games. The joystick is a lever that can be moved any direction from vertical. It sends a *byte* to the computer, the numeric value of which indicates its position. A joystick is thus capable of reporting up to 256 positions, though few are engineered to such precision. Also has some application in industrial control systems and in aircraft.

Julian date A common form of calendar repesentation within a computer system. The Julian date indicates the year and the number of elapsed days in the year; e.g., 82.299 was October 26, 1982, the 299th day of 1982.

jump To deviate from the normal sequential execution of *instructions* in a computer program and resume processing elsewhere within the program. Also called a *branch*; used as both verb and noun.

jumper A wire or other form of external conductor that joins two otherwise unconnected circuits on a *printed circuit board*. Jumpers are used to activate options; sometimes they also correct design errors.

jumper selectable An option or feature activated by means of a *jumper* in electronic circuitry.

jump vector A list of the *memory addresses* where various *modules* (sections) of a program are located. Generally, each module performs a distinct function, e.g., clear the display screen, read data from a *file*, etc. When the program needs to perform such a function, it obtains the location of the module from the jump vector and then *branches* to that address. The jump vector thus serves as an index of services available to the program.

justification   The alignment of data within a *field*, usually to the extreme left or the extreme right. Justification is usually an automatic operation, with alphabetic letters *left justified* and numerics *right justified* within the allowable space of the field. For example, if an alphabetic field has room for 21 characters and an item of data is only 14 characters long, it might be positioned—justified—to the extreme left, leaving the rightmost seven character positions blank.

K

K Abbreviation for *kilo-*, meaning thousand. In computer parlance 1K equals 1024, the nearest round number in *binary* to 1000. This leads to a discrepancy in expressing sizable quantities in terms of K. For example, a *memory* of 64K actually holds 65,536 *bytes* (64 × 1024 = 65,536). The term is one of the most familiar measurements of quantity used in data processing.

KBD Abbreviation for keyboard (used only in writing).

kernel (1) A *software* product sold with the understanding that it must be modified by the buyer before he or she can use it on a specific machine. The kernel is usually, but not always, accompanied by other programs that facilitate customization.

(2) Sometimes used in the sense of *nucleus,* the central and indispensible portion of a computer *operating system*.

key (1) In reference to a piece of *hardware*, any switch or button.

(2) In a *sort*, a *field* (item) of data evaluated in determining the order into which *records* are rearranged. Often called a *sort key*.

keyboard On a terminal, similar to a typewriter keyboard.

keyboard lockup A situation in which entries typed on a keyboard are ignored. A keyboard lockup is not physical; the keys continue to operate mechanically, but they have no effect. May be caused by a failure, but can also be done deliberately by *software*; for instance, to prevent unauthorized use of a terminal.

key bounce   In some keyboard terminals, several repetitions of the same character sent during one *keystroke*. This can be caused by mechanical bouncing due to worn or weak springs in the key, or because of faulty design. In the latter case, the key constantly generates a character while depressed, and because the computer repeatedly checks the keyboard for a character, it reads the same one over and over while the key is held down (even if only momentarily, since the computer is much faster than a typist). See also *debounce*.

keycap   The physical button on a keyboard that generates a signal corresponding to a character when depressed.

keypad   A cluster of special-purpose keys on a terminal keyboard to one side of the normal typing keys. An example is a numeric keypad, which furnishes a ten-key adding machine function.

keypunch   A machine with a keyboard, used to punch *cards* for input to a computer.

keystroke   The keying of one character on a keyboard. The counting of keystrokes is one means of measuring the amount of work done to prepare data for input to a computer.

key-to-disk   A data input device similar to a *keypunch*, except that data typed at the keyboard is written directly onto *disk storage*.

key-to-tape   A data input device similar to a *keypunch*, except that data typed at the keyboard is written directly onto *magnetic tape*.

keyword   A word or a pseudoword (a group of letters and numbers in a specific order) that has special significance.

keyword parameter A *parameter* that is identified by a *keyword* label, usually with an equals sign linking them. For example, under a data security system a *password* is required to perform certain functions. This might be specified PASSWD = SKLRGX. In this case, PASSWD is the keyword and SKLRGX is the parameter.

keyword search A method of filing and retrieving information (usually text) by the use of keywords that describe the contents of individual records. Keywords in this context are analogous to index tabs on file folders, but more versatile in that several keywords can be used to categorize and access a single item in various ways. In a law enforcement information system, as an example, descriptions of crimes might be filed with keywords as follows:

Case 1	ROBBERY	MURDER
Case 2	RAPE	MURDER
Case 3	ROBBERY	DRUGS

A Keyword search on MURDER alone would produce Cases 1 and 2; on ROBBERY alone, Cases 1 and 3. A search on ROBBERY AND MURDER would turn up only Case 1. If instead a search were done on MURDER BUT NOT ROBBERY, only Case 2 would be pulled. In this way, a computer can be used to store vast amounts of information and highly selective searches can be done.

kilo A thousand. In computerese, kilo- stands for 1024, the nearest round number to 1000 in *binary*. One kilobyte is therefore 1024 *bytes*. Abbreviated *K*.

kludge See *kluge*.

kluge (1) A group of similar computers physically adjacent to each other and connected together electronically in order to function as a single unit, somewhat in the same sense as an association of people. In a kluge, one processor acts as the leader, doing some of the work itself and assigning work to the others.

(2) Any jury-rigged arrangement of *hardware* and/or *software* that could be described as "held together by bailing twine and chewing gum."

KSR   Keyboard Send and Receive. A *dumb interactive* terminal that functions as a remote keyboard and printer in communication with a computer. A KSR has no ability to store messages that will later be sent.

L

label (1) In reference to a *file* saved on *tape* or *disk*, a *record* indicating the name of the file, its date and time of creation, its *attributes*, and other control information. Also called a *header record*.

(2) In a computer program, a symbolic name given to an *instruction* or to a part of the program for reference purposes. For example, the section of the program that prints output might have the label PRINTO. The programmer can then write instructions such as GO TO PRINTO. The *language processor* translates labels into *memory addresses*.

LAN See *local area network*.

land The area of a printed circuit board available for mounting electronic components. Also called *real estate*.

language processor A *utility* that translates human-written *source* programs into a form that can be executed on a computer. Every language processor is designed to accept one *programming language* (e.g., PASCAL, COBOL, BASIC, etc.) and translate it into the *machine language* of a specific *CPU* type (e.g., Zilog Z80, IBM 370-series, etc.) The language it accepts is called the *source language*; the machine type for which it produces output is the *target CPU*. There are three general kinds of language processors: *compilers, assemblers,* and *interpreters*.

large-scale integration *Semiconductor chip* technology. The placing of thousands of microscopic circuits, transistors, resistors, etc., on a tiny piece of semiconductor material (usually silicon). The degrees of refinement in this technology are LSI (large-scale integration), VLSI (very large-scale integration), and ULSI (ultra-large-scale integration).

laser memory   A fairly new type of extremely high-*density* data storage. *Bits* are literally burned into a smooth surface as tiny pits by a high-power laser beam. They are later read by a low-power laser that scans the surface, detecting bit patterns by the degree of reflectivity (the pits not being reflective). Once recorded upon, the surface is not erasable or reusable. Because of the high densities possible, however, billions of characters can be held on an inexpensive surface the size of a phonograph record. This technology is widely used for video disks and is beginning to appear in computer storage devices.

laser printer   An extremely fast electrostatic printer. As paper travels through the printer, it passes a laser that forms character images in *dot matrix* patterns as dots of static electricity. A metallic dust then blows across the paper, sticking to the static dots and falling off uncharged areas. A heat process melts the powder, fusing it to the paper to form inked printing. Laser printers can typically print upwards of 2 miles of paper output per hour.

latch   (1) A mechanical lock that secures a moving part.
   (2) An electronic circuit that reverses and holds its state each time power is applied; the first time it latches on, the second time, off, third time, on again, etc. Latching circuits are controlled by *flip-flops* and often activated by push-on/push-off buttons.

latency delay   Delay in reading or writing data on a *storage device* due to mechanical action. In accessing *disk,* the *head* must move to the desired *track* and then wait until the appropriate point on the surface rotates under it. The combination of such delays is latency.

layered architecture A concept applied chiefly to the design and control of very large data-communications networks. Layering is closely allied with the notion of *hierarchy*, in which all components of the network fit at one level or another within a pyramidal control structure; the higher the layer, the broader its span of control.

layered protocol The rules for passing communications among levels in a hierarchical network using *layered architecture*. Relates to the kinds of control information to be added to or deleted from messages as they pass among layers.

LDM Limited-Distance Modem. A low-cost device used to send and receive data signals over short-haul lines (typically less than 5 miles).

leading edge A buzz word implying technological leadership: "On the leading edge of technology." Applies to vendors who pioneer new developments in products; also to client companies who are willing and eager to buy such products.

leading pad Characters used to fill unused space on the left end of a *field* of data. In the seven-digit field 0000329, the zeros are a leading pad. SPACE characters are also often used.

leading zeros See *leading pad*.

least significant bit The rightmost *bit* in a *byte*, which has the lowest numeric place value in *binary* just as the rightmost digit (the 7) has the lowest value in the number 4237.

LED (Usually pronounced as a word) Light-Emitting Diode. A solid substance that glows as electricity passes through it. Often used for indicator lamps because it is more dependable than a light bulb. Also used for numeric displays, in which the images of digits are formed by selectively turning on several of seven long LED's arranged in two cubes, one atop the other.

left justify To shift the contents of a *field* so that the first printable character appears in the first (leftmost) position. Most *programming languages* automatically left justify alphabetic text. The term also applies to page format; a typewriter produces left justified copy because every line (unless deliberately indented) begins the same distance from the left edge of the paper.

legal Acceptable under the *software* rules of a computer system.

level set A revision to a *software package* that replaces most or all of the executable program(s) with improved software.

levels of nesting In programming, *nesting* involves placing similar *constructs* one inside the other, as the variously sized mixing bowls of a set are stacked. This is often done in *loops*. In a text processing program, one loop (the "outer" loop) might read a line at a time from a *file*; an inner ("nested") loop then scans through the line character by character. When the inner loop completes work on the line, the outer loop reads the next line, and so on. The inner loop repeats many times for each pass of the outer loop. In this example there is one level of nesting. If the nested loop in turn contained a smaller loop, there would be two levels of nesting. Also applies to other programming constructs such as *functions*, *procedures*, and *subroutines*.

lexicon See *data dictionary*.

LF Line Feed. A control character that causes the paper in a printer or the *cursor* on a display to advance to the next line.

librarian A person working in a computer center who has the responsibility for the physical and administrative maintenance of *tapes*, *card decks*, and other data storage.

library (1) A *tape* library is a collection of reels of tape kept at a computer center.

(2) A documentation library is a collection of printed material such as equipment manuals, program listings, etc.

(3) On *disk storage*, a library is a collection of related *files*, such as computer programs.

license contract A document and the accompanying payment of money to a vendor, entitling the purchaser to run a *software* product on his or her computer. A license contract usually also commits the vendor to provide assistance and fixes when problems occur, updates to the product, etc., and provides legal safeguards to prevent the buyer from selling or giving a copy of the software to someone else.

LIFO Last In, First Out. A technique of handling events in reverse chronological order. See *FIFO*.

light-emitting diode See *LED*.

lightning cutover See *big-bang implementation*.

light pen A device used for marking a position on a *display* screen. It looks like a pen on a string. When the tip of the light pen is placed near the surface of the screen, a signal is emitted that is picked up by the control electronics of the *CRT*, translated into an *XY address*, and passed as such back to the computer. Used for marking one of several choices in a *menu*, for sketching changes in a *graphic* display, and for other applications where a savings in time or keying data can be realized.

lightwave communications See *fiber optics*.

limited-distance modem See *LDM*.

linear amplification The changes in the output signal strength are directly proportional to the input signal strength, as in being multiplied by a constant factor.

line analyzer A device used to measure the transmission characteristics of a telephone line, either by electronically observing signals or by performing active tests.

line driver   An alternative term for *limited-distance modem*.

line editor   An *interactive* computer program that permits a terminal user to enter, view, and *edit* information one line at a time.

line feed   See *LF*.

line of code   A *statement* in a *programming language*, in most cases occupying one line of text. Lines of code are a general measurement of the size of a program: "That program has three thousand lines of code."

line pitch   The density of characters on a printed line, usually expressed in terms of characters per inch. Ten pitch means ten characters per inch.

line printer   A printer that produces an entire line of type at a time, rather than printing serially as a typewriter does. See *drum printer*.

line switching   As in a telephone switching center, where lines are electrically connected together in random patterns. Contrasts with *message switching*.

line trace   A computer program that records and time-stamps all traffic passing between a communications line and a computer. Used to troubleshoot problems.

line turnaround   In *half-duplex* transmission (the ability to transmit in both directions, but not simultaneously), line turnaround is the time it takes the line to prepare to reverse the direction of transmission.

link   (1) To combine program *modules* into a single executable program using a *linkage editor*.
   (2) A data-communications line connecting two or more *intelligent* machines.

linkage   Between computer programs, establishing common points of reference for purposes of communications. A *utility* called a *linkage editor* builds these points of reference into the programs as *memory addresses*. Linkage can also be accomplished by external means, such as passing *files* between programs, or by the use of predetermined memory locations (see *COMMON*).

linkage conventions Agreed-upon methods for accomplishing *linkage* between programs.

linkage editor A *utility* program that combines two or more related computer programs into one. The input to a linkage editor is *object modules* produced by a *compiler* or *assembler*; its output is a *machine language* program in a form suitable to be executed on a computer. Large programs are often developed in pieces called modules, which refer to each other. The linkage editor resolves these references by replacing them with the actual *memory addresses* it assigns in the process of arranging the modules into a single, monolithic program.

linkloader A *linkage editor* that, upon completing the linking phase, loads the program into *memory* to begin execution.

LISP LISt Processor. A *high-level programming language* that is especially suited for text manipulation and analysis.

list device The *target* output device for a computer program. Normally either a printer or a display.

listing A printed report produced by a program.

load (1) To place data in a *register* or *memory*.
(2) To move an executable program into memory in preparation for running it.

loader A *system control program* that moves a program into *memory* and prepares it for execution.

load module A *machine language* program capable of being brought into *memory* and executed without further preparation.

local (1) Limited in its effect to a single phase of a program's overall execution. Contrasts with *global*; a global variable, for example, appears repeatedly throughout the program, whereas a local variable exists only while some smaller part of the program is being run, e.g., in a *subroutine*.

(2) Attached directly to the computer system via *house cable* and treated by the system as a *peripheral*. Contrasts with *remote*, which is connected through data communications.

local area network An in-house data-communications system, usually within a single building, connecting a number of microcomputers together. Abbreviated LAN (pronounced either as a word or letters separately). A LAN often includes a large *mainframe* computer as well, thus permitting the micros to act both in a *stand-alone* mode and as terminals. The micros can share devices and *files* using the LAN, so that equipment costs are held down by pooling such expensive resources as printers and *hard disks*. The LAN is the basis for *office automation*.

logical page A unit of *memory* consisting of an arbitrary number of *bytes*, usually a multiple of 256 (since round numbers in *binary* occur every 256 counts). A logical page seldom has any significance except as a convenient measure of memory usage.

logical record A complete unit of information describing something, e.g., an invoice. In an invoice *file* containing 1000 invoices there are 1000 logical records, one for each.

logical unit Any component in a data-communications network that has its own *address*. A *physical unit* might consist of one logical unit (e.g., a printer only), several logical units (e.g., a keyboard, a display, and a printer in one housing), or none (if it is not directly accessable to the computer). A logical unit is assumed to be a self-contained machine possessing a set of defined *attributes*.

logic circuit An electronic circuit that performs switching and control functions based on logical concepts such as *AND*.

logic error A programming error caused by faulty reasoning on the part of the programmer. The *instructions* in the *programming language* are correct and executed as written, but because the process is wrong the results are wrong.

logic gate An electronic switching component that evaluates two or more inputs and produces one output based upon a rule of logic. The inputs are usually *bits* arriving simultaneously. If the logic rule is *OR*, the output will produce a 1 bit if any input is a 1. Logic gates are always identified by the rule they operate under. See *AND, OR, NAND, NOR, XOR*.

logic high A logic high is the electrical representation of a 1 *bit*, and a logic low is the electrical representation of a Ø bit. Conceptually, digital circuitry operates on the precept that a 1 bit is a pulse of electricity and a Ø bit is the absence of a pulse. In fact, this is not so in most computers. Instead a 1 bit is a high voltage and a Ø bit is a lower voltage, thus providing for the positive reception of Ø bits and the reassurance that the circuitry is working.

logic low See *logic high*.

logic operation The manipulation of two pieces of information according to the rules of logic, thus leading to a result. In electronics, these rules are called *AND, OR, NAND, NOR,* and *XOR* (exclusive OR).

logic-seeking print head A *bidirectional* printing mechanism that optimizes its motion for more efficient printing. In bidirectional printing, the first line is printed left to right, the second right to left, etc. In advancing from the right end of one line to the right end of the next, a logic-seeking print head jumps directly to the final character position in the next line and begins its leftward travel from that point.

LOGO   A *programming language* developed chiefly for teaching young children elements of computer programming. LOGO is a simple and rather limited language strongly oriented toward *graphics* and of no value for general data-processing use. It is highly *interactive*, permitting children to learn quickly how to draw geometric patterns and pictures on the screen.

log off   To end a work session at a terminal and remove the terminal from active status in the computer system. A *command* (typically, LOGOFF or BYE) is entered at the terminal keyboard, thus notifying the system that the terminal is no longer active. The system will then ignore the terminal until a command to *log on* is entered.

log on   To initiate a work session at a terminal and place the terminal in active status within the computer system. A *command* such as *LOGON* is entered at the keyboard, and the system then prompts the user for identification and commands, thus establishing active status.

longitudinal redundancy check   See *check character*.

lookalike   One product that copies another. When a vendor enjoys success with a product, its competitors offer lookalikes.

loop   A programming term describing a sequence of *instructions* that is repeated until some task has been completed. Because data processing involves many repetitious operations, the loop is one of the most common programming techniques. For example, suppose we want to print ten characters. Rather than writing the print instructions ten times, once for each character, we write them once and repeat them ten times, thus creating a loop. The program example below, written in 8080 *assembly language,* illustrates a loop that accomplishes this purpose. The *comments* (preceded by semicolons) help to explain the program.

With few exceptions, all loops have four stages: initialize, process, alter the control variable, and test. In this case, initialization is done in the first two instructions (determine the location of the output data and its length). The actual loop begins with the process, which is the next three instructions (get a character, print it, point to the next). The instruction DCR C *decrements* (subtracts one from) the control variable, in this example a value indicating the number of characters still waiting to be printed. Testing is the last instruction; if the control variable is not yet zero, the program loops back to the process and repeats. When the control variable reaches zero, the loop is completed and the program continues with the next instruction (not shown in the example).

```
; LOOP INITIALIZATION
    LXI H,OUTPUT        ;LOCATION OF OUTPUT DATA
    MVI C, 10           ;LENGTH OF OUTPUT DATA
; LOOP TO PRINT 10 CHARACTERS AT 'OUTPUT'
LOOP: MOV A,M           ;GET NEXT CHARACTER
    OUT PRINT           ;PRINT IT
    INX H               ;POINT TO NEXT
; LOOP CONTROL
    DCR C               ;COUNT
    JNZ LOOP            ;REPEAT UNTIL THRU
```

The condition for ending the loop in this case is that the control variable (the number of characters left to be printed) must reach zero. The loop repeats until this condition is satisfied.

A program is said to be "in a loop" (*looping*) when the exit condition is never reached. The loop continuously repeats for infinity, making it appear that the computer (though, in fact, it is stuck in the loop) has "gone to sleep," or produces an endless printout of the same information, or otherwise causes undesirable results. This is a fairly common programming bug.

In more complex programs, loops often contain other loops, which contain yet smaller loops, and so on. Such constructions are called *nested loops*, and they form a powerful tool in computer programming.

loopback switch   A switch at the end of a telephone line that, when closed, "loops back" the line so that received signals are reflected back to the sender. Used in testing the line.

looping   A program is said to be looping when it becomes trapped in a *loop* from which it cannot escape. This is a programming error causing the program to execute the same sequence of *instructions* forever. It can only be halted by *canceling* the program.

loop technology   A method of connecting communicating machines together in a network. See *daisy chain*.

loosely coupled systems   Two or more physically adjacent computers that share *peripherals* and communicate with one another for the purposes of coordinating efforts, sharing *files*, and helping each other when one is overloaded.

low core   The lowest *addresses* of the main *memory* in a computer, starting at Ø. In most *operating systems*, low core is used for the storage of control values needed to run the computer system, and for other critical information and *instructions*. The actual program *code* of the operating system is located in *high core* (the top of memory), with workspace for *application programs* situated in middle core.

low-order   Numerically less significant than *high-order*, e.g., in the number 58, the 8 is the low-order digit.

low side   The portion of a *remote controller* that "faces" away from the computer with which it communicates. For example, a *device cluster controller* handles communications between a *host* computer and a number of terminals; the *high side* handles host communications, and the low side handles the terminals.

lower case   Noncapitalized alphabetic letters.

lowlight   The normal intensity of *video display* characters. Contrasts with *highlight*, which makes characters stand out by increasing their intensity.

LPI   Lines Per Inch on printed or displayed output, measuring vertically.

LRC   Longitudinal Redundancy Check. See *check character*.

LSB   See *least significant bit*.

LSI   See *large-scale integration*.

M

M68ØØØ   A *microprocessor chip* manufactured by Motorola. The M68ØØØ is a *16-bit CPU* chip developed specifically for small computers, rather than a general-purpose processor adapted to computers, as was the case for most first-generation (*8-bit*) chips.

machine check   A *hardware* failure within a computer that causes it to stop running.

machine cycle   The period of time it takes for a computer to perform a given number of internal operations. See also *cycle*.

machine language   The *binary code* read by the *control section* of a *central processor* and translated into electronic actions. All *programming languages* ultimately resolve into machine language, the patterns of *bits* that make the computer function. Every CPU type has its own machine language, and there is very little portability of machine languages from one CPU type to another. For this reason, when a program is moved from one vendor's machine to another's (e.g., from an IBM to a Honeywell, or from a Radio Shack to an Apple), it must be re*compiled* from its *source* form in order to develop the machine language executable by the new computer.

macro   In an *assembly language* a macro is a single *instruction* that symbolizes a predetermined set of assembly language instructions. During assembly, these instructions are inserted at the point where the macro is "issued" (written into the program). A macro has a unique name, e.g., FILEREAD, by which it is specified in the program. The actual instructions (*macro expansion*) are either defined elsewhere in the program or in an external macro *library* where the assembler can find them by name and obtain the instructions. Standardized macros are used to save the time of writing frequently performed routines in assembly language. One can, in a way, view all *high-level programming languages* as an elaborate system of macros.

macro assembler   An *assembler* capable of performing the substitutions of actual *assembly language instructions* for a symbolic *macro* instruction.

macro expansion   The *assembly language instructions* generated by a *macro* and inserted into a program as though they had actually been written there.

macroinstruction   (1) A macro.
   (2) Any single *command* or programming *instruction* that triggers several resulting actions.

magnetic core   A tiny iron ring used in obsolete computer *memories*. See *core*.

magnetic ink character recognition   See *MICR*.

magnetic tape   A recording tape used to store data. The *bits* representing each character are written across the width of the tape in the form of magnetized spots. The reading and writing of tape is done by moving the tape's surface across the read/write *head* of a *tape drive*. Tape is an economical and popular *medium* for storing large amounts of data in a machine-readable form.

mag tape   See *magnetic tape*.

mainframe   (1) Specifically, the rack(s) holding the *central processing unit* and the *memory* of a large computer.

(2) More generally, any large computer. "We have two mainframes and several minis."

main storage   See *memory*.

maintainability   Refers to the ease with which changes can be made to a computer program.

maintenance   (1) With reference to *hardware*, used in the conventional sense of maintenance.

(2) In *software* the ongoing effort of correcting *bugs*, making minor modifications, and updating computer programs to meet changing conditions.

maintenance contract   A business contract between a client and a repair service vendor for the maintenance of *hardware*.

maintenance pack   A *disk drive* on which copies of computer programs are kept for the purpose of applying and testing *maintenance* changes.

make-busy   A switch that, when activated, makes a dial telephone line (or a group of lines) appear to be busy to prevent incoming calls. Used with dial lines that access computers to prevent calls from arriving while the computer is "down."

male connector   An electrical connector with protruding contacts for mating with a *female* receptacle.

management information system   A coordinated system of *hardware*, *software*, and data whose purposes are to solve business information needs and to furnish summary information on business activities for management review and decision making.

manifest constant   In a computer program, the assignment of a value to a symbolic name at the start of the program, that value not subject to change during execution. Also called a *global declaration*. Manifest constants are useful for easing the task of modifying a program. A program might, for example, deal with numerous *files*, all having a *record length* of 80 characters. At the start of the program, the manifest constant RECLEN = 80 could be declared, and everywhere that the record length is specified in the program it is stated by the symbol RECLEN (not 80). If the record length is later expanded to 100 characters, the programmer simply changes the declaration to RECLEN = 100 and re*compiles* the program, thereby changing the record length everywhere.

mark   A 1 *bit*. Contrasts with *space* (a 0 bit).

mark-sense   A method of encoding data using a lead pencil, as is done on standardized achievement tests for school children. Defined spaces are provided for selecting alternatives, the selected space to be filled in with a lead pencil. The data are then read by a *mark-sense reader*.

mark-sense reader   A data input device that reads *mark-sense* documents. The mark made by a soft lead pencil conducts electricity. A mark-sense reader tests each possible marking location on the document for conductivity and, where the test succeeds, converts that location into a *byte* that is sent to a computer as input data.

mask   A fixed pattern of *bits* or characters that is combined with variable information to produce some result. An *encryption* mask, for example, is a fixed set of *bytes* that is mathematically applied to information to conceal its content by making it unrecognizable. The content can later be retrieved by applying the same mask under an obverse process that ''undoes'' the scrambling. See also *test under mask*.

Mass Storage System   Abbreviated MSS. A *peripheral* device intended to accomplish the same purpose as a *tape library*—i.e., to store vast amounts of information—but to make the information quickly and automatically accessible.

All *files* under control of the MSS are indexed as to location, so that they can be immediately found and retrieved. Technologies vary. The most widely used MSS is the IBM 3850, in which files are stored on small cylinders, each capable of holding 100 million characters. Hundreds of these cylinders are held in a honeycomb. When a file is needed, its honeycomb *address* is looked up in the index and a mechanical arm plucks the cylinder out and places it in a read/write station, where it *emulates* a *disk drive*.

massage   To process data.

master file   The current *generation* of a *file* containing all information relevant to, and thus serving as the central point of reference for, an *application system*. In a bank, for example, the "savings master" contains all records of savings accounts current as of today.

master scheduler   In a *job entry system,* the program that prioritizes *jobs* submitted for execution. See *job scheduling*.

master unit   When two *intelligent* devices are connected, it is sometimes necessary for them to establish which one is in control. This becomes the master unit, the subordinate device the *slave* unit.

matrix   A conceptualized *array* of numerous items of related information, arranged by rows and columns. Each individual element is *indexed* by the use of subscripts indicating its row and column numbers.

MB   MegaByte.

mean time between failures   Abbreviated MTBF. A measure of the reliability of a class of devices, indicating the average frequency of failure. For example, if we measure 900 of some type of device over a month, we have $900 \times 1 = 900$ device-months. If 15 failures occurred, MTBF is calculated as $900/15 = 60$ months, or, in other words, the average device in this group fails once every five years.

mean time to repair Abbreviated MTTR. A measure of a repair organization's responsiveness to failures. Time-to-repair is the interval from reporting a problem to its resolution. MTTR is the average of these intervals over some reporting period, and is typically expressed in hours and minutes.

mechanization The application of machinery (usually computers) to the resolution of information needs. Interchangeable in most instances with *automation*.

media A generic term for all surfaces used for recording data in machine-readable form, such as *disk, cards, tape,* and *drum* storage. ''Media'' is the plural form of *medium.*

media failure When data are unreadable due to a defect in a magnetic recording surface.

medium A surface on which data can be written in machine-readable form, such as *tape* or *disk.* Plural is *media.*

Meg Short for *megabytes.* ''That machine has 8 meg of main memory.''

mega One million. In computerese, mega- is the square of *kilo-* (1024), and therefore actually equals 1,048,576. This is the nearest round number in *binary* to 1,000,000.

member A separate complete *file* belonging to a *partitioned file* (a collection of related files grouped under one name). Each member has a unique name by which it is identified in association with the name of its partitioned file. For example, if a company has a weekly payroll, it might have a partitioned file called TIMECARDS, with a member for each day of the week. The Sunday member would thus be identified within the computer system as TIMECARDS(SUNDAY). This member can be read, written, and altered without affecting the other members of the partitioned file.

memo post To write transactions into a temporary file as they are received in the computer system. From time to time the accumulated memo postings are processed as input data to update other files. Similar in concept to jotting down notes to oneself.

memory   In general, memory is the ability and the devices that enable a machine to store information subject to recall. In its broadest sense, memory refers to any *hardware* capable of serving that end, e.g., *disk, tape, semiconductor storage*, etc. More specifically, in common usage memory is the high-speed working area associated with the *central processor* of a computer, where it writes and reads information immediately useful to the tasks in execution. Both the program being run and the data it is currently processing are kept in memory for the duration of the program run. Memory is divided into "boxes" that correspond to characters. Each such "box" has a numeric *address* that the CPU specifies when it reads the content of the location or writes new information into it. The speed of information movement in and out of memory generally corresponds to the speed of the CPU itself. Each action the CPU takes in some way or another involves the memory, and thus it is an integral part of the computer.

Most computer memories are semiconductor *chips* called *RAM* (for Random-Access Memory). Older computers used instead *core* memory. Both technologies function the same as far as capabilities are concerned, but semiconductor memory is cheaper by several orders of magnitude and more reliable.

The size of a computer's memory is expressed in *K* (for kilobytes), 1K being equal to 1024 *bytes*. Thus, a 64K memory in a microcomputer has 65,536 bytes of space. In large computers, the size of memory is expressed in *MB* (for *megabytes*), 1MB equaling 1,048,576 bytes (1024 × 1024).

For special purposes, such as having a frequently used program immediately available (rather than having to bring it into memory each time it is needed), a type of memory called *ROM* (for Read-Only Memory) is sometimes installed in a computer. A ROM has memory addresses and, in some cases, makes the corresponding numeric addresses unavailable in RAM. It is different from RAM in that its addresses can only be read; data cannot be written into them. The program it contains is "burned" into its locations and is not lost when power is removed.

ROM is thus non*volatile* memory, whereas RAM is volatile (loses its contents when power is removed).

Memory is also called *main storage*, immediate memory, *core*, working storage, and direct memory. These terms are all interchangeable.

memory cycle The amount of time required to move one *byte* of information into or out of *memory*.

memory dump A printout showing the contents of *memory*. Used for troubleshooting problems in programs.

memory expansion card A *printed circuit board* containing additional *memory* that can be plugged into a computer to increase the memory capacity.

memory refresh See *dynamic RAM*.

memory map An *image* in *memory* of information appearing elsewhere, maintained for purposes of control. In a *display* device, for example, there is a memory map of the screen, with one memory location corresponding to each character position on the display. When a program "prints to the screen," it actually modifies memory locations in the map, and the control electronics of the display causes these modifications to appear visually.

menu In an *interactive* program, a list of choices from which to choose an action that the program will perform.

menu-driven A program that relies heavily on *menus*, thus providing the user with total control over the way the program proceeds.

merge   To combine two or more separate *files* into one. A merge is similar to a *sort* in that it usually rearranges information from the files into an order as determined by the content of individual records, thus mingling ("merging") records from different sources into one ordered file.

message   A unit of information sent from one device to another in a form understandable to the receiving machine so that it can act upon it. A message can be either human-oriented information, such as text or numbers, or it can be control information useful only to the involved machines. In data communications a message usually consists of three parts: a header indicating the destination, source, time, sequence number, etc., of the message; the actual content of the message; and a trailer signifying the end of the message and perhaps containing a *check character*.

message blocking   The dividing of *messages* into blocks of a fixed number of *bytes* in order to provide consistent work units, thus simplifying the design of data-communications networks.

message handler   A computer program that processes incoming and/or outgoing data-communications *messages*.

message header   The first part of a data-communications *message*, indicating the destination and source of the message, its length, the date and time sent, and other control information.

message queue   In data-communications *software*, a *queue* (prioritized list) of messages that need to be processed.

message switch   A computer that receives data-communications *messages* from originators and relays them to their destinations. A message switch differs from a line switch (e.g., *crossbar*) in that it does not electrically connect lines, but rather receives messages, stores them temporarily, and then redirects them to the appropriate lines.

message trailer The last part of a data-communications *message*, perhaps containing control information such as a *check character*, but mainly signifying the conclusion of the message.

metered device A piece of data-processing equipment for which the user is charged on the basis of usage, rather than by a flat rental fee. Metered printers measure paper footage; most other metered devices measure time in operation.

MG Motor Generator. A generator installed in a data-processing center to convert commercial power into the special electrical requirements of large computers. Standard *street power* has a frequency of 60 *Hz*, but some computers require 400 Hz; commercial power therefore turns the motor generator, which developes the appropriate frequency for local use.

MHz MegaHertz. One million cycles of alternating current per second.

MICR (Pronounced "miker") Magnetic Ink Character Recognition. The ability of a machine to read human-legible *alphanumerics* by detecting the shapes of their magnetic fields. MICR is used mainly on bank checks. The account number and other information is printed across the bottom using a special metallic ink. When the check is processed by a machine, it is first magnetized and then the characters are read by sensing their magnetic fields. This information then passes to a computer as input data.

micro Short for *microcomputer*.

micro- (1) One millionth. A microsecond is 1/1,000,000 of a second.
   (2) Smallest, as a *microcomputer* is the smallest kind of computer, a *microprocessor* the smallest kind of *CPU*, etc.

microcode A term used mainly by IBM to mean *firmware*; a computer program permanently "burned" into *read-only memory*.

microcomputer A small, inexpensive computer. Because of wide differences among various makes and due to the rapid development of technology, it is difficult to define a microcomputer precisely and to say where the line is between micros and the larger *minicomputers*. Despite the lack of a consensus, however, it is generally agreed that a micro is a computer that an individual can afford and that will satisfy most of his or her personal computing requirements.

microelectronics Electronic technology involved with *semiconductor chips* using *large-scale integration*.

microfiche See *fiche*.

microform See *fiche* (terms interchangeable).

microprocessor A small limited-capability *central processing unit* contained entirely on one *semiconductor chip*. Used in microcomputers and also in other devices under program control.

microwave An extremely high-*frequency* radio communications technology. Microwave communications relies on line-of-sight (point-to-point) beams aimed using dish antennas. Frequently used for long-haul telephone circuits.

microwave hop A *microwave* radio channel between two dish antennas aimed at each other.

milli- One one-thousandth. A millisecond is 1/1000 of a second.

mini Short for *minicomputer*.

minicomputer A small- to medium-sized computer, usually able to execute several programs concurrently. There is no clear-cut distinction between a large microcomputer and a small mini, except that the mini is expandable to a much greater extent than a micro.

minidisk A small (5¼″ diameter) *floppy disk*.

minimum configuration (1) A "bare-bones" *hardware* system with no extra-cost options.

(2) The minimum numbers and kinds of hardware and *software* elements necessary to perform a specific data-processing activity.

MIP rate See *MIPS*.

MIPS Millions of *Instructions* Per Second. A measure of the speed of a large *CPU*. Refers to the average number of *machine language* instructions that the CPU performs in 1 second. The IBM 3083, as an example, is a "seven-MIPS machine" because it does about 7 million operations per second. Also called *MIP rate*.

MIS See *management information system*.

mixed-mode Alphabetic and numeric data mixed together.

mixed vendor environment An installation where equipment from different vendors is combined to form a computer system.

mnemonic (Pronounced "num-ON-ic") An abbreviation usually (but not always) consisting of letters extracted from, and thus suggestive of, the word or phrase it symbolizes. *Assembly language instructions*, for example, are mnemonics: BNE for *Branch* if Not Equal, LDA for LoaD *Accumulator*, XCHG for eXCHanGe two registers, etc.

MOD Abbreviation for *modulo*; the remainder after division. As an example, the programming *instruction* 9 MOD 2 returns a value of 1, since 9/2 = 4 with a remainder of 1.

mod Short for modification. Specifically applies to changes made in the *operating system* by a computer user, as described under *hook*.

modem (Pronounced "moe-dehm," with an equal stress on both syllables) MOdulator-DEModulator. A device placed between a communicating machine and a telephone line to permit the transmission of digital pulses. A phone line is not capable of carrying digital signals as produced by computer-related equipment, having been designed instead to carry the *alternating current* of voice-type signals. The modulator converts the pulses of *bits* into tones and sends them on the line; the demodulator changes the received tones back into corresponding bits. Also called a *data set* (mainly by the Bell System). Virtually all modems utilize the standard *EIA interface* (*RS-232*) to ensure compatibility and interchangeability.

modem eliminator   A device that "tricks" two communicating machines into believing they are connected via *modems* and a telephone line. Used between two such machines located within the same room or very near to one another. Each machine's standard modem *interface* is plugged into the modem eliminator, whose electronics simulate the appropriate control signals and pass data between the machines.

modular   Using, or consisting of, building blocks (*modules*). A modular device, for instance, is one that is built, tailored, and expanded by connecting various mutually compatible components.

modular compilation   To *compile* individual parts of a program separately. When all parts have been compiled (translated into *machine language*), they are combined into a single program by a *linkage editor*.

modular programming   To break the writing of a large computer program into several smaller, related units called *modules*. Each module under such an approach generally has a distinct function (e.g., data input, computations, output, report creation, etc.). This enhances the *maintainability* of programs by making it easy to locate the single point of change, rather than having to make many changes scattered throughout the program for one modification. See also *modular compilation*.

modulate To convert information into a form suitable to be transmitted over a communications facility. See *modem*.

module A major individual component of a larger whole; a building block.

modulo See *MOD*.

monadic (1) A *logical* operation having only one *operand*, such as negation. Synonymous with *unary*.

(2) A *Boolean operator* involving one value, e.g. NOT.

(3) In "monadic processor," a stand-alone, *single-thread* computer with one *CPU*. Contrasts with *dyadic*.

monitor (1) To observe a system, line, or component as it operates, for purposes of diagnosing problems or gathering performance statistics.

(2) A device (or sometimes *software*) that performs the functions described in (1).

(3) The viewing screen of a *video display* device.

(4) A primitive *operating system* for a small microcomputer that is not equipped with *disk drives*.

monochrome display A *video display* capable of producing only one color against the background, e.g., green-on-black.

monolithic Complete and all in one piece. For instance, a *linkage editor* combines several fragmentary program *modules* into a single monolithic program.

most significant digit The leftmost and therefore numerically highest-value digit in a number. In the number 31,491, the '3' is the most significant digit. The same concept applies in "most significant *bit*," in which the first or leftmost bit in a *byte* has the greatest numeric value.

mother board A *printed circuit board* into which other printed circuit boards plug, for purposes of conducting power and electronic signals among the boards. See also *backplane*.

motor generator   See *MG*.

MP   See *multiprocessor*.

MSB   Most Significant Bit.

MSC   See *multisystem coupling*.

MSS   See *Mass Storage System*.

MSSG   Abbreviation for message.

MTBF   See *mean time between failures*.

MTTR   See *mean time to repair*.

multidimensional array   An *array* (or *matrix*) of data that has more than the usual two dimensions of rows and columns.

multidrop circuit   A single telephone line that connects three or more points.

multimode device   A machine capable of *emulating* several other machines, or capable of adapting its operation to fit any of several situations.

multiplexer   A device that combines several separate communications signals into one and sends them out on a single line. When receiving mutiplexed signals, the multiplexer performs the reverse process by breaking out separate signal components from the stream and redistributing them to their appropriate destinations. See also *frequency division* and *time division multiplexing*. Multiplexers are used in data communications to save line costs, by enabling numerous devices at two points far apart to communicate over one line. Multiplexers are also used in computer *channels*, so that one channel can control several *peripheral* devices with a minimum of cabling within the computer room. Abbreviated "mux."

multipoint circuit   See *multidrop circuit*.

multiprocessor A *processor configuration* in which two *CPU*s share the same *memory*, thus doubling the capacity of the machine. A multiprocessor differs from an *attached processor* in that the attached processor is wholly dependent on the primary CPU for direction and communications with *peripherals*, whereas in a multiprocessor each CPU is able to function independently of the other. A multiprocessor differs from a *kluge* in that, in a kluge, each CPU has its own memory, while in a multiprocessor there is one memory for two CPUs. Also called a *tightly coupled system*.

multiprogramming The concurrent execution of two or more unrelated programs by the same computer. Multiprogramming is controlled by the *operating system*, and consists of periodically suspending work on one program in order to proceed with another, as for example when the currently running program is waiting for an input/output operation to conclude. Multiprogramming increases a system's *throughput* by productively utilizing *CPU* time that would otherwise be lost waiting for relatively slower external devices. The "multiprogramming level" of a computer system refers to the number of programs it can run concurrently.

multisystem coupling A general term referring to the electronic connecting of two or more physically adjacent computers in order to make them into one logical machine. Numerous approaches exist to this end, e.g. *loosely* and *tightly coupled systems*, *attached processors*, *multiprocessors*, and *channel-to-channel adaptors*.

multisystem network A data-communications network with two or more *host* computers, so that a terminal is able to select the computer with which it wishes to communicate.

multitasking The concurrent execution of two or more dissimilar *tasks* by a computer, i.e., running a *batch* job and at the same time conducting an unrelated *dialog* with a terminal user, while also keeping a printer busy with the output from a previous program.

multiuser   Generally refers to the ability of a computer to support several *interactive* terminals at the same time, with the appearance that each terminal user has the exclusive use of the computer system. Because of the relatively slow input/output speed of terminals the *CPU* in fact, divides its time among them.

multivolume file   A *file* too large to be contained on a single reel of *tape* or on a single *disk*, so that it spans between two or more such storage *media*.

Murphy's laws   A set of humorous, pessimistic "laws" based on the precept that "whatever can go wrong will go wrong at the worst possible moment": "The light at the end of the tunnel is only another train coming this way on the same track"; "The program that runs perfectly during testing will inevitably fail catastrophically as soon as it is placed in production"; etc. Murphy's laws are well suited to the nature of data processing, and after a bad day, one is apt to hear that "Murphy was busy today."

mux   Abbreviation for *multiplexer*.

MVS   Multiple Virtual Storage. The actual name is OS/VS2 -MVS; the primary *operating system* for large IBM and IBM-compatible computers.

N

NAK Negative AcKnowledgement. In data communications, a control character returned from the receiving machine to the sending machine to indicate that the preceding *block* of data contained errors. See also *ACK* and *check character*.

naming convention A standard for assigning symbolic names to such data-processing elements as programs and *files*. A naming convention specifies how names are to be structured: so many characters long, first two characters mean this, next two that, etc. Naming conventions are usually developed and enforced by the data-processing organization, rather than by the vendor, to suit local requirements.

NAND A *logic* operation in which two *bits* or electrical pulses are combined, producing one resulting bit according to the following rules:

$$\emptyset \text{ NAND } \emptyset \longrightarrow 1$$
$$\emptyset \text{ NAND } 1 \longrightarrow 1$$
$$1 \text{ NAND } \emptyset \longrightarrow 1$$
$$1 \text{ NAND } 1 \longrightarrow \emptyset$$

Note that this is precisely the opposite of logical AND, hence the term NAND meaning "Not AND." See *AND* for further discussion.

nano- A billionth. One nanosecond is 1/1,000,000,000 of a second. Light travels approximately one foot per nanosecond, electricity slightly less, consequently placing a physical constraint on the speed of computers.

native mode   The mode of operation when a device is "being itself" and not *emulating* another device.

negative-going voltage   An electrical current of negative polarity (less than 0 volts).

nested loop   A *loop* in a computer program that is contained inside another loop. See *levels of nesting*.

nested subroutine   In a computer program, a subroutine that is called by another subroutine. See *levels of nesting*.

network   A group of communicating devices, usually terminals and one or more computers, connected via telephone lines for the purpose of moving information from place to place.

networking   The design of networks.

nibble   Half a *byte*; the first or second 4-*bit* grouping of a byte of data. An 8-bit byte is considered to consist of two 4-bit *binary* numbers (nibbles), and since 4 bits can represent any of 16 values, a nibble can be represented by its corresponding *hexadecimal* digit. In the byte 01001100, the *high-order* nibble is 0100 (hex 4), and the *low-order* nibble is 1100 (hex C); thus, 01001100 is shown as X'4C', representing its two nibbles.

nixie tube   A vacuum tube used to display legible numbers. A nixie tube has several grids inside, each structured to glow in the shape of a digit when power is applied to the appropriate electrical contact.

node   In a data-communications network, a device that performs control functions and thus influences the operation of the network. A node is often remote from the *host* computer and acts on its instructions, much as in human organization where the local manager acts on instructions issued from a headquarters located elsewhere. A *device cluster controller* is an example of a node.

noise The various noninformational electrical disturbances present on a communications facility that have no relation to, or contribute nothing to, the signal.

noise distortion The loss of signal on a communications facility due to excessive *noise*. A certain amount of noise is always present, and standards govern acceptable levels. Noise distortion occurs when the standards are violated and the noise "drowns out" the signal.

nondeletable A message appearing on a display screen, that cannot be erased from the screen, except by entering a specific command to do so. For example, nondeletable messages are used to advise the computer operator that an error has occurred, and also to request permission to perform certain operations such as changing critical system *files*. In many *operating systems*, nondeletable messages do disappear from the screen of the system *console*, but they are placed in a pending file and can be redisplayed and acted upon at the operator's convenience. See also *nonscrollable*.

nongraphic character A character (*byte*) that, when sent to a printer, does not produce a printable character image. Used for control purposes, e.g., carriage return, line feed, tab, etc.

nonlinear distortion One of the most important principles in communications is that of *linear amplification*, in which an output signal rises or falls in direct, predictable proportion to the strength of the input signal. Nonlinear distortion occurs when the output signal varies in other than a linear fashion, thus causing loss of information due to screeching or unacceptably weak signal strength. An example is "feedback" in a public address system, when the amplifier picks up its own output via the microphone and reamplifies it, then reamplifies that higher signal, etc., until it screeches.

nonprocedural language A *programming language* in which the programmer does not need to specify the actual steps required to solve a problem (open the *file*, read data, add this to that, etc.). Rather, the programmer states the rules and objectives, usually in English, and the programming language by implication develops the necessary procedures to achieve the desired results.

nonrotating disk   A special *memory* that *emulates* a *disk drive* for high-speed input/output. Also called *semiconductor disk.*

nonscrollable   A message or a portion of the screen that does not *scroll* off the top as new information is written at the bottom of the display. In some *operating systems*, nonscrollable messages are used to advise the computer operator that a serious problem has occurred. A nonscrollable message will advance to the top of the screen as new information appears, but it remains there, even if the following lines scroll. This is similar to *nondeletable*, except that nondeletable messages scroll off the screen and are subject to recall; nonscrollable messages do not disappear until the operator enters a specific command to erase them from the screen.

nonswappable   A program that cannot be *swapped out* (execution cannot be suspended for an indefinite period) in a system that runs several programs concurrently. See *job swapping*. A *job* must be explicitly identified as nonswappable at the time it starts in order to be granted this priority, otherwise the *operating system* may swap it out as the system becomes heavily loaded. Normally used only for crucial jobs that merit top priority.

nonvolatile   A *memory* or data storage device that does not lose its information content when electrical power is removed. *Storage media* such as *tape* and *disk* are nonvolatile, while most computer memory is volatile.

nonwrap mode   On a display screen or a printer, information that extends beyond the end of the line is not carried to the next line. In most systems, nonwrapped data are present, but simply not shown. Some nonwrapping printers overstrike all the characters that exceed the available line length in the last printing position of the line. Nonwrap displays ignore such information.

no-op Stands for "no operation." A *machine instruction* that causes the *CPU* to do nothing. A no-op simply advances the *program counter* to the next instruction. No-ops are used to reserve space within the program for the insertion later of additional instructions.

NOP (Pronounced "no-op") A *mnemonic* in most *assembly languages* signifying a do-nothing *instruction*. See *no-op*.

NOR A *logic* operation in which two *bits* or electrical pulses are combined, producing one bit according to the following rules:

$$\emptyset \text{ NOR } \emptyset \longrightarrow 1$$
$$\emptyset \text{ NOR } 1 \longrightarrow \emptyset$$
$$1 \text{ NOR } \emptyset \longrightarrow \emptyset$$
$$1 \text{ NOR } 1 \longrightarrow \emptyset$$

This is the opposite of *OR*, since NOR signifies NOT OR. The circuitry that performs this operation is called a NOR *gate*. See *AND* for further discussion.

NOT A *monadic Boolean operator* that checks for a condition of TRUE or FALSE in an *IF . . . THEN . . . statement*, and controls subsequent execution based on its findings. For example, in *PASCAL* the *function* EOLN means "end of text line"; it is TRUE if the end of the line has been reached and FALSE if not. Thus a program can contain an instruction IF NOT EOLN THEN (continue work on the line) ELSE (read the next line).

nucleus The essential portion of an *operating system*, often contained in the lowest part of the computer's *memory*, where it stores control information and perhaps the fundamental *instructions* that keep it running.

null parameter   Same as *dummy parameter*.

null file   Same as *dummy file*.

number crunching   Mathematical or scientific computing in which the majority of a program's activities involve calculations.

Numeric variable   The symbolic name of a numeric data element that changes during the execution of a program. In the *instruction* X = A + B, the value called X is a numeric variable since the *memory* location it signifies will hold a sum that is determined by the values of A and B, which themselves might also be numeric variables calculated elsewhere in the program.

O

object code The *machine language* resulting from the *compilation* or *assembly* of a computer program, which can be executed as it is or can be converted with little additional effort into executable form.

object module A *file* containing *object code*; the output of a *language processor* such as a *compiler* or *assembler*.

OCR See *optical character recognition*.

octal A numbering system to the *base* 8. Octal numbers are Ø, 1, 2, 3, 4, 5, 6, 7, 1Ø, 11, 12. . . . Octal was a popular numbering system for early computers, but it is seldom used in modern machines.

odd parity The setting of an extra (redundant) *bit* in order to have an odd number of 1 bits in a group. See *even parity* for discussion.

off the shelf Generally refers to a standard, mass-produced *software* product that does not have to be tailored by the vendor and is thus readily available at the vendor's; does not need to be specially written for a customer's requirements.

office automation The deployment of personal computers as *word processors* and employee workstations, the use of *local area networks* for electronic interoffice mail, and other such new technologies to increase the productivity of office workers.

off-line   Not communicating with a computer. An "off-line machine" does data-processing related work, but not in direct contact with a computer; rather, data must be presented in the form of *tapes*, *floppy disks*, *punched cards*, etc. On the other hand, when "the machine is off-line," its normal communication with a computer has been disabled. To "take the machine off-line" means to turn off its communications capability.

off-line storage   The storage of data that are not directly accessible to a computer system, e.g., on *tape* or *punched cards*.

offset   The number of character positions or *memory* locations away from a point of reference. The point of reference has an offset of Ø, the next position has an offset of + 1, the next of + 2, etc. Synonymous with *displacement*.

OLRT   On-Line Real Time. A system that communicates interactively with users. The results of data processing during an interaction are returned immediately to the computer user.

on the fly   A modification made to *systems software* while the system is running is said to be "made on the fly." (Ordinarily, changes are made only when the system has been idled.)

one-dimensional array   A list of related data elements, arranged so that the entire list has one symbolic name and each entry is referred to by its numeric position (subscript) in the list. Used in many *programming languages*.

one-pass compiler   A *language processor* that passes through a *source* program one time and produces an *object module*. Many compilers for *structured programming* languages such as *PASCAL* are one-pass compilers.

on-line   Communicating, or in a condition capable of communicating. A device is said to be on-line when its communications path is open to a computer. Similarly, a computer is on-line when it is capable of communicating with terminals.

on-line tab setting A feature in some printers that permits tab stops to be changed and set under commands issued by the computer that controls the printer.

opcode OPeration CODE. The portion of an *assembly language instruction* that specifies an action to be taken by the *CPU*. An opcode is usually a *mnemonic*, and it is sometimes followed by one or more *operands*.

open To establish a flow of information between a program and a *file* so that the program can read and/or write data in the file.

operand Information in an *instruction* or *command*. In the human command "eat the apple," the verb 'eat' is analogous to an *opcode*, and 'the apple' is the operand; it tells what the operation is performed upon. Similarly, in the *assembly language* instruction MOV E,A the *mnemonic* MOV is an opcode indicating a movement of data, and the operands E,A specify that the move is between two *registers* called E and A.

operating environment The conditions, technology, *hardware, software*, etc., in which a system functions.

operating system The master control program that governs the operation of a computer system. The operating system is a large and highly complex program. Unlike other computer programs, it does not run through a predefined sequence of operations and then quit; rather, it is always present and active while the computer is running. Operating systems vary widely in their capabilities, depending on the size and complexity of the system they control, but most include the following:

•Job entry control: Furnishes a means for *jobs* to be started via operator commands or other methods.

- **Input/output services:** A set of prewritten routines that programs can call upon to handle the details of obtaining input or producing output (e.g., *disk* reads/writes, sending reports to the printer, etc.).
- **Convenience services:** Prewritten routines available to programs for access to miscellaneous features of the machine, such as setting *timers*, reading the system time-of-day clock, etc.
- **Data management:** Furnishes standardized methods for storing, retrieving, indexing, and organizing data.
- **Supervision:** Manages the computer system by controlling *memory*, the jobs in execution, access to data, error-handling, etc. Also cleans up after programs have ended ("*housekeeping*").

Operations In an organizational sense, the department responsible for the actual running of computers.

Operations Support In an organization, a department associated with *Operations*, responsible for various auxiliary functions having to do with data processing. These might include the distribution of computer-produced reports, liaison with other deparments that use data-processing services, technical support, planning, etc.

operator (1) A person who controls a computer or a computer-related machine.

(2) A mathematical or logic symbol indicating an action or a relationship between two values, e.g., $+$, $-$, $=$, $<$, $>$, XOR, etc.

optical character recognition The visual recognition of letters, digits, and other symbols legible both to a machine and to a human. Abbreviated OCR (letters pronounced separately). In OCR, a printed document is passed through a scanner that reads from the page and translates the shapes of symbols into *binary* codes that are then passed as input data to the computer.

optical fiber   A fine strand of clear material suitable for transmitting light over great distances. See *fiber optics*.

optical memory   See *laser memory*.

optical scanner   A device for reading documents using *optical character recognition*.

optimized code   The *compiled code* of a computer program that has been reworked to remove inefficiencies and unused or unnecessary *instructions* so that the program runs faster and requires less storage space.

optimizer   A *utility* program that processes executable programs and produces *optimized code*.

option switch   (1) In *hardware*, a *DIP-switch* or *jumper* that turns on an optional feature.

(2) In *software*, a *parameter* that activates a feature by overriding a *default* value, thus serving much the same purpose as a hardware option switch.

option toggle   Same as an *option switch* in *software*.

OR   A *logic* operation in which two *bits* or electrical pulses are combined, producing one resulting bit according to the following rules:

$$\emptyset \text{ OR } \emptyset \longrightarrow \emptyset$$
$$\emptyset \text{ OR } 1 \longrightarrow 1$$
$$1 \text{ OR } \emptyset \longrightarrow 1$$
$$1 \text{ OR } 1 \longrightarrow 1$$

The effect of OR is exactly the opposite to that of *NOR*. For further discussion, see *AND*.

ORG   An *assembler directive* denoting the *origin* of a computer program or a portion of one.

ordered array   An arrangement of data elements into a specified order. An order array differs from an *ordered list* in that data elements are organized into rows and columns so that each element is individually accessible. Thus, a group of customer records might be placed in an ordered array; they are organized into account number order (the 'rows'), with 'columns' indicating the account number, the customer name, and the current balance. In an ordered array, a balance could be read, modified, and written back into the array without having to reference the other associated elements (account number and name). In an ordered list, on the other hand, an action involving any one element must involve the others as well, since a list is a one-dimensional ('rows' only) array.

ordered list   A list of data elements in a specified order, using a one-dimensional *array*. See also *ordered array* for more discussion.

orderly shutdown   See *graceful shutdown*.

origin   The first *memory address* of a program or of a portion of one; i.e., the first *instruction* to be executed. The mnemonic in most *assembly languages* is ORG, followed by an *operand* indicating the address. When this *directive* is encountered, the *assembler* resets its address calculations accordingly.

OS   (Letters pronounced separately). Abbreviation for *operating system*.

OS/MVS   (Letters pronounced separately, slash omitted in speech) Operating System/Multiple Virtual Storage. The primary *operating system* for large IBM and IBM-compatible computers.

outage   An out-of-service condition. During a power outage, there is no electricity; a planned outage usually means that the computer system is taken out of service for maintenance.

outage analysis   A statistical report indicating periods, percentages of time, and reasons for a computer being out of service, usually as related to *up-time* objectives.

output (1) The results of data-processing activity, e.g., a printed report produced by a program.

(2) A device that produces computer output.

(3) The signals or indications produced by circuitry.

output class The indicator of the priority of printed output. In a *multiprogramming* system where several *jobs* are running concurrently, output is written to a system *file* called the *spool* rather than directly to a printer (since a printer can only serve one job at a time). As the printer finishes a report, the *operating system* inspects all output held in the spool and selects the next report to be printed based upon their relative priorities (output classes).

overflow A condition in which a value becomes larger than the *word length* of the computer. If a microcomputer has a word length of 16 *bits* (or 2 *bytes*), it can represent a maximum value of 65,535. When computations result in a larger number, overflow occurs. *High-level programming languages* have a facility to handle overflow; in some languages this occurs automatically, and it others it is programmer-controlled through a mode called *double-precision arithmetic*.

overhead The amount of processing required to accomplish some task, with reference to the consumption of computing resources. A "high-overhead function" is one that "burns up a lot of *cycles*," or, in other words, places heavy demands on the computer.

overlapping I/O A phenomenon occurring in large computer systems as a result of the wide discrepancy between the speed of a *CPU* and the speeds of *peripherals*, which is utilized to advantage in enabling a computer to execute several programs at the same time. If a CPU executes one million *instructions* a second and a *disk drive* takes a tenth of a second on the average to complete a write operation, the CPU can execute 100,000 instructions while waiting for the disk to finish its job. Thus, during this period the CPU suspends work on the program that has issued the disk write, and works on another instead. In the course of those 100,000 instructions, it usually encounters another I/O operation, so it initiates that action before the first (disk) write is done. It now has two 'overlapping' I/Os in progress, with both programs waiting for their completion, so the CPU picks up a third program, and so on. When the first disk write is finished, an *interrupt* is received at the CPU to signal that fact, and in due course the CPU resumes work on the first program until it initiates another I/O or until another interrupt from a different I/O. In this way, the CPU "keeps several balls in the air" and productively uses the time it would otherwise waste waiting for the relatively slow peripherals.

overlay (1) As a verb, to write information over existing information in *memory* or on a data *storage medium*. When a *magnetic tape* is reused, it is usually not first erased; instead the new data overlay the old.

(2) In programming, a technique for minimizing the amount of *memory* a program occupies as it executes. It often happens that the entire program does not have to be in memory at the same time (as, for example, when some parts of the program are run only at month-end closing, others weekly, others daily, other annually, etc.). In such cases the main part of the program (the *nucleus)* remains in memory, and other parts are brought in from *disk* as they are needed. A section of memory called the overlay area is set aside for this purpose by the nucleus, so that different portions of the program reside in the same place at different times.

override To force a preexisting value to change in *software* by superseding it. Many software systems have options that govern their behavior. It is usual practice to set *defaults* that preselect certain options, thus saving the trouble of specifying the options each time the software is run. If an option is not stated, the default automatically prevails; the default is overridden by specifying a different choice during a given execution.

overrun A condition that occurs when the amount of data is greater than the amount of space allocated for them. If 80 *bytes* of *memory* have been set aside and 90 bytes of data arrive, an overrun occurs. This can have catastrophic consequences.

owner (1) In a *data security* system, the person or organization "owning" data; i.e., having unquestioned authority to create and use certain *files* and other information.

(2) In *software*, a program that has control of a device is said to be its "owner."

P

PABX (Letters pronounced separately) Private Automatic Branch eXchange. A computer-controlled telephone switching system as used by large businesses.

pack To compress two digits into a single *byte* to conserve storage space. In both the *ASCII* and *EBCDIC* data representation *codes*, the first four *bits* indicate that the byte is a decimal digit, and the second four bits (the *low-order nibble*) contain the value in *binary*. In packed format, the binary value bits of two consecutive digits are combined to form a single byte, thus reducing storage space by half.

package (1) Another term for *chip* (seldom used).

(2) A *software* product usually designed to appeal to a wide range of data-processing customers with similar interests; e.g., a general ledger accounting package for corporations, an inventory control package for manufacturers, a portfolio tracking package for investment bankers, etc.

packed decimal Decimal digits in a *packed* format to reduce storage space and handling *overhead*. In packed decimal, the last four bits of a string of packed digits is a nonnumeric value indicating the sign (positive or negative).

packet switching A discipline for controlling and moving messages in a large data-communications network. Each message is handled in a manner comparable to the way the post office moves parcels; i.e., as complete units containing the addresses of the recipient and the originator. Using this method, messages can be routed through several *message switching* computers en route from the point of origin to the destination.

padding The inclusion of meaningless characters in data in order to fulfill length requirements. For example, if a *record* is expected to be 160 *bytes* long but there are only 125 bytes of data, the remaining 35 bytes might be padded with zeros.

page An arbitrary unit of *memory* in a computer, consisting of some round number (in *binary*) of memory locations. In a microcomputer, as one example, a logical page of memory is 256 *bytes* since that number is "round" in binary (B'100000000', or in *hexadecimal* notation X'100'). For similar reasons, in larger computers pages occur at intervals of 2048 or 4096 bytes. Except in *virtual storage systems*, the notion of a page has no real significance, but it serves as a convenient point of reference or a measure of memory utilization.

pageable memory The portion of a computer's main *memory* that is subject to *paging* under a *virtual storage system.*

page boundary The point at which *memory addressing* progresses from one logical *page* to the next.

page data set In *virtual storage systems*, a *file* maintained by the *operating system* to store the images of *memory pages* so that, when needed, they can be restored to memory for further processing.

page frame In *virtual storage systems*, a logical *page* of *memory* treated as a unit that can be taken out of memory and saved in a *page data set* and later, as needed by the program it belongs to, restored to memory.

page skip Same as *form feed*; a control character that causes a printer to skip the rest of the current page and move to the top of the next page.

pagination   The breaking of a printed report into units that correspond to pages.

paging   The movement of *page frames* between *memory* and the *page data set* in a *virtual storage system*. In virtual storage each program potentially has an *address space* larger than the entire real memory of the computer. This is accomplished by dividing memory into arbitrary, fixed-sized units called *pages*. The *operating system* monitors the usage of each page. When a page is not used for some period of time, it is automatically moved to the page data set on *disk*. When the program that ''owns'' the page attempts to access it, the page is copied back into memory. This movement in either direction is called paging.

paging rate   The number of *pages* moved by a *virtual storage system* between *memory* and the *page data set* per second. See *paging*. The paging rate is one measure of system performance. At some point (depending on the system) the paging rate progresses from an acceptable level to the point where it degrades overall performance of the computer system.

paint   In computer *graphics*, to fill a selected area with a solid color.

panel   A screen of information and/or dialog in an interactive computing system using *video display* terminals. Roughly equivalent to a page of printed information on paper.

paper tape   A *medium* for storing information by punching round holes in a paper strip. The *bits* of each character or *byte* are punched across the width of the paper tape. Used mainly in connection with obsolete teleprinters.

paragraph   In the *COBOL programming language*, a complete, logical unit of *instructions* needed to perform a definable function or task.

parallel interface   A connection between two devices in which all the information exchanged between them is sent at the same time over separate electrical conductors. Thus, the information *bits* and the control signals travel along parallel paths.

parallel test   The "acid test" of a new piece of *software*, in which the same data are processed by the old software and the new, and the results are compared in order to verify the accuracy and correctness of the new programs. This is a customary way of introducing major changes in data processing.

parallel transmission   A means of implementing the signaling method described under *parallel interface* on a communications line. In parallel transmission, the signal on each conductor is assigned a certain tone *frequency*, and all tones are sent at the same time over one line. At the distant end the tones present on the line are converted back into electronic pulses.

parameter   A piece of information that serves to govern the operation of *software*, establish limits, select options, or otherwise control the behavior of a computer system or one of its constituent parts. A parameter is very similar to an *operand* in that it explains an expected action. Parameters, however, do not always modify a command in the sense that the predicate modifies a verb, as do operands. Much of the effort in installing an *operating system* involves building an elaborate set of parameters that establish the "marching orders" for the operating system and thereby directing how the system will function. In another usage of the term, when control passes from one part of a program to another, the routine that is relinquishing control gives the receiving routine parameters to indicate the location of data that is to be processed and other required information. In general, a parameter is therefore any piece of information needed for purposes of control. Usually called a *parm* in computerese.

parameter driven   A software system whose functions and operations are controlled chiefly by *parameters* is said to be "parameter driven."

parent   A *file* whose contents are required and in some cases are the only source of information available to create new records. An example is the day-to-day "balance forward" on an account, in which today's balance is calculated by applying subsequent transactions to yesterday's balance. The balance from yesterday is the parent; today's is the child.

parent/child relationship   The passing of information from one *generation* of data to the next, in which older information is necessary to create new or to establish continuity.

parity   The addition of one or more redundant *bits* to information to verify its accuracy. As an example, in the *ASCII code* seven bits are used to represent the value of a character and the eighth bit is for parity. To determine the setting of the parity bit, the seven information bits are scanned and the 1 bits are counted. If even parity is to be used, there must be an even number of 1 bits in the character; thus, if the information bits contain an odd number of 1 bits, the parity bit is set at 1, otherwise, it is left as 0:

ASCII 'W'	1 0 1 0 1 1 1	1 bits = 5
Parity bit	—> 1 1 0 1 0 1 1 1	(Even parity)
ASCII 'G'	1 0 0 0 1 1 1	1 bits = 4
Parity bit	—> 0 1 0 0 0 1 1 1	(Even parity)

The above is character parity, also called *vertical redundancy*. By prior arrangement, parity may be either even, as shown, or odd (every character is forced to have an odd number of 1 bits).

  Block parity is also used in lieu of, or in addition to, character parity. In block parity (or *longitudinal redundancy*), an entire block of data is scanned and a *block check character* (BCC) is created. All the first bits are scanned and the 1 bits are counted, then all the second bits, etc., and the check character is added to the block. In the following example, the block consists of the word 'MESSAGE' and even parity is used to calculate both character parity and the block check character:

	MESSAGE	1 bits	BCC
(Parity)	0 1 0 0 0 0 1	2	0
	1 1 1 1 1 1 1	7	1
	0 0 0 0 0 0 0	0	0
	0 0 1 1 0 0 0	2	0
(Info)	1 0 0 0 0 0 0	1	1
	1 1 0 0 0 1 1	4	0
	0 0 1 1 0 1 0	3	1
	1 1 1 1 1 1 1	7	1

Note that the block check character corresponds to the ASCII charcter 'K'; in this case, however, it does not carry that value since the system "knows" that the last character of a block is the block parity indicator.

Parity is used in almost all transmissions of data, both within a computer (e.g., from *disk* to *memory*) and in communications. The sending and receiving devices both calculate parity the same way, and the receiving device compares its parity calculations with those transmitted by the sending device. An error is assumed whenever the two disagree. This is ordinarily resolved by requesting a retransmission of the block (see *ACK* and *NAK*).

parm See *parameter*.

parmlib (Pronounced "parmlibe") A large number of system control *parameters* that have been accumulated in a *file* that establishes the way the *operating system* of a computer performs.

parse To scan a stream of information such as a *command* or text, looking for selected words (or *strings*). Parsing is a fundamental activity in much of data processing, e.g., in translating *programming languages*, interpreting operator commands, etc.

parser   The portion of a computer program that *parses* input information and signals other portions of the program when a specified *string* is found.

partially populated   When some, but not all, of the possible electronic components are mounted on a *printed circuit board*, leaving room for additional components, the board is said to be partially populated.

partition   (1) To create arbitrary subdivisions of a greater whole. See partitioned file, also the following.

(2) In some *virtual storage operating systems*, the computer's *memory* is divided into regions called partitions. Each of several programs running concurrently is assigned a partition in which to execute. The program then "owns" its partition and confines both its *instructions* and its data to this area.

partitioned data set   An IBM term; same as *partitioned file*.

partitioned file   A *disk file* that is divided into subdivisions, each of which is a complete file unto itself. A partitioned file is used to group these related files (*members*) under one heading; it is sometimes also called a *library*. A partitioned file contains a directory indicating the names and other information about each of its members. Frequently used for storing programs and other control information, less often for data storage. See *member* for further discussion.

Pascal   A *high-level programming language*, PASCAL was originally developed as a tool for teaching the concepts of *structured programming*. In recent years, however, it has become very popular for writing business and scientific programs, and consequently PASCAL has evolved into a powerful general-purpose language.

passive device Any electrical device placed within a circuit that passes signals without altering them. A connector is one example. Another is a signal *monitor* that observes signals but does not change their characteristics.

password In a data security system, a specific password is required to gain access to protected information.

patch (1) A modification made to *machine language* without re*compiling* the *source program*. To implement the change, the actual *binary instructions* are replaced. A "soft patch" changes the program while it is in *memory*, and thus prevails only for the duration of this run of the program. A "hard patch" modifies the stored copy of the program and is therefore permanent. A patch and a *zap* are the same thing.

(2) To rearrange cable connections, usually between a set of *modems* and a *communications control unit*.

patch panel A switchboardlike set of plugs and cables that enable the connections between a group of *modems* and a group of *ports* to be rearranged. A double-ended patching cable is plugged between the receptacle for the modem and the receptacle for the port. If modems are later reassigned to different ports, these patching cables can be moved, thus saving considerable trouble.

path length (1) In software, the number of *instructions* that must be executed in order to perform some task.

(2) In hardware, the physical distance a signal traverses to move between two points.

p-code Pseudocode. A method used in microcomputers to aid in making programs *portable* from one machine type to another. In p-code, a program is translated into an *intermediate language level* that can be placed on any computer. Another piece of *software* then adapts the p-code to the particular computer type. This is an attempt to deal with the uncontrolled proliferation of microcomputers and the resulting chaos of incompatibilities.

PC register   A *register* within the *central processing unit* that keeps track of the *memory address* of the next *instruction* to be executed. PC stands for Program Counter.

PCM   See *pulse code modulation*.

PDM   See *project development methodology*.

PDU   See *power distribution unit*.

peak second algorithm   A sophisticated mathematical *algorithm* that attempts to predict, in a communications system, how many transmissions will be in progress at the busiest instant of time during some study period. This figure is useful for defining the number of circuits and other elements required to handle the expected traffic load of the network.

pedestal   A table or other physical support for a terminal.

pending I/O   An input/output operation that has been started but has not yet completed, so that the *CPU* is either idled while awaiting completion, or else services other programs and tasks while the I/O is pending. See *overlapping I/O*.

PERFORM   In the *COBOL programming language*, a PERFORM is a *subroutine* (equivalent to a PROCEDURE in some other languages, such as *Pascal*); a portion of the program that can be executed upon command by other portions of the same program.

performance analysis   The measurement of how well a computer system performs as a whole, and how well its components interact with each other. Performance analysis attempts to find and correct deficiencies and "bottlenecks," thereby improving the return on investment in computing resources.

performance monitor   A sophisticated *software package* that measures a wide range of internal *events* within a computer system, categorizes them, and reports the results of its observations. Performance monitors are of two basic types, statistical and event-driven. A statistical monitor samples all activities in progress on a periodic basis and extrapolates its findings within a statistically acceptable range of accuracy to cover periods when observations were not made. An event-driven monitor actually counts every occurrence of the events it measures to provide an absolute record of all activities. The information reported by a performance monitor is used in *performance analysis, capacity planning,* and data-processing management.

perfs Perforations in paper to facilitate removing pin-feed edges and bursting continuous paper into separate pages.

peripheral A generic term encompassing the input/output and data storage devices attached to a computer, and located adjacent to it. Used as both a noun and an adjective: a computer and its peripherals comprise a *hardware* system. Includes printers, *disk drives, tape drives, card readers,* etc., but excludes remote devices connected via data communications.

permanent error On *disk packs* and *floppy disks,* data are written in concentric circles called *tracks,* and each track is divided into some number of *sectors,* each of which is marked to show its *address,* whether it is in use, and other control information. A permanent error occurs when this sector mark is erroneously modified by writing data over it. The only way to recover from the error is to re*initialize* the device (to run a *utility* program that wipes the disk clean and rewrites all the track and sector marks).

personal business computer A professional-quality micro-computer suitable for handling most of an individual's computing needs (e.g., an engineer or a manager) in a business setting.

personal computer A microcomputer; called a personal computer because it serves the computing needs of one person at a time.

PF key Program Function key. A key on the keyboard of a terminal such as a *CRT* that has no predefined function. Instead, a program can assign that key a function that remains in effect while the program runs. In an interactive system, operation of a PF key might mean the user wants to review the previous *panel*; in an *editor* it might mean, "Cancel the last change I made and put things back the way they were before." Most terminals have several such keys, usually marked PF1, PF2, etc.

PFK See *program function key*.

phase jitter Brief and unexpected *phase shifts* in a signal arriving over a communications line that, when severe enough, cause loss of information.

phase modulation A sophisticated technique for conveying information on a fixed-frequency *carrier signal* by the deliberate introduction of *phase shifts*. Different *bit* patterns are implied according to the relative durations of the shifts. This technology, because of the exotic circuitry involved, is seldom used except in very high-speed data communications.

phase shift A very brief interruption in a fixed-frequency signal. As shown below, a tone of some single frequency is sent over the line for a period of time, and then an instant

PHASE SHIFT

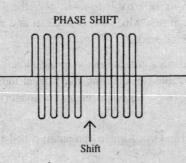

Shift

of silence occurs and the tone reappears at the same frequency. When unwanted phase shifting occurs, it is called *phase jitter,* which can distort a signal beyond recognition. The introduction of phase shifts of varying durations can be used to convey information, e.g., a shift of one-half *hertz* means *binary* Ø1, of one hertz means binary 1Ø, etc. This is called *phase modulation.*

phosphor A substance used in cathode-ray tubes such as TV picture tubes and *video displays*. Phosphor glows when struck by an electron beam, thus patterns such as character images and pictures can be constructed by selectively directing a beam at the phosphor coating on the back side of the tube's viewing surface.

photosensor A device that detects the presence of light and emits a signal indicating that light has been sensed.

physical path length The physical distance an electronic signal must travel between the originating and receiving points. In computers operating at speeds measured in *nanoseconds*, physical path lengths become a critical design factor.

physical record See *block*.

pico A trillionth. One picosecond is 1/1,000,000,000,000 of a second.

piggyback board A small *printed circuit board* mounted on another, larger board in order to add a feature whose circuitry requires more space than the larger board has available, or whose circuitry was not included in the layout of the larger board.

pin A protruding electrical contact on a male connector or on a semiconductor *chip*.

pin feed A type of paper advance mechanism in a printer in which protrusions on two wheels engage evenly spaced holes along the edges of the paper and draw it forward by turning.

pin-outs Descriptions for engineering purposes of the signals sent out on the *pins* of a semiconductor *chip*.

pioneer An organization that uses a new, untried product in its data-processing activities.

piracy Occurs when a person or organization purchases a *software* product and then either sells or gives away copies of the product to others without remunerating the vendor.

pitch The density of printed copy. Pitch usually refers to the number of characters printed per horizontal inch ("10 pitch" meaning ten characters per inch), but it can also indicate the number of rows measuring vertically.

pixel (Pronounced "pixl") Acronym for picture element. A small graphic shape on a display screen. Several pixels are combined to form a character image, or they may be combined in various ways to make up *graphics*.

PL/I (Pronounced as "P-L-1") Programming Language/I. A *high-level programming language* developed to embody the best of both *FORTRAN* (a mathematical language) and *COBOL* (a *file* processing language). PL/I is an extremely powerful language that lends itself well to the concepts of *structured programming*.

place value The magnitude of a digit with respect to its position within a number. In conventional *decimal* numbering, working from right to left, the place values are units, tens, hundreds, thousands, etc. In *binary* the place values are units, twos, fours, eights, sixteens, etc.

plain vanilla Without special modifications or customization. The term usually applies to *systems software*. "We're running a plain vanilla system" means that the *operating system* has been installed as delivered from the vendor and has not been changed to accommodate local whims.

platen The roller, as in a typewriter, that advances the paper and serves as an impact-absorbing surface when *slugs* strike the paper.

platter A round, flat, metallic plate covered on both surfaces with a brown magnetic substance. Several platters are mounted on a common axis to form a *disk pack* that is mounted in a disk drive and serves as a high-speed data storage device.

plotter A machine that draws pictures, graphs, schematics, and other such pictorial representations under computer control. There are basically two types of plotters, drum and table. A drum plotter has a cylinder around which the paper is wrapped; drawings are made by rotating the drum to and fro under a pen, which moves laterally. The combination of motions is coordinated to create lines, curves, etc. A table plotter holds the paper on a level surface, and a carrier moves the pen about much as a hand draws.

plug-compatible When two competing pieces of equipment can be exchanged without having to make other changes to accommodate their differences, the devices are said to be plug-compatible.

PM Preventive Maintenance. Used as both a noun and a verb. "They're going to PM the tape drives tonight."

pocket computer A small computer of very limited capabilities that, though it resembles an electronic calculator, is able to process small amounts of data under the control of complex stored programs.

pointer A data element that indicates the *address* of (or points to) a piece of information. A pointer might show where to find information that has been saved in *memory,* or it might give the location of a specific *record* stored on *disk.* *Software* usually reserves an area for noting pointers as it processes data, so that it can later "recall" where things are by retrieving the pointers. This is rather like doing research and noting down the page numbers of relevant passages in a book for later reference; the page numbers are "pointers." See also *data base*.

point-of-sale device   A machine such as a cash register or a credit-verification terminal that captures retail sales information at the point of sale and furnishes these data as input to a computer.

point-to-point circuit   A communications line between two (and only two) locations.

Poisson theory   A statistically based mathematical method for estimating the number of lines needed to handle a given amount of communications traffic.

polarity   (1) The orientation of a magnetic field (north or south pole).
   (2) The direction of flow of an electrical current (positive or negative).

polling   An organized method for controlling the flow of traffic in a large, multi*node* data-communications network. Ordinarily the *host* computer in the network polls each node on a periodic basis by sending out the *address* of the node and a request for traffic. The node then either sends a message it has stored, or it sends a "no-traffic" response. The host then proceeds to the next node, and so on around the network until it returns to the first node again.

pool   A group of similar *peripherals*; e.g., the *DASD* pool is all the *disk drives* associated with a given computer, the *tape* pool all the tape drives, etc.

population   The electronic components on a *printed circuit board*. Dense population means the board has many compo-

nents and probably little room for adding more; sparse population the opposite. Fully populated and partially populated
mean the same, respectively.

port A communications connection on a computer or a
remote *controller*, suitable for attaching a single line.

portability Refers to the ease with which a program can be
moved from one computer type to another.

POS device See *point-of-sale device*.

position The numbered location of a single character within
a group of characters, such as a line of print, in which the
first (leftmost) is position 1, the second is position 2, etc.
Contrasts with *offset*, in which the numbering of positions
starts with 0.

positional parameter One of several *parameters* in a group,
the significance of which is not specifically identified, but is
instead implied by its position within the group. As an example,
to rename a *file* the *command* might be REN (old) (new). If
we have a file named TODAY.DATA and we want to call it
YESTERDAY.DATA, we would enter the command:
     REN TODAY.DATA YESTERDAY.DATA
These file names are positional parameters since it is necessary to specify them in the proper order to achieve the desired
result. Contrasts with *keyword parameter*.

positive-going voltage Opposite of *negative-going voltage*.

post To record a transaction in a *file*, thus updating the
records related to the affected account.

pot *Potentiometer*.

potentiometer A rheostat; a device for adjusting the amount
of current in a circuit by moving an electrical contact along a
high-resistance surface, thus increasing or decreasing the flow
of current by varying the overall resistance of the circuit.

power check An automatic halt of a computer when a significant fluctuation in internal electrical power occurs.

power distribution unit Abbreviated PDU. A piece of equipment located in or near a computer room. It receives the main electrical power as a single high-voltage current and breaks it down to the appropriate levels for distribution to the *CPU* and *peripherals*.

power-line monitor A device that observes and records levels of electrical power on a continuous basis. Some power-line monitors draw a continuous graph; others only report on deviations from an established norm.

power supply Circuitry within a *hardware* unit that converts incoming electrical power into the voltages needed for internal consumption by the unit's electronics.

precedence of operators Establishment of the order in which mathematical operations are handled in a complex instruction, e.g., all additions are done, then all subtractions, then all multiplications, etc. Because the precedence of operators varies from one programming language to another, or even between different versions (*dialects*) of the same language, most programmers override precedence by the liberal use of parentheses, which have the same effect as in higher mathematics.

precompiled module A standardized program *module* that is used by many different programs, and has therefore been separately developed and *compiled*. This module can then be *linked* into any program by the *linkage editor*, thus saving the programmer the trouble of redeveloping frequently used *instructions*. Some examples are a routine to fetch and interpret the date from the system calendar, screen control instructions for a specific type of *video display*, and an *interface* to communications control *software*.

predecessor job   A *job* whose output becomes the input to another job, and which therefore must run to normal completion before the other job is started.

predefined function   A sequence of *instructions* built into a *high-level programming language* as a convenience to programmers. Predefined functions do such tasks as computing sines, cosines, logarithms, and other advanced mathematical calculations, and manipulating text in various ways. With predefined functions, the programmer merely specifies the function he or she wants performed and the value(s) required, rather than having to personally *code* the requisite instructions.

price/performance analysis   A comparison of several alternative products (*hardware* or *software*) that attempts to determine which product delivers the most speed, features, flexibility, etc., per dollar of cost.

primary registers   Any general-purpose CPU register with an *address* in *assembly language,* where data can be loaded from *memory*, operated upon, and written back to memory using program instructions. A CPU normally reserves some registers for its exclusive use in controlling the computer that the programmer cannot directly utilize; these are excluded from the primary registers.

prime registers   Some *CPU*s have a duplicate set of general-purpose *registers*, and the active set can be selected by a program *instruction*. The Zilog Z80 microprocessor is an example. In such a CPU, the set of registers inactive at the moment is called the prime registers.

primitive   A noun describing a sketchy specification for some action within a program. A primitive sets out a general outline of how the action occurs, but omits details; these are usually developed later, or they are of no relevance. A primitive is a little better than a note, but not as good as a specification.

print density   The number of printed characters per unit of measurement on a page.

print driver   The segment of a computer program that routes output to a printer and usually also contains printer control functions, e.g., pagination, margins, page headers, etc.

printing pitch   See *pitch*.

printout   A printed report produced by a computer.

print pool   In a computer room, an area where all the printers are located together.

print queue   A prioritized list maintained by the *operating system* of all printed output waiting on the *spool* for output. See *spool*; also, *output class*.

print train   The drum in a *drum printer* or the chain in a *chain printer* containing the *slugs* that are used to make character impressions on paper. Sometimes also used to mean the electronic character set that accomplishes a similar purpose in a *laser printer*.

print wheel   See *daisywheel*.

prioritized interrupts   An *interrupt* is a signal sent to the *CPU* by a device or a system component that needs attention. Each interrupt signal is accompanied by a numeric value indicating its relative importance. The *first-level interrupt handler* takes control each time an interrupt is received; it evaluates the priority of the interrupt with respect to the task that has been interrupted and decides whether the interrupt is important enough to handle right away, or if it can be deferred. For instance, it is more important that a *disk drive* has completed a read operation than that the printer has finished printing a line. Similarly, a component failure is more important than a disk read.

priority polling In data communications, a *polling* plan in which high-activity *nodes* are polled more frequently than those with only occasional traffic.

priority queuing The arrangement of things to be done in a list (a *queue*) according to their relative importance, the most pressing first and in descending order of priority thereafter.

PRIVATE When a *disk pack* is assigned for the exclusive use of one *application* or one user, it is declared as PRIVATE so that the *operating system* will not attempt to *allocate* space on that device for others.

privilege class The assignment of *authorization* to a specific program to use *privileged instructions*.

privileged instruction A *machine language instruction* that alters the status of the computer system as a whole, or otherwise affects all users of the system. Under sophisticated *operating systems,* such as IBM's *OS/MVS,* a privileged instruction can only be issued by an *authorized* program, such as the operating system itself, thereby limiting who can control the system.

probe Usually a pencil-like electrical contact held in the hand, used to test the voltages and other characteristics of circuits by touching the probe against the bare conductor.

PROC (Pronounced ''prock'') Stands for *procedure*. In *Job Control Language (JCL),* a prewritten set of JCL *statements* that can be executed in the manner of a *subroutine* by a different set of JCL statements.

procedural language A *programming language* in which the processing steps are specified in the order in which they are to occur, and in which the programmer must issue *instructions* for every action. Most programming languages, including all the ''old standards'' such as COBOL, BASIC, FORTRAN, ALGOL, Pascal, etc., are procedural languages.

procedure   (1) With reference to *JCL*, see *PROC*.

(2) In a computer program, see *procedure declaration*.

(3) Any written set of instructions that tells a human how to perform a data-processing-related task.

procedure declaration   In some *programming languages*, a procedure is the name used for *subroutine* (a set of *instructions* that can be executed by a single statement elsewhere in the program). The procedure is declared (given a name and written as a segment of the program), and then whenever that action must be performed, the procedure name is given as an instruction. Procedures are useful for reducing the length of programs by developing a single standardized set of instructions to perform a routine task that might be needed at several points in the program. In the pure sense of the term, a procedure is a subroutine that causes an effect external to itself; this contrasts with the other type of subroutine, a *function*, which returns a value mathematically derived from a known value but has no other, external effect.

procedure division   In a *COBOL* program, one of the four required divisions. The procedure division contains the actual *instructions* that comprise the computer program.

process   (1) As a noun, any complete self-contained sequence of operations that yields a result. This result is then input to another process, etc. Computer programs consist of many processes.

(2) As a verb, the generalized activity of operating computers, running programs, and producing information.

process control   The use of computers and programs to operate machinery in manufacturing. See also *CAM*.

processor bound   See *CPU bound*.

processor complex   Very large computers such as the Control Data Cyber series and the IBM 3081 consist of several *central processors* working in concert within a single housing. Although this housing is normally called simply "the *CPU*," it is, in fact, a processor complex because of its multiplicity of *CPU*s.

PROCLIB (Pronounced "prock-libe".) PROCedure LIBrary. A collection of prewritten *Job Control Language (JCL)* routines saved in a *disk file*. These routines, which start and control *jobs*, can be executed by entering a *system command* that names the desired routine, thus saving the trouble of reading in *punched cards* containing the *JCL statements* each time a job is to be run.

production Routine operation of a data-processing system, excluding the development and testing of new programs. A "production system" is a group of fully developed, related computer programs in regular use.

program A program is a complete set of *instructions* that tells a computer how to do something. It starts at some point and runs to completion at another point, and contains all the directions necessary to fulfill its purpose. As a verb, "to program" means to write computer programs.

program check An error in a computer program that causes the computer to halt, or to cease work on the program containing the error.

program counter See *PC register*.

program function key See *PF key*.

program library A related set of computer programs, usually stored as *members* of a *partitioned file*.

programmable device Any piece of *hardware* that operates under the control of a stored program. The term usually refers specifically to a device whose program(s) can be changed or replaced by the user (rather than by the vendor).

programmer A person professionally responsible for computer *software*. Although it is generally supposed by those outside the data-processing field that all programmers do basically the same thing, in fact, that is not so. The profession has a number of well-defined specialties, some of which differ so greatly that they have little (aside from a computer orientation) in common. The two major occupational groupings are *systems programming* and *applications programming*. Systems programmers specialize in the *operating system* and other *system control programs* that give overall direction to a data-processing installation. Applications programmers are much closer to the common conception of the profession. They design, develop, write, test, and maintain programs that process data. Under the umbrella of applications programming, however, there are two widely differing areas of specialty, called business and scientific programming, and these persuasions are further broken down into systems analysts, coders, programmer analysts, data base administrators, and others.

programming language A human-oriented language for telling a computer what to do, and how to do it. Most programming languages consist of a finite number of English-like verbs (e.g., PRINT, READ, ASSIGN, SAVE, OPEN) and implied verbs (e.g., +, −, =, etc.), that are combined with symbolic data names according to certain rules (the *syntax*) in order to form *statements* that make sense to a human. When a program is written in the language, another program (a *compiler, assembler,* or *interpreter*) translates the statements into *machine language* instructions that the computer is able to act upon. There are many programming languages, going by names such as BASIC, COBOL, FORTRAN, Pascal, ALGOL. Some programming languages are *application oriented,* meaning that they are suitable for only a narrow scope of data-processing activities, while others are general-purpose languages; those mentioned above are in the latter category. Among general-purpose languages, however, each has strengths and weaknesses, so that FORTRAN is good for mathematics but poor for *file* processing, and COBOL is just the opposite. Often, in developing a new program, considerable thought goes into the selection of the appropriate programming language.

program status word Abbreviated PSW. The contents of the *CPU registers* and *status flags*, which are saved as a unit of data when a program is interrupted. Execution of the program can later be resumed at the point of interruption by restoring the PSW to the CPU registers.

program trace A report that traces the flow of execution through a computer program, showing each *statement* that was executed and the order in which it occurred. Traces often show the effect of instructions on the data, also. Used for *debugging* programs.

project development methodology Abbreviated PDM. A disciplined, structured set of procedures for controlling the development of computer programs by a large organization. The purposes of a PDM are to provide a consistent approach to the complex and often highly individualized tasks of programming, to bring some degree of accuracy to cost and time projections for new projects, and to furnish a means for keeping management apprised of progress. Unfortunately, PDMs are often dogmatically bureaucratic, keeping programmers busy filling out reports rather than writing programs, with the result that benefits tend to be canceled out by decreased productivity.

PROM (Pronounced as a word) Programmable Read-Only Memory. A *memory* device whose contents are not lost when power is removed, and which can only be read. It takes a special device called a *PROM burner* to write on a PROM; once information is recorded by the PROM burner, it cannot be erased. Used to save *machine language* programs that become part of the *hardware* of a computer, as for example the program that starts up the computer when power is first turned on.

PROM burner See *PROM*.

prompt A message output by *interactive software* to request instructions from a person at a terminal or to ask a question that needs an answer before the software can continue.

propagation delay The amount of time required for a signal to travel from one point to another. Although of no significance to the human ear, propagation delay can seriously affect data communications. In satellite communications, for example, the propagation delay is on the order of a quarter of a second, a very long time in comparison with computer speeds.

proportional spacing Variations in the spacing of characters on printed copy, so that the amount of horizontal space for each character is proportional to its width. The letter w is wider than the letter i, so more space is given to it. Typewritten copy has fixed spacing, while typeset copy (such as this book) has proportional spacing.

proprietary software *Software* that has been developed and is sold as a product, to which the vendor retains proprietary rights under copyright and trademark laws.

protocol The rules and formats for conducting communications on a large network. The protocol governs such matters as the way messages are addressed and routed, master/slave relationships among network *nodes*, *polling*, the exchange of control information, and *hierarchy*. See also *HDLC*.

protocol-level timer A *timer* within a communicating device that synchronizes and sets deadlines for *protocol*-related activities. A protocol-level timer issues a high-priority *interrupt*.

pseudo-op In *assembly language*, a *directive* that does not generate *machine language*, but instead causes the *assembler* to take some action. An example is DS, the pseudo-op to define storage; the directive DS 256 causes the assembler to set aside 256 *bytes* of *memory* as a data workarea. The pseudo-op END signifies the end of the program.

pseudorandom number generator A built-in function in many *programming languages* that generates random numbers according to a fixed mathematical process. Although the numbers generated are apparently random, they are predictable if one knows the starting value and the *algorithm*, thus the prefix "pseudo."

p-system A *software* system that translates *p-code* into the *machine language* appropriate to a specific *CPU*.

PSW See *program status word*.

PUBLIC A *disk drive* assigned to the general *pool* of data storage and on which any program can obtain space is said to be a PUBLIC pack. Contrasts with *PRIVATE*.

public domain software Any uncopyrighted computer program.

public network A communications service that is open to anyone, usually on a fee basis. Telephone service is a public network. There are also public data networks.

pulse-code modulation Abbreviated PCM. A technique for converting *analog* signals into a digital form. In PCM, the *amplitude* (voltage) of an analog signal is periodically sampled. This voltage is represented by a numeric value sent across a high-speed line. At the receiving end, the analog signal is reconstructed from the values. PCM usually samples a number of signals concurrently, combining their digital representations on a single line; it is thus a form of *multiplexing*. Widely used for long-distance telephony.

punch   A hole in a *punched card*.

punched card   The most familiar face in data processing; a piece of thin cardboard punched with holes representing characters or digits.

punched paper tape   An oiled ribbon of paper punched with holes representing information. Used chiefly in connection with obsolete teleprinters.

purge   To erase a *file*.

PUT   A programming *instruction* that causes data to be written into a *file* from computer *memory*.

Q

QA See *quality assurance*.

QBE See *Query By Example*.

quad density A data recording format on a *floppy disk* that accommodates four times as much information as would normally be contained on the diskette.

quality assurance A comprehensive system of measurements and planning methods intended to improve the performance of a data-processing operation.

quantum slicing level In *amplitude modulation*, the measurement of a signal component's strength at a given instant to determine the information value it conveys.

Query By Example (Letters pronounced separately) Abbreviated QBE. A method and a *programming language* for searching large amounts of data for information that satisfies user-specified formats or ranges of values. The commands that initiate searches under QBE are English-like "for instance" statements that indicate the desired results. These are then interpreted by *software* as *search arguments*, and the information is extracted.

queue A list of things to be done, such as messages that are awaiting processing, *jobs* that need to be run, data to be filed, etc. Queues are built and maintained by *software* when there is more work to be done at the moment than can be accomplished. The software stores its backlog in a queue and as tasks are completed it pulls the next item from the queue. To place in a queue is to *enqueue*; to remove from it is to *dequeue*.

queue-driven   A *software* system that maintains many *queues* for tasks that are in various stages of processing is said to be queue-driven. Such systems are usually very large, complex, and efficient, perhaps capable of handling several hundred data-communications messages per second, or of controlling the execution of several programs at the same time.

quiesce   To restrain the computer system from starting new *jobs*, so that as the current jobs reach completion, the system gradually winds down until nothing is running. A system is usually quiesced in preparation for a planned outage.

QWERTY   (Pronounced as a word.) The standard arrangement of a keyboard such as that on a typewriter. So called because the top row on a standard keyboard starts with the letters Q-W-E-R-T-Y.

R

rack mounted   Equipment modules bolted into a standard-width metal rack (usually 19″) or a cabinet with similar mountings.

radians   A measurement of angles based on π rather than on degrees. A straight line (180-degree angle) has an angle of π (3.1415927 radians); a 90-degree angle is 1.5707963 radians, or half π. Trigonometric functions in many *high-level programming languages* work on radians instead of degrees.

radio frequency interference   Disturbances caused by high-frequency signals in the environment or emitted by a computer that adversely affect other electronic devices.

radix   Same as *base* in a numbering system.

raised flooring   Elevated flooring used in computer rooms so that cables can be laid directly between equipment units and so that chilled air can be distributed to machinery. Raised flooring consists of 2-foot-square metal tiles whose intersections rest on pedestals. The tiles can be lifted out to gain access to the space beneath.

RAM   (Pronounced as a word) Random-Access Memory. A common term for the semiconductor *memory* of a computer.

rampage through core   When a program error causes the program to write data in the wrong places or otherwise alter *memory* locations improperly, it is said that "the program went rampaging through *core*."

random (1) In no particular order.

(2) A *file* organization in which individual *records* can be read or written directly no matter where they are in the file, without searching through other records.

random access The ability to read or write at a particular location in *memory* or a *file* without having to pass sequentially through preceding locations. See also *random*, definition 2.

randomizing A method based upon a *random number generator* for spreading *records* evenly throughout a large *direct-access file*. Each time a new record is added, the location where the data are to be written is calculated using a random number within some specified range.

random number generator A built-in *function* in a *programming language* that produces numbers at random.

range check A data validation check that determines if an input value is within an expected range. For example, if hourly pay rates for employees are entered, a range check would reject negative amounts and pay rates in excess of perhaps $30 per hour.

raster scan A means of constructing an entire line of *dot matrix* characters on a *video display* as one unit, rather than a character at a time. As shown in the drawing, a beam travels the width of the line, illuminating all the top-row dots for the character to be displayed, then sweeps across again forming

RASTER SCAN

all the second-row dots, etc., until the set of characters in the line is complete. The beam then moves to the next line of display and repeats the process, thus constructing a full screen. Raster scanning is also used in *laser printers*.

rated speed The absolute maximum operating speed of a data-processing device or a line. Rated speed is usually expressed in characters per second (cps) for equipment and in *bits* per second (bps) for a communications facility. For example, the rated speed for a printer might be 100 cps, meaning that while it is actually printing characters the printer can achieve 100 characters in a second, but no more than that. Rated speed is seldom sustained in any device because of periodic pauses for various reasons, e.g., carriage return/line feed on a printer. Consequently, rated speed is reduced by these pauses to arrive at an effective speed.

rated thruput The maximum amount of data that can be "put through" per unit of time. See *rated speed*.

RBA See *relative byte address*.

reader (1) A *peripheral* device that reads *punched cards* as input to a computer.

(2) In *software*, a program that *emulates* a punched card reader by fetching data from a *file* and feeding it into another program as though it had come from cards. Usually called an internal reader.

reader-sorter A machine that prepares *punched cards* for input to a computer. A deck of cards in random order is placed into a *hopper*. The reader/sorter then reads each card and routes it mechanically into one of many slots, depending on the value of the information read, thus sorting the cards into order. A reader/sorter only sorts on one *column* at a time, so if cards are to be in account number order and the account number has ten digits, the cards must be resorted ten times, once for each digit. A reader/sorter is an *off-line* device, meaning that it does not communicate directly with the computer. After cards are sorted, they are physically carried to a *card reader* to be read in.

read-only memory   Abbreviated ROM. A semiconductor *memory chip* whose contents can be read but can be written only by special means. See also *PROM, EPROM, EEPROM*.

read/write head   A device that both records and reads data on a moving magnetic surface such as *tape* or *disk*. The magnetic surface passes across the read/write head. If a 1 *bit* is sent to the head by the computer, it generates a magnetic field stored as a charge of static electricity on the recording *medium*. Later when a read command is sent to the head and the surface passes across it, it senses the static charge and sends a 1 bit to the computer. In this way, data are written to and read from storage media in the form of tiny magnetic spots.

real estate   The area on a *printed circuit board* or a semiconductor *chip* available for electronic circuitry. Also called *land*.

real number   Any number capable of expressing a fractional value (i.e., with a decimal point or in scientific notation). Real numbers and integers (whole numbers) are usually treated differently in computers. Also called *floating-point numbers*.

real storage   Actual physical *memory* consisting of some number of *addresses*. Used to express both the amount of memory available ("This machine has eight *megabytes* of real storage") and the amount of memory needed by a program ("This program takes 64*K* of real storage"). Contrasts with *virtual storage*.

real time   A method of data processing in which data are acted upon immediately instead of being accumulated and processed in batches. In an on-line real-time system, for example, as a terminal user keys data, the system does calculations on it, updates records, and returns the results to the user so that they are immediately available.

reboot A function similar to "reset" on a home appliance; to reboot a machine means to reload the *systems software* so that the machine makes a fresh start. A reboot usually occurs by human intervention as the result of a problem. The term most often applies to *controllers* and small computers. In large computers the comparable function is called *IPL*.

RECFM (Pronounced "wreck-F-M") RECord ForMat. Chiefly an IBM acronym.

record format A specification indicating the way information is formatted in the *records* of a *file*, e.g., fixed- or variable-length, *blocked* into units of several records each, *spanned* from one record to another, etc.

recording density The maximum amount of data recorded per physical unit of space on a storage *medium*. For example, a recording density of 6250 *bpi* on *tape* means there are 6250 *bytes* per inch.

record length The number of *bytes* per data *record* in a *file*. For instance, in Digital Research's CP/M® *operating system* for microcomputers, every record ends with a carriage-return–line-feed sequence. Therefore, if records each contain 60 characters of data, their record length is 62 bytes.

recovery Overcoming a problem.

recovery routine A piece of *software* that gains control when an error occurs and attempts to resolve it automatically without crashing the system or otherwise wreaking havoc. An example is a recovery routine for division by zero; if a program attempts to divide by zero, the recovery routine replaces the divisor with a very small value (maybe .0000001) and issues an error message, then allows processing to resume.

recursion Self-utilization; an intriguing concept more easily understood by example than by definition. Recursion is the use of computers to design computers. When a window washer applies his or her weight to a differential hoist to raise and lower his or her weight, that is recursion. Another more relevant example is the "bootstrapping" of a *compiler,* in which the compiler program is written in the *language* it translates. Thus extensions, new features, and modifications to the compiler are added to its *source* program and then the compiler recompiles itself. There are many examples of recursion in data processing; one way to compute the fourth root of a number, for instance, is to call a routine that calculates the square root, and then have that routine call itself to calculate the square root of the first square root.

recursive Pertaining to *recursion.*

red-green-blue monitor A high-resolution color display unit.

redirected I/O In a program, the simplification of input/output alternatives by assuming that all I/O devices are the same. The *Pascal programming language,* for example, treats a printer, keyboard, and display as *files.* When an input is desired Pascal "reads" the keyboard "file" just as it reads a *disk* file. In output, it "writes" to a "file" (actual or an output device) by merely signaling the *operating system* to indicate the destination for the data being sent.

reel A spool of *magnetic tape.*

reentrant In *multiprogramming,* a reentrant routine is a segment of *systems software* that can be used concurrently by two or more independent programs.

reflective spot A piece of metallic foil embedded in a *magnetic tape* to indicate the physical end-of-*reel.* As the tape approaches the read/write head of a tape drive, a light shines on it. When the reflective spot appears, it bounces the light onto a *photosensor* and the drive, alerted by the sudden increase in light, stops advancing the tape.

refresh Periodic reconstruction of information in place. In *dynamic memory*, the *capacitive* charges representing *bits* begin to decay after a few milliseconds, so it is necessary to refresh the memory periodically by reading the charges and writing them back into the same *addresses* before they become too weak to detect. On a display, the *phosphor* glows for only a brief time after being struck by an electron beam. Consequently, the beam constantly scans the display, refreshing it by rewriting the same patterns.

region size The size (in number of *bytes*) of the *address space* in which a program executes.

register A small special-purpose *memory* within a *central processing unit*, where information is held temporarily and manipulated according to program *instructions*. Depending on its size and capabilities, a CPU might have anywhere from six to sixteen registers. All registers in a CPU are of the same length; in most microcomputers they are 8 *bits* in length, while very large computers have 32- or even 64-bit registers. In addition to the general-purpose registers used directly by programs, the CPU has several special-purpose registers for its own use in controlling the system (e.g., the *PC register*).

register-to-register instruction A programmatic action that moves information from one *CPU register* to another.

register-to-storage instruction A programmatic action that moves information from a *CPU register* to a location in *memory*.

reinitialize To restore a program back to the condition it was in at start-up time, i.e., close all *files*, reset all totals to zero, erase data saved in *memory*, etc., so that nothing is left over from previous executions of the program. To "reinitialize a system" is to *reboot*.

relational operator   A symbol indicating a mathematical operation or a relationship between two values, e.g., $+$, $-$, $<$, $=$, $>$, etc.

relative address   A location expressed with reference to another point. In "the third house from the corner," the relative address is 3. Usually used to specify the position of a character or *field* within a larger grouping of information, using the start of the grouping as a reference point: "The customer name begins at the 25th character of the *record*."

relative byte address   A *relative address* expressed in terms of *bytes* as an *offset* from a point of reference. In a *record*, if the account number begins at the first character position, its relative byte address (RBA) is Ø; if the date of the transaction starts in the sixth position, its RBA is $+5$. The RBA is added to the address of the point of reference to determine its actual address in *memory* or on a storage device.

relink   See *linkage editor*.

relocatable code   A computer program in which the *addresses* specified in *instructions* can be changed if the *origin* (the starting point) of the program is changed, thus permitting the program to be relocated to any point in *memory* without affecting its operation.

remark   Same as *comment*.

remote   Located at a distance from, but connected to, a computer, usually at the other end of a communications line. Also used as a noun: "The remotes are all up and running." Also as a verb: "We remoted that terminal."

remote job entry   See *RJE*.

removable media   Data storage *media* that can be removed from the drive that reads/writes it. *Magnetic tape* and *floppy disks* are removable media. Some disk drives (those with *demountable packs*) also have removable media, but some (*Winchester disks*) do not.

repeater An *amplifier* built into a communications line.

repeat key A keyboard button that, when pressed at the same time as a character key, causes the character to be repeated until one of the keys is released.

report Any document produced by a computer program; usually printed, but sometimes displayed.

request A message sent to the *operating system* by a program that needs a system control function performed. This is usually accomplished by setting up the appropriate *parameters* and then *branching* to an entry point in the operating system. Upon receiving the request, the operating system interprets the parameters and attempts to act on them. It then returns control to the program, sending a message to indicate whether or not the request was successfully completed and, if so, passing back appropriate control information.

rerun To run a *job* that has already been run using the same data, starting from the beginning.

reserve An *operating system* indicator that a *peripheral* is in use; a concept similar to a busy signal on a phone line. When the operating system of a large computer initiates an input/output to a device such as a *disk drive*, it "places a reserve" by setting an indicator in *software*. This indicator remains on until the I/O is complete. If other I/Os are requested involving the same device during this time they are denied, just as an incoming call is denied by a busy signal. Sometimes a disk is reserved for a long period, as when the data on it are being reorganized (*compacted*). Reserves are also placed on printers, *tape drives*, and other attached devices.

reserved word In a *programming language*, a word (or any defined sequence of letters and digits) that has a special, unique meaning and cannot be used for any other purpose. For instance, many programming languages have the *instruction* PRINT; this is a reserved word because it cannot be used as the symbolic name of a variable, *file,* or *procedure,* or for anything else except to instruct the system to print output.

reset   (1) In general, to *reinitialize*.

(2) To reset a *file* is to wipe out its contents and prepare it to receive entirely new data. This is ordinarily done by writing an *end-of-file mark* at the start of the file. (In *Pascal,* however, RESET means the opposite: prepare the file to be read, not written.)

(3) To reset a *bit* is to change its value to 0.

(4) To reset a small computer or a *controller* is to operate a mechanical switch that forces the machine to halt its current activities and *reboot*.

reside   To be permanently stored, or active, at a specific place. In a large computer system, certain *libraries* must reside on a specific *disk drive* (designated as the *system residence*). When a program must start at a stipulated point in *memory* in order to execute properly, it is said to reside at that *address*. The term usually applies to executable programs but not always; occasionally someone says that data reside at a given point, or that a data *file* resides on such-and-such a storage unit.

residence   The data storage unit on which the *file* referred to is stored.

resident   Refers to programs that are located in the main memory. Most commonly, a program that is "resident in *core*" is a *machine language* program that remains at a fixed point in *memory* no matter what other activity is occurring in the system. Normally resident programs are portions of the *systems software* that must always be present in memory to control the system.

resistance (1) Opposition to the flow of electricity. Some amount of resistance is an inherent property of all circuits and conductors, and thus is accommodated in design. Measured in ohms.

(2) A work-performing device placed in a circuit; the device resists the flow of electricity by converting its energy into useful work.

resistor An electrical component placed in a circuit to adjust the level of current downward by some specified amount.

resolution (1) The fix for a problem.

(2) The focus and clarity of a *video* display.

resource management See *performance analysis*; also, *capacity planning*.

resources A collective term covering computers, *peripherals*, *memory*, programs, data, and anything else that immediately contributes to data-processing activity. This term does not usually include the physical environment of the computer room (air conditioning, power distribution, etc.), but rather encompasses *hardware*, *software*, and data that are directly and intimately controlled by computers.

resource sharing The connecting of *peripheral* devices to two or more computers so that they share the devices and the data stored on them.

response time In an *on-line real-time* system, the elapsed time in seconds that the system takes to respond to an entry made at a terminal. Average response time is one of the primary factors used to measure the performance of an online system.

restart To resume the running of a *job* that has failed or halted for some reason, recommencing execution at an intermediate point in processing instead of restarting from the very beginning.

restart procedures Step-by-step documentation written for a computer operator, explaining how to *restart* a *job*.

restore (1) To restore a *file* is to recreate it from a *backup* copy. This is done under either of two circumstances: (a) the file was damaged during processing and is no longer usable, or (b) the file was *archived* to *tape* and now for some reason its contents need to be brought back to *disk* for further processing.

(2) As a program *instruction*, RESTORE means to reset the data *pointer* at the start of the data. Many *languages* have this or a similar instruction.

results The product of data processing.

RETURN A program *instruction* that serves as the exit from a *subroutine*. On encountering RETURN, the system *branches* back to the instruction following the one that called the subroutine.

return address The *memory address* to which a *subroutine* returns control when it has finished (upon encountering a *RETURN instruction*). The return address is normally the location of the instruction following the one that called the subroutine.

return code A numeric indicator issued by a program upon completion, whose value shows whether the program completed successfully ("ran to *EOJ*") or if it ended abnormally due to an error. Also called *completion code*.

RETURN key A key on a terminal keyboard that, when pressed, causes a print mechanism or a display *cursor* to advance to the start of the next line. Called ENTER on some keyboards.

reverse channel Same as *aux channel* or *side channel*.

reverse Polish notation Abbreviated RPN. A form in which many *programming languages* internally represent mathematical operations. In RPN, two *operands* are grouped with their *operator* immediately following. For example, x + y is represented as xy + . More complex operations can also be represented this way, with computation groupings becoming the operands of further operators. The formula:

$$(m + a) \times (n + b)$$

is noted as:

$$ma + nb + \times$$

So called because it was developed by the Polish mathematician Lukasiewicz.

reverse video   Reversal of the normal characteristics of a screen display; i.e., if the screen usually displays white characters on a black background, in reverse video mode black characters appear against a white background.

RFI   See *radio frequency interference*.

RF shielding   The enclosure of a cable or a physical space (e.g. a room) with a shield that stops radio frequency radiation from entering or leaving.

RGB monitor   See *red-green-blue monitor*.

ribbon cable   A flat cable in the form of a wide ribbon, in which the conductors are side by side in parallel.

ribbon cartridge   An inked printer ribbon enclosed within a housing that can be snapped in place in the print mechanism.

right-justify   To move an item of information to the right end of the space (*field*) that has been set aside for it. Columns of numbers are usually right-justified.

ring network   See *daisy chain*.

RJE   Remote Job Entry. The submission of *batch jobs* from a remote terminal using a communications line, so that the job is treated by the system as though it had been entered through a local *reader*. An RJE terminal often has a *card* *reader,* a *card punch,* and a printer, and some have a *CRT* as well, enabling the device to function as an extension of the computer room.

R/O   (Letters pronounced separately) Receive-Only in connection with a terminal. Read-Only in reference to a *file* (cannot change the contents).

roll paper   Printer paper in continuous form on a spool.

roll your own   A program developed by a computer user to fit specific requirements, rather than buying a generalized *package* for the purpose.

R/O terminal   A communicating machine capable only of receiving, and not of transmitting. Most printers are R/O terminals.

ROM   (Pronounced as a word) Read-Only Memory.

ROMable code   A computer program specifically developed to be "burned" into a ROM.

room circuit   A communications line within a computer room.

room power   Electrical power on the computer-room side of a *motor generator, power distribution unit,* or other conditioning/isolating device. Room power is usually fed into the computing machinery and not the lighting.

rotate   An operation performed on data in a *CPU register.* In right rotation, as shown below, all the *bits* in the register

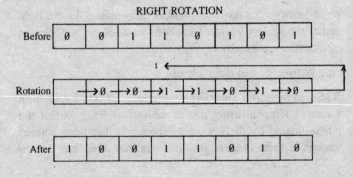

RIGHT ROTATION

are shifted one position to the right. The rightmost bit is shifted out, so it is carried around and placed in the leftmost bit position, thus "rotating" the register contents. A left rotation is similar, but opposite in direction.

rounding error A slight discrepancy in the result of a mathematical operation that arises because of the *truncation* or *round off* of fractional values. For instance, 15 percent interest on a balance of $3216.12 comes to $482.418. When this amount is rounded to $482.42, a rounding error of − .002 occurs. By itself such an error is insignificant, but when thousands of interest calculations are performed, the accumulated rounding errors can amount to several dollars and cause accountants to have headaches.

round off To truncate the least significant digits of a number and adjust the remaining value upward or leave it alone, depending on the amount truncated.

routine A sequence of *instructions* in a program that can be identified as a complete, discrete task having an entry point, a job to perform, and an exit point. Programs consist of many routines; one reads data from a *file*, another calculates the current balance, another prints a line of output, etc.

row A horizontal line of print on a display, or a horizontal grouping of data *elements* in an *array*.

RPG Report Program Generator. A *high-level programming language* intended chiefly to format and print the finished results of data-processing programs.

RPN See *reverse Polish notation*.

RPQ Request for Price Quotation. An RPQ is initiated by a customer who wants a vendor of data-processing equipment to make a custom modification or install a nonstandard feature on *hardware*. The term has been extended by usage to include not only the request, but the product as well, so that an unusual device or characteristic of a computer is often described as an RPQ.

RS-232 A standard of the Electronic Industries Association (EIA) describing the most commonly used *interface* between communicating data-processing equipment and *modems*.

runaway tape As a result of a *hardware* malfunction, a *tape reel* spins rapidly and out of control, often breaking the tape or sometimes unrolling it.

run documentation Detailed instructions written for a human operator, describing how to run a specific computer program.

run-time error A program error not detected in the process of translation, but that causes a processing error to occur during execution.

run-time error handler A *systems software* facility that intercepts, diagnoses, and issues error messages concerning *run-time errors*.

run-time library A set of *utility routines* furnished by a *language translator* that *interface* the program with a specific *operating system*.

R/W Read/write. A written abbreviation only.

rx Written abbreviation for receive.

S

S-100 bus   A 100-conductor *bus* adopted as a standard for microcomputers by the Electronic Industries Association. Because of the rapid development of micros, not all manufacturers have adhered to the S-100 design, and as a consequence there is little standardization among small computers.

S and P   Systems and Programming. The name in many corporations for the department that is responsible for *applications programming*.

saturation   A communications term meaning that a network is "full" in the sense that no further traffic can be handled without increasing the number of lines and/or reconfiguring the network layout.

scalar value   An *integer* declared as such in a *programming language* and possessing a value within a fixed range. In many microcomputers, for example, a scalar is any integer between -32767 and $+32767$.

scheduler   (1) A person working in a computer room who is responsible for making sure all *jobs* are run at required times.

(2) A *system control program* that sequences jobs and automatically submits them for execution at preset times. When dependencies exist among jobs, a scheduler makes sure the *predecessor job* has been completed successfully before it releases the next job in the series.

(3) See *master scheduler*.

scientific computing   A form of data processing that concentrates chiefly on large, complex calculations.

scope   The portion of a program in which a *declared* value is valid. See *local*; also, *global*.

SCP   System Control Program.

scramble   To rearrange the *bits* within each *byte* of a message or of stored data according to a prearranged pattern, thus making the data unrecognizable unless the pattern is known and can be reversed.

scratch   (1) To remove all data from a *file* by writing the *end-of-file marker* at the beginning.

(2) A scratch *tape* is a *reel* that is uncommitted, i.e., its contents are no longer useful and the tape is available for reuse.

scratchpad   An area set aside in *memory* for saving intermediate computational results, control values, and other information that needs to be kept temporarily during processing.

screen   The viewing surface of a *video display*, normally a *CRT*, similar to a television set.

screen format   The way information is presented on a display.

screen image buffer   An area in the *memory* of a computer that contains an *image* of the information seen on a display. A program writes information into the screen image buffer and then sends this buffer as a message to the display, thus altering the viewed output.

screen refresh   See *refresh*.

screen size   Normally, the diagonal measurement of a *video display screen* in inches. A 12″ screen measures that distance from one corner to the opposite corner. Screen size is sometimes also expressed in numbers of *rows* and *columns* (e.g., 24 × 80) or in numbers of *pixels* (e.g., 320 × 160).

scrolling A characteristic of a *video display* that, as new lines are written at the bottom, the other lines are "pushed up." The top line is said to "scroll off the top," and in most cases this line is lost to view.

scrub To pass through a large amount of data, eliminating duplicate or unwanted items of information.

SDLC Synchronous Data Link Control; an IBM variant on *HDLC*.

SE See *system engineer*.

search argument See *argument*.

secondary allocation A data storage area assigned to a *disk file* when the primary *space allocation* is insufficient to hold the entire file. In some *applications* it is very difficult to predict the amount of data from day to day. The programmer can thus request a reasonably large space, and then provide an overflow for unusually heavy volume by specifying a secondary allocation that will only be used by the system if necessary.

sector A subdivision of a *track* on a *disk*, constituting a unit of data storage space. On a *floppy disk*, as an example, the disk might have 77 tracks, with each track subdivided into 26 sectors of 128 *bytes* of data apiece. An *address* on disk consists of the track and sector numbers.

seek time The amount of time it takes to position a *disk drive*'s read/write head over a specific *track*. Seek time varies according to the distance the head has to move, and is determined by the *head stepping rate* times the number of tracks that have to be crossed between the point of origin and the destination.

segmentation (1) Breaking a long communications message up into smaller messages that are sequence-numbered.

Between segments other messages are transmitted on the network, the purpose of segmentation being to prevent a long message from monopolizing the network by blocking other traffic. The receiving machine pieces the segmented message back together.

(2) Breaking a very large computer program into smaller functional units by using an *overlay* structure. The main portion of the program (root segment) *resides* in *memory* all the time the program is executing and other parts (overlay segments) are brought into memory and executed as needed.

semantic error The mistaken use of the wrong symbolic name in a computer program. Semantic errors are not detected by the *language processor,* but rather must be ferreted out by the programmer when it is found that the program returns incorrect results. A semantic error would occur when the programmer meant to add A to B and instead added A to C.

semiconductor A material whose resistance to the flow of electricity can be varied by the presence of an adjacent electrical field, magnetism, or light. Highly refined semiconductor materials are used for the manufacture of extremely small, dense circuits in electronics. The most common material is silicon.

semiconductor disk A large *memory* designed to *emulate* a *disk drive*. The *operating system* reads and writes to semiconductor disk as though it were a normal rotating device, but the actions occur much more rapidly and thus improve performance. Semiconductor disk is very expensive per unit of storage space as compared with real disk, and as a result it is used sparingly by systems that have it. Also called *nonrotating disk*.

semiconductor memory The most common form of *memory* used in modern computers. The memory consists of thousands of *capacitors*, each capable of storing one *bit* arrayed on *chips* that are mounted on *printed circuit boards*

sentence A complete *instruction* in the *COBOL programming language*. Because COBOL reads very much like English, instructions are written as sentences and grouped into *paragraphs*. An example of a COBOL sentence might be "ADD OVERTIME TO BASE-PAY GIVING GROSS-PAY."

separator page In a computer printout, a page preceding and another page following the actual report, showing the name of the *job* that produced it, the time and date, and other information useful for identifying the output.

sequence numbering The numbering of *records* in a *file*, of messages, of *statements* in a *source program*, and of other such entities in data processing to show their order. Sequence numbers are placed at fixed positions, and though they are in ascending numeric order they are not necessarily in strict numeric progression. It is acceptable, for example, to number the statements in a program 100, 110, 112, 119, 120, 125, 132, etc. Their purpose is merely to indicate order and not to count items.

sequential access A *file* organization in which *records* are read and/or written one after another, and jumping around is not permitted. To read the 984th record in a sequential-access file, it is necessary to read the preceding 983 records.

serial I/O The most common form of data transmission, in which the *bits* of each character are sent one at a time over the line. In data processing, serial I/O is almost always performed in accordance with the *EIA RS-232 interface* standard.

serially reusable A program or *routine* that *reinitializes* itself at the end of execution is said to be serially reusable. This routine can then be executed again without danger of being *corrupted* by results left over from the previous execution. Most *resident systems software* routines are serially reusable, since they are executed repeatedly by different programs.

service bureau   A business firm that sells data-processing services.

service objective   A formal agreement between a data-processing organization and a client organization, establishing deadlines for delivery of processed results, *response time,* system availability, error tolerance, and other quality-of-service targets. Service objectives are usually stated in terms of percentages or other numeric indices, and the performance of the data-processing organization is measured against these indicators.

session   Active connection of a terminal device to a *host* computer system, during which interactions actually occur or can occur without the terminal having to reidentify itself (sign on) to the system. When a terminal is activated it "initiates session," and when it is deactivated it "breaks session."

set   (1) A collection of related values, as in the mathematical sense of set.

(2) To set a *bit* is to force its value to *binary* 1; contrasts with *reset*.

(3) An *instruction set* is all the actions a *CPU* is capable of performing in response to programmed instructions, or all the possible instructions that can be issued by a *programming language*.

(4) A *working set* is the *resources* required by a program in order for it to function.

set up a job   To prepare a *job* for execution in a large system by ensuring that all the *files* are available, *coding* the appropriate *job control statements*, and otherwise making certain that everything is in place for the job to run properly.

shared DASD *Disk drives* and/or *drum storage* shared by two or more independent, adjacent computers. (DASD [Direct-Access Storage Device] is pronounced "daz-dee".)

sharing device A small, inexpensive *multiplexer* or *concentrator* that allows two independent data signals to share the same communications line.

shell A computer room, exclusive of the computing machinery itself. See also *empty shell*.

shielded cable A cable connecting two devices, with foil or other sheathing around it to stop *radio frequency interference* and magnetic fields from entering and leaving the cable.

shielded pair A pair of conductors within a cable that is individually shielded as described under *shielded cable*.

shift To move information right or left within a *memory* location or a *register*. A shift is similar to a *rotation*, except that the *bit* that is shifted out is lost and not carried around to the other end.

DOUBLING A VALUE USING A LEFT SHIFT

Before	Ø	Ø	1	Ø	Ø	1	Ø	1	= 37

Left Shift ⟵

Result	Ø	1	Ø	Ø	1	Ø	1	Ø	= 74

Shifting is a convenient and efficient way of doubling and halving numbers in *assembly language* programming. The figure above shows how the number 37 (in decimal) is doubled using a left shift.

In the figure on the next page the same value (37) is divided by 2 using a right shift. In this case, the *low-order* bit is shifted out and lost, thus *truncating* the result (37/2 = 18) and ignoring the remainder. If the programmer wants to keep the remainder

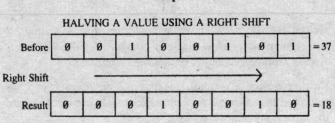

HALVING A VALUE USING A RIGHT SHIFT

(a 1 bit representing a value of .5), he or she must check the *CPU status flags* to find out whether a bit was shifted out and, if so, take some further action to handle the situation.

shop A data-processing installation. "This is a high technology shop."

shop standards Written standards governing data-processing methods in an installation. Shop standards define the *conventions* for the naming of programs and *files*, the procedures for implementing new *jobs*, the uses and purposes of *job classes*, documentation requirements—in short, they define the structure within which the data-processing organization functions.

SIB See *screen image buffer*.

side channel Same as *aux channel* and *reverse channel*.

sieve of Eratosthenes See *Eratosthenes' sieve*.

sift To extract certain desired items of information from a large amount of data.

signal-to-noise ratio The ratio of signal strength to the level of *noise* on a communications line. Expressed in dBRN.

signed decimal A form of *packed decimal* numeric representation in which the *low-order nibble* of the last *byte* contains a value indicating whether the number is positive or negative.

sign flag A *flag* in the *CPU status byte* that indicates the sign (positive or negative) of the result of an arithmetic operation.

significance   See *place value*.

sign off   To enter a command from a terminal that ends the current *session* between that terminal and the *host* computer. Same as *log off*.

sign on   To enter a command from a terminal that initiates a *session* between the terminal and the *host* computer. Same as *log on*.

silicon   An element occurring in nature (in sand and rocks) that, when refined, has the property of being a *semiconductor*. Silicon is widely used for this purpose.

Silicon Valley   The Santa Clara Valley south of San Francisco, so called because it holds one of the highest concentrations of electronics firms in the world.

simulation modeling   The representation of reality by means of mathematical models, so that the effects of changes can be predicted by adjusting the values of certain reality factors. Simulation modeling is a powerful use of computers because it allows engineers and scientists to conduct "experiments" that might otherwise not be possible due to expense or time, such as determining the depth at which a submarine will collapse from water pressure or the effects of erosion over several thousand years.

single thread   The ability to do one and only one thing at a time.

SIO   See *serial I/O*.

"size"   The "size" of a computer in data-processing usage has nothing to do with its physical dimensions; for those the term *footprint* is used. Rather, size, in general, refers to the capabilities of a machine: its upward limit on *memory*, how many million *instructions* per second it executes, the number of *channels* it supports, and various exotic features that fall under the broad heading of *architecture*. As machines become faster and thus "bigger" in this sense, they must become smaller in physical size because the distance a signal travels within the computer becomes a limiting factor on its speed, and therefore on its size.

slave unit   Any device acting under the control of another external machine (the *master*).

sleep   Word used to describe the computer's apparent inactivity when an error has caused an *endless loop*.

slew rate   In a *logic-seeking* printing mechanism, the speed with which the print head advances to the next line and finds the position where it is to begin printing. The faster the slew rate, the less time is lost between lines of print, and consequently the greater the *thruput* of the printer.

slot-bound   A physical limitation on the expandability of a computer. Expansion is accomplished by plugging more *printed circuit boards* into the machine's *bus*; when all the slots on the bus are filled, the machine becomes slot-bound.

slug   A metal casting that carries the image of a printable character. The slug prints by striking the paper.

small business machine   A micro- or minicomputer suitable for performing all the data processing for a small company.

SNA   (Letters pronounced separately) Systems Network Architecture. A comprehensive product offering of *hardware* and *software* by the IBM Corporation for integrated data-communications/data-processing systems.

soft error   An error occurring in automatic operations that does not recur when the operation is attempted a second time; a recoverable error. Most automatic operations are set up to retry automatically several times. If a *disk* read fails the first time and succeeds the second time, a soft error has occurred.

soft failure Any failure that can be overcome without having to have someone with specialized knowledge repair the failing device, or any failure from which a full recovery can be made. If a *controller* halts and someone pushes its RUN button, whereupon it resumes normal operation, a soft failure has occurred. Contrasts with *hard failure*.

soft key Same as *PF key*.

soft patch A change made to a program's *machine language code* while the program is in *memory*. A soft patch endures only while the program remains in memory; if the program ends and a fresh copy is later fetched from storage, the soft patch is lost. A soft patch is therefore a temporary, one-time program change. Contrasts with *hard patch*.

soft sectored diskette A *floppy disk* on which the *sector* locations are identified by control information written on the diskette (sector boundaries), rather than by some physical means. The recording format and *density* of a soft-sectored diskette can be changed by moving the sector boundaries.

software A generic term for computer programs. All computer systems consist of *hardware* (the physical equipment required to accomplish data processing) and software (the instructions that direct the hardware in performing work). Software is broken down into three categories:

1. Systems software performs overall control and direction of the computer system by telling it how to start programs, how to communicate with the hardware devices under its control (*disk drives,* printers, etc.), and how to do other such functions basic to the operation of a computer. (See also *operating system*.)

2. Utility software encompasses a variety of general-purpose programs that operate on data, and that are available to save the programmer the trouble of writing a special program to do some frequently needed task. Utilities perform

such tasks as *sorting* data, transferring data from one place to another, and managing *data bases*. *Compilers*, which translate human-written programs into the computer's internal language, are also utilities.

3. Applications software are programs written to solve a specific problem or to do a particular job, such as producing payroll or determining the status of a customer's account. Many computer users write their own applications software, and it consumes the vast majority of programming effort in the data-processing industry.

software configuration   The kinds of, and the relationships among, *system control programs* installed on a computer system.

software engineering   A fancy term for programming.

software floating point   Special *routines* built into *high-level programming languages* to enable them to perform *floating-point arithmetic* on computer *hardware* designed for integer arithmetic. Because most machines are integer-oriented, software floating point is extremely sophisticated and consumes a great deal of *overhead* in processing.

software integrity   The reliability of *software*.

software path length   The number of *machine language instructions* that must be executed in order to perform some task: the more instructions, the longer the path length, and therefore the more time required to complete the task.

software piracy   See *piracy*.

software QA   Quality Assurance. An administrative review process aimed at improving and maintaining the reliability of software. Most data-processing organizations have some form of software QA to ensure that new software is exhaustively tested before it goes into production and is soundly designed, and to review the performance of existing software in an effort to find and correct weak spots.

solder track An electrical conductor on a *printed circuit board*, made by applying molten solder to the board.

solid state Referring to the use of semiconductor technology in electronic devices.

solid-state disk See *semiconductor disk*.

sort To rearrange data *records* according to the contents of some part (*field*) of each, as to alphabetize or place in numeric order. A sort may be into either ascending (lowest to highest) or descending (highest to lowest) order. Sorts can also be done on multiple fields with a precedence of fields defined; e.g., if the sort is by last name and several customers have the same name, the order is determined by their account numbers. See also *collating sequence*.

sort algorithm The method for sorting data, i.e., the internal procedure followed by the computer according to program *instructions*. There are numerous ways to accomplish sorting, some more efficient than others. Certain sort algorithms have become standards (e.g., the ''bubble'' and the Shell-Metzner methods). Because sorting is a complex activity that is basic to information processing, a great deal of care and attention goes into the selection and design of sort algorithms, and heavy learned tomes have been written on the subject.

sort key A *field* within a data *record* that is evaluated in sorting the records into order. The location, length, and characteristics of sort keys, and what is to be done with them, are specified to the sort program as *parameters*.

sort/merge To combine two or more similar *files* into one file with all *records* sorted into appropriate order.

sortworker A temporary file created by a sort program to hold intermediate results when the amount of data to be sorted is larger than the available *memory* workspace. When very large amounts of data are being sorted, the sort program creates several sortworkers and then combines them with a *sort/merge* to produce a single final product in the specified order.

source (1) The origin of data moved to a new destination.

(2) Data, or text written in a *programming language*, from which further processing proceeds. "Source data" is original information that has been processed and serves as the basis for the present results.

source code The *statements* of a computer program written in a *programming language*.

source listing A printout of a computer program.

source module A portion (*module*) of a computer program in human-written form.

source program A program as written by a person for translation by a *language processor*; the form of the program before *compilation*.

space allocation The amount of data storage space assigned to a *file* on a *disk drive*.

space request A *parameter* accompanying the creation of a new *file*, usually in *job control language*, specifying the amount of *disk storage* space to be assigned to the file. The *operating system* attempts to satisfy the space request; if it cannot, it halts the job before starting execution of the program that needs the file space. A space request always specifies a primary *allocation* expressed in units of disk space. Some also request a *secondary allocation* to be used in case the primary allocation is too small to hold all the data.

spanned records A method of organizing data. When a set of related items of information (a *logical record*) actually occupies two or more physical records in a *file*, it spans the record boundaries. This is roughly analogous to a multipage printed form, in which all of the information required is more than a single page can hold.

special forms Preprinted forms (e.g., bank statement) on which computer output is printed.

special-purpose register A *CPU register* dedicated to a particular function and available only for that purpose. Contrasts with *general-purpose register*. The *PC register* is an example.

specs Specifications.

speech synthesizer A computer *peripheral* that converts output signals into an artificial human voice that "speaks."

speed-matching buffer A small *memory* that adjusts speeds between two devices operating at different data-transfer rates. The first machine writes into the *buffer* at its own rate, then signals the second machine that a message is waiting. The second machine reads the buffer at its own rate and replies by writing a message into the buffer, etc.

spike A brief sudden surge of electricity.

spindle A complete rotating unit of disk storage, same as *disk pack*. Usually used in connection with quantities: "This system has sixty spindles." One does *not* say that data are "stored on a spindle."

split screen A mode of operation on a display screen. The screen is subdivided into zones, each containing the contents of a different *file*, or with one zone containing data and the other system messages, or with one zone displaying output and the other reserved for prompts and input, etc.

spool   A *file* maintained by *systems software* where printed output is temporarily held if a program attempts to print while the printer is busy. The *operating system* accepts the output issued by the program and writes it to the spool. When the printer finishes the present report, the operating system then routes the spooled report to it. In this way, programs are not held up by the printer, which is always much slower than the computer. In large systems where several programs are running concurrently, many reports might be spooled at the same time and a system of priorities (*output class*) determines the order in which they are routed to the printer.

spooler/despooler   A *system control program* that controls the *spooling* and printing of reports.

spreadsheet   A powerful, screen-oriented, interactive program enabling a terminal user to lay out financial or other numeric data on the screen. A spreadsheet totals rows and columns, applies user-defined factors and formulas to calculate tax breaks and other complex operations, does statistical analyses of the data, projects future trends, etc. It is a *simulation modeling* tool most useful to business management, but applicable to any numeric manipulations of rows and columns of numbers.

squish   Same as *compaction*; the reorganization of stored data to reduce *fragmentation*.

SRC   (1) Abbreviation for source.
  (2) See *stored response chain*.

SSD   Solid-State Disk. See *semiconductor disk*.

SSDD   Single-Sided Double-Density. A data recording format on *floppy disk* storage.

SSSD   Single-Sided Single-Density. A data recording format on *floppy disk* storage. This is the base format, to which other formats are compared (e.g., *SSDD, DSDD*).

stack An area in *memory* for the temporary storage of values, such as the contents of *registers*, where they are set aside for the moment so that the register can be used for other purposes, and from where they can be readily retrieved when needed again. The stack is an *architectural* feature of some *CPU* types, most notably in microcomputers. It is an *FIFO* (first-in, first-out) *buffer* controlled by a special register called the *stack pointer* that maintains an *address* pointing to the next location in the stack. The stack works from the top down, so that values are PUSHed onto it and POPped off it (PUSH and POP being the *assembly language instructions* that control movement of data to and from the stack, respectively). In Z80 assembly language, for example, the instruction PUSH BC takes the two *bytes* from CPU registers B and C and writes them one below the other at the addresses indicated by the stack pointer, then adjusts the stack pointer downward by two. Later these values are retrieved from the stack by the instruction POP BC, which reads them from the stack back into registers B and C and adjusts the stack pointer upward by two. Because other values might be written onto the stack between the PUSH and POP instructions, it is important that the programmer manage the stack pointer so that it does not get out of phase and fetch the wrong values.

One of the most important uses of the stack, other than simply to set aside register contents for brief periods, is in the calling of *subroutines*. When a subroutine is called, the address of the instruction following the CALL is placed on the stack automatically, and control passes to the subroutine. When a *RETURN* instruction is encountered, the two bytes above the current stack pointer setting are POPped into the *PC register*, thus returning control to the instruction following the CALL.

standalone An adjective describing a data-processing device capable of operating independently (outside the control of a computer). Examples of standalone machines are *keypunches* and *reader/sorters*.

standard function   Same as *built-in function*. A feature of a *high-level programming language* that calculates a complex mathematical function (such as a logarithm or a cosine) without the programmer having to code the actual instructions that perform the computation.

star network   As shown below, a communications network configuration in which all lines converge on a central *host* computer that controls all traffic.

STAR NETWORK

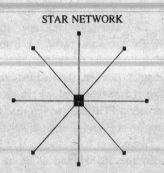

start bit   In *asynchronous* data communications, a *bit* prefixed to a *byte* (character) as an alert to the receiving device. A start bit has no information value; it simply notifies the receiver that information is being sent.

started task   A program that, though not a part of the *operating system*, is made *resident* and treated as though it were. Examples of started tasks are data-communications control *software* and *automated scheduling systems*.

start/stop   Same as *asynchronous* communications.

state-of-the-art   A catchy phrase that implies being up to date in technology. A ''state-of-the-art shop'' is a data-processing organization that uses current *hardware, software*, and methods of operation.

statement A line of text in a *source* program. A statement may be either a *comment* or an *instruction*.

statement label A symbolic name or a line number of a *statement* in a program, which is translated into a *memory address*.

statement number See *statement label*.

static RAM A type of semiconductor *memory* that does not need to be *refreshed*. Data stored in static RAM (*random-access memory*) remains there until changed or until power is removed. Contrasts with *dynamic RAM*.

statistical monitor In this case, a monitor is *software* that measures the performance of a computer system. A statistical monitor is one of two types (the other being *event-driven*). It periodically samples activity in the system (e.g., *disk* operations in progress, number of programs being executed concurrently, lines of print waiting for output, etc.) and, on the assumption that this and many other such samples accurately reflect system activity at any given moment, it averages and extrapolates its measurements to construct a statistically acceptable profile of the performance of the system.

status byte A *byte* of storage that contains neither data nor a *machine instruction*, but instead indicates one or more alternative conditions (*flags*) used to control execution of a program. In some status bytes each *bit* has a unique significance, thereby indicating up to eight different "on/off" conditions. For example, the *CPU* maintains a status byte in a *register*, with individual bits indicating whether the value being worked on is positive or negative, whether the preceding operation resulted in a carry or borrow, whether two compared values are equal or not. As another example, the

CP/M® *operating system* for microcomputers maintains an I/O status byte in which the first two bits indicate the location of the printer *port*, the last two provide information about the system *console*, and the central four bits show the disposition of various auxiliary *peripherals*. The CPU status byte register is controlled by *hardware*, but status bytes in memory operate and have meanings and structures as the programmer has specified.

status line   A conductor on the *bus* of a computer on which an *addressed* component indicates its status to the *CPU*. As an example, when the CPU is preparing to move a value into *memory* it sends out a "write memory" command and the address of the destination. That memory location then sends back a pulse on the status line saying "I'm ready," whereupon the CPU issues the value to be saved.

stop bit   In *asynchronous* data communications, one or two *bits* sent after a character to create a pause so the receiving machine has time to act on the character (print or otherwise process it) before the next is sent.

storage allocation   The assignment of some specified amount of *memory* or data storage to a program. Storage allocation is performed on *request* by the *operating system*.

storage capacity   The maximum amount of data that can be stored on a device (e.g., *disk*) or held in a computer's *memory* at one time.

storage device   A computer *peripheral* on which information (programs and data) is held in a magnetic form that can be readily read and written by the computer. The main storage devices are *disk*, *drum*, *tape*, and *floppy disk drives*.

storage medium   Any surface (or semiconductor circuitry) for reading and/or writing information in a machine-readable form, e.g., *disk*, *punched cards*, *tape*, etc.

storage pool A group of similar data storage devices; the *tape drives* in a computer installation are collectively referred to as the tape pool.

storage-to-register instruction A *machine language* instruction that moves a *word* of data from *memory* into a *register*.

storage-to-storage instruction A *machine language* instruction that moves a *word* of data from one place in *memory* to another.

store (1) To write data from a *CPU* register into *memory* or onto a storage device.

(2) To save data in a *file*.

(3) In British usage (less commonly in the United States), the *memory* of a computer, or any storage device. "Data are held in the store."

store and forward An operational characteristic in some data-communications systems. An incoming message is temporarily saved by a computer (*message switch*) and later sent on toward its destination. "Later" is usually as soon as the complete message has been received, but it could be held for an extended period if the path toward the destination is busy or if the receiving machine is unable to accept the message for some reason.

stored program Any program placed into the *memory* of a computer and executed by a *CPU* reading and acting on its *instructions*. The concept of the stored program is fundamental to all data processing.

stored response chain Abbreviated SRC; letters pronounced separately. A fixed sequence of responses to *prompts* issued by an interactive program, stored in a *file* to save the terminal user the trouble of always keying the same commands for some frequently repeated function. When the user starts the interactive program, he indicates the name of the SRC file.

As the program runs, at points where it normally requests instructions from the user it instead reads the next line from the file and acts on that line as though it had been entered at the terminal.

strain relief   A strap, bracket, or other means of securing a cable so that it does not accidentally become disconnected.

strapping option   A means of enabling/disabling *hardware* features by rearranging *jumpers* on a *printed circuit board*.

streaming   A malfunction in a communicating device; the device constantly sends data (gibberish or the same character over and over), thereby locking out all other devices on the line.

street power   Commercial power as delivered by the public utility ''from the street.''

stress test   To test new *software* (and sometimes *hardware*) under ordinary or unusually heavy work loads. Used as both a noun and a verb.

string   (1) Any group of *alphanumeric* characters treated as a unit of data by a program, e.g., a customer name, a line of text, or a command. Most *high-level programming languages* treat string data as a special *type* on which mathematical operations cannot be performed.

(2) A group of storage devices connected in series and sharing a *port* on a *controller*, e.g., a string of *disk*.

string variable   In a *high-level programming language*, a symbolic name for an *alphanumeric field* of data, for example, EMPLOYEE-NAME.

strip off   To extract selected information from a larger collection of data.

strobe   Any signaling pulse of a very short duration. In the definition of *status line*, the "I'm ready" signal sent by an *addressed memory* location is a strobe.

structured programming A disciplined approach to the development and organization of computer programs. The fundamental concept of structured programming is that all information-related activities can be accomplished by the combination of three logic *constructs* called DO, DO-WHILE, and IF . . . THEN . . . ELSE.

1. DO is a straight-line nonrepeating sequence of program *instructions*.

2. DO-WHILE is a *loop*, a sequence of operations repeated while some condition remains true (WHILE X < Y) and terminated when the condition becomes no longer true (X ≥ Y).

3. IF . . . THEN . . . ELSE is a decision that influences the sequence of activities based upon some situation or condition dynamically occurring and evaluated during processing.

Structured programming asserts that because all programs can be written using these three simple constructs, no other flow of logic ought to be used. Most specifically, structured programming discourages the use of *GOTO* logic (jumping around), which has earned it the nickname "GOTO-less programming."

Furthermore, structured programming presents a methodology for thinking and planning during the development phase that is based on the three logic constructs. This is intended to simplify complex processes and, if properly followed, will lead naturally into the writing of clear, concise structured programs.

In connection with the program-planning phase, structured programming employs a concept known as *top-down design*, in which the starting point is a broad statement describing the purpose of the program. This statement is broken down into successively more detailed steps incorporating the basic logic constructs until ultimately a fully detailed description of the program exists, which can then be directly translated into the instruction set of a programming language.

STX Start of TeXt. A control character in a message, delineating the boundary between the *message header* and its text.

submit To enter a *batch job* into a computer system for execution.

subparameter The variable item(s) following a *keyword parameter*; an *argument*.

subprogram A vague term generally referring to any of several major program segments that combine to form a complete computer program. A subprogram is usually a fairly complete sequence of *instructions* that accomplish a broadly stated purpose such as "update the status of the customer's account from recent activity" or "scan all the input data and report on any items that contain obvious errors." Frequently, but not always interchangeable with *module*.

subrange A subset of a range of permissible values. If the range of A is 1 to 100 and the range of B is 1 to 20, then B is a subrange of A.

subroutine A set of *instructions* in a computer program that can be executed anywhere in the program as though they were a single instruction. A subroutine is invoked by a *call* instruction that transfers control to the subroutine. When a *return* instruction is encountered in the subroutine, control reverts to the instruction following the call, thus making it seem as though all the actions of the subroutine were performed by a single instruction placed in the position of the call. Subroutines are often—but by no means always—actions performed at two or more points in the program; since the instructions in a subroutine are only written once and executable by calls scattered throughout the program, the subroutine is an efficient means of simplifying and economizing on the size of a program.

Subroutines are also useful for breaking a program up into logical activity units (e.g., "read the next *record*," "compute the current balance," "print column headings"). For this reason, many programmers make extensive use of subroutines. They also ease the *debugging* of a program, since it is usually fairly easy to detect in which subroutine an error has occurred.

Some *programming languages* rely heavily on subroutines. In *Pascal* and other *structured programming* languages subroutines are called *PROCEDURES* and *FUNCTIONS*, and they are virtually indispensible in any but the simplest programs. In *COBOL* a subroutine is called a *PERFORM*, and it constitutes one of the most powerful features of the language.

subscriber loop   The portion of a phone list that connects the customer's premises with a telephone company's central office.

subscript   The *index* of an *array* of data, indicating the specific element referred to. In the symbol MAT(3,2) the bracketed numbers are the subscript for an array called MAT and point to the element in the third row, second column.

subscripted variable   A symbolic name for an *array* of variables, requiring the use of a *subscript* to identify the specific element referred to.

subset   Used in the same sense as in mathematics: a group of information items that is part of a larger grouping.

successor job   A *job* that accepts as input the output of a previous job (*predecessor*), so that it cannot be started until the predecessor has completed successfully.

supermini   A minicomputer whose processing power approaches that of a large-scale *mainframe* computer.

superscript   Exponential notation.

superset   Ordinarily used to describe the *implementation* of a *programming language*, in which the standard *instruction set* of the language has been extended to include extra features. "This version is a superset of standard *Pascal*."

supervisor The portion of the *operating system* that supervises (controls) the execution of programs.

supervisor call Abbreviated SVC; letters pronounced separately. A standard *subroutine* furnished by the *operating system* that any program can call for certain system services, e.g., *memory allocation*, time of day, open/close *files*, etc.

suppress Inhibit. For example, to suppress printing is to accept print requests from a program by the *operating system* and to respond appropriately so that the program "thinks" printing is being done, but in fact to ignore the request. To "suppress leading zeros" is to convert all zeros to the left of the most significant digit of a number into space characters.

SUPV Abbreviation for *supervisor*.

surface analysis A program that writes a known series of characters onto a magnetic data storage *medium* and then reads them back to determine whether, and where, flaws exist.

surge protector A device placed in an electrical circuit to prevent surges and *spikes* that might injure electronic equipment from passing.

SVC See *supervisor call*.

S/W Abbreviation for *software* (written only).

swapping See *job swapping*.

switch selectable addressing The ability to set *DIP* switches in a *peripheral* or terminal device to establish the *address* by which the device is known to a computer system. Usually done by a technician when the device is installed.

switched line A dial telephone line.

switched network The dial telephone network.

switching node A point in a network where either lines or messages are switched.

symbol In general, this term follows conventional usage. More particularly, a symbol in a *programming language* is the representation of a *memory address* or a value by means of a letter or a group of *alphanumerics* that ordinarily suggest the meaning of the quantity represented. For example, NET-PAY symbolizing a numeric value, or PAY-CALCULATION representing a *subroutine*.

symbol table A list of *symbols* used in a program, cross referenced to the values they represent.

symbolic debugger A programming aid for *debugging*, that shows the symbols for variables along with the values they represent at each step of the program.

synchronous A data-communications term describing the way signals between machines are timed. Contrasts with *asynchronous*. In synchronous communications, a prearranged number of *bits* are expected to be sent across the line per second, e.g., 4800 *bps*. To synchronize the sending and receiving machines, in addition to the data signal a secondary frequency is sent on the same line by the transmitting machine. This is called the clocking signal, and it sets the pace for both devices. For each cycle of the clocking signal some number of bits is sent on the data signal. In synchronous communications there are no *start* and *stop bits*; all the bits either have information value or are *parity* bits used for error-checking. Synchronous communications is usually found at the higher end of the speed spectrum, from 2400 bps upward.

synchronous data link control Abbreviated SDLC; letters pronounced separately. An IBM adaptation of *hierarchical* data link control, which the reader should see for further discussion.

synergistic Greater than the sum of its parts. A popular data-processing buzz word.

syntactic error Same as *syntax error*.

syntax The rules for forming *statements* in a *programming language*. Syntax is comparable to the grammar of a human language, but much more precise and less complex. It defines such things as the language's *reserved words* and their meanings, the proper ways of writing mathematical expressions, the formation of variable names, etc. In brief, the syntax describes what the *language processor* will (and by inference what it will not) accept as valid statements, and how to write programs using the language described.

syntax error An improperly formed *statement* in a *programming language* that the *language processor* rejects as being incoherent.

syntax scanner The *subprogram* performing the first phase of the translation of a program into executable form by a *compiler* or *interpreter*. The syntax scanner checks the program's *statements* to make sure they conform to the *syntax* rules of the language. When errors are detected, the syntax scanner reports this fact by printing the statement and a *diagnostic message* indicating (as best it can determine) what is wrong. In most compilers (but not interpreters) the syntax scanner attempts to detect and report on every error in the program so that the programmer can make all the necessary corrections at once, and then recompile. In interpreters, syntax errors are usually reported by the syntax scanner at the time the interpreter attempts to execute the statement, and the program halts.

SYSCTLG (Pronounced "sis-catalog") SYStem CaTaLoG.

SYSGEN (Pronounced ''sis-jen'') SYStem GENeration.

system (1) Any group of individual components working together to form a unified whole, e.g., computer system, *application system*, etc.

(2) The usual term used in data processing for a computer. (It is not fashionable among ''insiders'' to refer to a computer as such.) ''The system will be shut down for maintenance.''

system calendar A date-and-year calendar automatically maintained by a computer system. Programs can determine today's date by a *supervisor call* to the *operating system*, which returns the calendar setting. System calendars vary from one system to another; some indicate the date/year in both *Julian* and *Gregorian* notation, as well as the day of the week, while others show only the Julian date.

system call Same as *supervisor call*.

system catalog A master index of all *files* under the control of a large computer's *operating system*; analogous to the card catalog in a public library. The system catalog shows the name of every file, its creation date, date of last access, location, and *attributes*. It is the primary reference for data management in a system.

system clock (1) An electronic circuit in the *CPU* that issues a steady high-frequency pulse signal by which all internal components are synchronized. See *clock, clocking, clock frequency*.

(2) The *time-of-day clock* of a computer system.

system control program Abbreviated SCP; letters pronounced separately. Any piece of *systems software* that furnishes overall direction and control to a computer system (rather than solving specific information problems).

system engineer A highly trained data-processing professional, usually employed by a vendor, whose job is to

provide technical advice to customers and technical suppor
for sales personnel. Often called an *SE* (letters pronounce
separately).

system generation　Abbreviated SYSGEN; pronounced "sis
jen." The process of preparing, configuring, and installing a
operating system or other *system control program*. System
generation is normally a highly complex project requiring th
participation of several *systems programmers*. See also *gen*.

system initialization　Most often to *IPL* or *reboot*, whic
resets the system to a start-up condition.

system-level timer　A *timer* used by the *operating system* t
set deadlines for events, to remind itself to take an actio
after a certain interval, and for other such "alarm clock"
purposes. A system-level timer has the highest priority of an
timer, since it is integral to the control of the compute
system as a whole.

systems and programming　A frequently used name for th
department that is responsible for *applications programming*
Abbreviated S and P.

systems integration　The combining of products from a num
ber of vendors, both *hardware* and *software*, to form a *turnke*
system tailored to a particular kind of business or *application*

systems network architecture　See *SNA*.

systems programmer.　A person professionally involved i
the writing, *generation*, installation, maintenance, repair
troubleshooting, and modification of *systems software*. Sys
tems programming is a highly specialized, lucrative occupation

systems software　A general class of programs whose pur
pose is to control a computer system. Systems software i
what turns a computer from expensive gadgetry into a usefu
functioning tool ready to solve information problems. It i

central and indispensible to the operation of all but the most primitive computing machinery. The basic foundation of systems software is the *operating system,* the master program under whose direction both the computer itself, its *peripherals,* and all other *system control programs* function.

system supervisor See *supervisor.*

T

T switch An electrical switch that connects one machine to either of two other devices. The switched device is terminated at the "lower end" of the "stem" and the alternatives are at the ends of the "top bar." An example is to switch a micro-computer *port* between a low-speed, high-quality printer and a high-speed, lower quality printer.

tab stop As in a typewriter, a column position to which the printing mechanism advances on receipt of the appropriate command.

table A cross-reference list showing symbols or reference values and their corresponding values, used for lookups.

table-driven A program that makes extensive use of *tables* located in *memory*.

table element An entry in a *table*.

table plotter A type of *plotter* operating under computer control. The paper is placed on an immobile flat surface and the pen moves over it. Contrasts with *drum plotter*.

tabulation (1) Summarization of data, such as developing totals and counts.

(2) Processing *punched cards*, often in preparation for input to a computer. A *reader/sorter* is tabulation equipment.

(3) Arranging printed results into columnar format using *tab stops* on a printer.

tag One or more characters attached to an item or *record* for purposes of identification. When data items are compressed (squeezed together to eliminate empty space), the individual items are often tagged to show that this is the account number, that is the customer name, etc.

tag sort A method of *sorting* data, where the *addresses* of *records* rather than the records themselves are rearranged during the sorting process. The result is a list of the addresses of records indicating the order in which they are to be printed or written out to a *file*.

tandem processors Two computers connected together and working on the same problem at the same time. If one machine fails the other takes over immediately.

tape See *magnetic tape*. Also used in the sense of a *file* stored on magnetic tape: "This is a tape of yesterday's receipts."

tape crease A wrinkle or fold in a *magnetic tape* causing an error in the reading or writing of data at that point.

tape drive An electromechanical machine operating under computer control that reads and writes data on *magnetic tape* in a manner similar to that of a voice tape recorder.

tape library The area in a computer room set aside for the storage of *magnetic tapes*.

tape pool A collective name for a group of *tape drives*.

tape rack A rack that holds reels of *magnetic tape*.

tape transport The portion of a *tape drive* that moves *magnetic tape* across the read/write head from one reel to the other.

target CPU The type of *central processing unit* (brand and make) for which a *language processor* produces *machine language* output. Every language processor (*compiler* or *interpreter*) has a target CPU; two *COBOL* compilers might translate exactly the same *source language statements*, but if the target CPU of one is the IBM 370-type CPU and the target of the other is the Z80 microprocessor, their outputs are entirely different and suitable for execution only on one CPU type.

target market   The industry or application for which a product has been specifically designed.

target pack   A *disk pack* set aside for the purpose of maintaining *systems software*. When a change is to be made to a *system control program*, the program is copied to the target pack and the changes are made there and tested using that copy. The updated program is then copied back into the *production library*.

task   (1) One of several programs currently in execution under the control of a *multiprogramming operating system*.
(2) Any major activity performed by a computer.

TDM   Time Division Multiplexer.

technical services   Same as *tech support*.

tech support   A data-processing organization that performs *systems programming* and furnishes other technical assistance to the data-processing operations department.

tech writer   A person professionally involved in the writing of technical documentation.

telecommunications   Voice and/or data communications using telephone circuits.

telemetry   Sensing and measurement performed by a remote instrument that transmits its signals via data communications to a computer.

teleprinter   A printer/keyboard machine specifically designed to be used in data communications.

teleprocessing The combination of *telecommunications* and data processing.

Teletype A teleprinter produced by the Teletype Corporation. The name, though protected by trademark laws, has fallen into generic usage and as such encompasses all teleprinters.

temporary file A *file* that is created during a program run to hold interim processing results. Data are written to the temporary file at one phase in the program's execution and read back at another phase for further processing. The file is deleted before the program ends.

terminal A generic term for any machine that enables a human to communicate with a computer, either on a direct-attached or a remote basis.

terminal block See *connecting block*.

test file A *file* of data used for testing a computer program during its development. A test file usually contains a relatively smaller amount of data than the corresponding production file, but the data in a test file are ordinarily carefully structured to represent the full range of possibilities that would ever be encountered in ''live'' data in order to exercise the program thoroughly.

test probe A pencil-like electrical contact attached to a measurement device by a cable. The probe can be used to reach inside tightly packed electronic devices to test circuitry.

test record A *record* in a *test file*.

test under mask To check the status of selected *bits* in a *byte* by comparing the byte as a whole with another byte in which the tested bits are set to 1 and all other bits are reset to Ø. If any of the selected bits is set to 1, this fact is sensed and a *status flag* is set.

text editor An interactive program developed to enable humans to key and edit text at a terminal, save and retrieve *files*, print text, etc. Word processing programs are text editors.

text processing The manipulation of alphabetic data (rather than numeric calculations) under program control.

thermal printer A printer that produces character images on paper by a heat process.

thimble A replaceable character set unit that spins in the printing mechanism of an impact printer. Character *slugs* are arranged around the perimeter of the thimble; as the slug for the character to be printed spins into the correct position, a hammer drives it forward to print the impression on paper. Similar to a *daisy wheel*.

thin film In a laminated structure, a layer of some substance laid down to a thickness of approximately one molecule. Very high-quality semiconductors are made using thin-film technology.

think time Idle time between periods of transmission in a *real-time* system, when either the terminal user is evaluating a system response and preparing to key, or the *host* computer is processing an entry made at the terminal and preparing to respond.

thrashing A situation in which a computer becomes overwhelmed with work. Thrashing is a phenomenon of *multiprogramming*; so many *jobs* are in concurrent execution and so many inputs are arriving at the same time that the *operating system* spends all its time trying to manage the overload, with the result that little headway is made against it.

threaded language A *high-level programming language* in which portions of a program are *compiled* into executable form as they are entered, and other parts are *interpreted* as the program runs. The *language processor* selects the alternatives based upon the complexity and thus the relative efficiencies of these different approaches with respect to the program's structure.

threshold value A "trigger point" beyond which something changes in the way a program executes. For example, if more than 40 errors occur in a minute, an *operating system* might reach a threshold value and shut down the system on the assumption that a *hardware* component has failed.

throughput The amount of data that can be processed, transmitted, printed, etc. (as appropriate) by a data-processing device per unit time. There are two fundamental measures of throughput: *rated* throughput is the maximum; *effective* throughput is the best one can expect on the average.

throw-away device Any electronic component not subject to service; if it fails, you throw it away and replace it.

thruput An alternative spelling for *throughput*.

tightly coupled systems Two or more *CPU*s that share common *memory*, and in which one CPU assumes control of the other(s). See also *multiprocessor*.

time division multiplexer Abbreviated TDM; letters pronounced separately. A device that *multiplexes* (combines the signals from) several independent transmission lines onto a single line. The TDM samples each incoming signal many times a second and constructs a *byte* representing the signal's voltage. These bytes, one for each line in a preset order, are continuously transmitted over a single line to a distant TDM. There they are used to reconstruct signals whose forms approximate those sampled, and from that point they are sent to their destinations.

timeout The expiration of some preset period of time, after which processing stops or an alternative action is taken.

timer An "alarm clock" in a computer system, usually provided by *hardware* but activated by *software*. A program sets a timer for some period and then goes about other activities; at the end of the period the timer generates an *interrupt* that signals the program that the period has elapsed. The intervals measured by timers vary widely. If a printer runs at 100 cps, the timer might be set to go off every 1/100 sec as a reminder to send another character to the printer. On the other hand, in data communications the remote device might be given 45 sec to respond to a message, so a timer would be set for that period when a message is sent. In another case, a *job* might be set up to start in 4 hours, and a timer measures that period.

time sharing A computing service in which many low-speed terminals share the resources of a high-speed computer. Time sharing is usually a business enterprise. Customers pay for "connect time" as a usage fee, and additionally for data storage space and other services furnished by the computer. Because of the wide discrepancy between the speed of a terminal and the processing power of the computer, many customers can be served at once and each has the impression that he or she has exclusive use of the system.

time stamp Information added to a message, *record*, or other unit of data indicating the date and time it was handled by a computer system.

timing loop A set of *instructions* in a computer program that does nothing, but whose execution time is known. If an action needs to be deferred for a brief period, the timing loop is executed an appropriate number of times to cause the appropriate delay.

tipping The painting or coloration of the raised lettering on a plastic card, such as a credit card.

TOD clock Time-of-day clock.

TOF (1) In an *editor*, Top Of *File*; the start of data.

(2) On a printer, a switch that positions the page at the top (Top Of Form).

toggle An on/off switch, either mechanical, in circuitry (a *flip-flop*), or in *software*.

top The start of a *file*.

top-down design A method for designing computer programs; one of the chief concepts of *structured programming*. In top-down design the programmer begins with a broad statement of the program's purpose and a general idea of how it should work. He or she then breaks this statement down into more finite and detailed steps, and then further divides those steps in successively more explicit levels of program specification. The end result is a complete plan for a program that can be translated directly into the *statements* of a *programming language*.

topology The conceptual layout of a complex data-communications network in a block-diagram form, showing the relationships of the various *nodes* of the network.

TP TeleProcessing.

trace A printed report that follows the execution of a program by identifying each *statement* in the order it was executed. A trace also often shows the effects of *instructions* on variables. It is useful for *debugging* programs during their development, but because of the voluminous amount of printout produced, it is usually used only when other methods of finding errors have been exhausted.

track A unit of storage space on a rotating data storage device (*disk* or *drum*). On a drum, a track bands the drum and corresponds to the location of a read/write head. On a disk, a track is one of many concentric circles of data written around the *platter* on one or both sides, and the read/write head positions itself over the track for access to it. It should be noted that a track is not physically isolated from the surrounding surface; it is merely the point where magnetic spots are recorded.

track access time In *disk* and *floppy disk* storage, the amount of time required for the read/write head to move mechanically from its present position to a desired track and to settle.

tractor feed A *pin feed* paper-advancing mechanism that mounts on top of a printer.

trailer (1) The last part of a data-communications message, indicating that the message is complete and, often, containing *block parity* character(s).

(2) A trailer *record* is written at the end of a *file* on *magnetic tape* to serve as an end-of-data indicator. It often contains a *block* count so that the program reading the file can determine whether it has read as many blocks of data as were originally written on the tape.

trailing pad Filler characters inserted after information in order to fulfill length requirements or for cosmetic purposes. In financial reports, for example, trailing pads of Øs are used to conform with standard monetary notation: $37.ØØ (instead of $37.), $23.5Ø (rather than $23.5).

transcendental function Same usage as in mathematics—a value that cannot be calculated using the arithmetic operations (addition, subtraction, multiplication, division). A transcendental function therefore transcends ordinary arithmetic. Examples are logarithm, sine, cosine, root.

transient (1) A surge of electrical power that occurs when a motor turns on or some other large resistance is suddenly placed in a circuit.

(2) An *application program* or any other type of program that remains in *memory* only while executing, and whose memory space is taken by another program when the first ends. Contrasts with *resident* program.

transistor A semiconductor switching device. Power flows across the transistor from an input to an output in proportion to the amount of power applied to a third lead. Thus, one circuit is used to control another by means of a transistor.

transparent (1) Not noticeable, or of no consequence. "When we switched the *on-line system* to the other *CPU,* the network operated the same, so it was transparent to the users."

(2) A transparent device is one whose effect does not alter the overall operation of a data-processing system, even if it has an essential function. A *modem* is a transparent device because it accepts *digital* information at one end of the line and delivers identical digital information at the other.

trap An *instruction* placed at a crucial point in a computer program to capture an error as it occurs. If the error does not occur the trap has no effect, but if it does occur, the trap stops the program and reports the error. Used in *debugging.*

trash heap A *memory* area owned by a program, in which the values are no longer useful and they therefore waste memory. Some programs contain *housekeeping routines* to reclaim this space for other purposes.

trifurcated Having three electrical contacts in series, all closed by the same mechanical switch. If any two contacts fail, the switch still works.

trinary Having three states. An electrical current is trinary since it may be positive, negative, or off.

TRUE A *Boolean* condition, the opposite of which is *FALSE.* The statement IF A = Ø generates a Boolean TRUE/FALSE condition, since A may be either equal to Ø (TRUE) or not equal to zero (thus FALSE). If A is .ØØØØØØ1, a human would be inclined to say it's as good as zero, but a computer will judge it as FALSE because it is not absolutely zero. Many comparisons in programs generate Boolean values (IF Z = I, IF J < = R), as do evaluations of control variables

(WHILE A < B . . .). In each of these cases a TRUE is generated as long as the condition is found to be as stated, i.e., as long as Z = I, J is less than or equal to R, A is less than B, etc. When the condition is not as stated, it is FALSE.

truncation To shorten a data item by simply "whacking off" some part of it.
>   THIS LINE IS NOT TRUNCATED.
>   THIS LINE IS TRUNCA

Truncation of numbers differs from *roundoff* in that no attempt is made to adjust the remaining value.

SOURCE VALUE	321.867
ROUNDED TO TWO DECIMAL POINTS	321.87
TRUNCATED TO TWO DECIMAL POINTS	321.86

truth table A problem planning aid in which every possible outcome of a given set of circumstances is graphically represented so that all the possibilities are anticipated in the program.

TTL Transistor-to-Transistor Link. A method of electronically connecting two devices so that the signals flowing between them are electrically isolated from their internal circuitry.

TTY Abbreviation for *Teletype*. More often used in writing than in speech.

tube A slangy way of referring to a *video display* terminal.

tuning The quasi-scientific art of improving the throughput of a computer system by adjusting *systems software*, modifying the *hardware configuration*, balancing work loads, and otherwise orchestrating the complexities of the system. Although based on careful measurement and observation of the system using *performance monitors* and statistical methods, tuning depends heavily on hunch, trial-and-error, and "feel." It is the most demanding and priestly of all data-processing skills, requiring expert knowledge of all aspects of system operation.

turnaround (1) The elapsed time from *submitting* a *batch job* to receiving its printed output.

(2) Of a line: The amount of time needed to reverse the transmission direction so that a line on which data were received is ready to be used to send back a response.

(3) A turnaround document is a document produced by a computer that is later used as input to the computer. The *punched card* sent out with a telephone bill and returned with payment by the customer is a turnaround document.

turnkey system A complete package of *hardware*, *software*, procedures, and training, sold as a unit so that all the customer has to do to get up and running is to "turn the key."

turnpike effect A phenomenon that occurs on highways, networks, within computers, and in other traffic-oriented situations; as traffic increases, bottlenecks and delays rise in an exponential progression, until at some point everything locks up.

turtle The term applied to *cursor* in the *LOGO programming language*; a cursor that has the properties of both position and direction.

tutorial Directions and hints issued by a conversational program to help guide the user in responding to *prompts*.

tweaking parameters Making minor adjustments in the performance of *systems software* to improve *throughput*.

twinax (Pronounced "twin-ax") Twinaxial cable.

twinaxial cable A type of cable in which two *coaxial* cables are enclosed within the same sheath. One side is used to transmit, the other to receive.

twisted pair The two wires of a signaling circuit, twisted around each other to minimize the effects of inductance (magnetic fields around a conductor, which can cause false signals).

twist-lock connector   A power plug and receptacle used for terminals and other electrical devices that could cause catastrophic effects if accidentally powered off because the plug was knocked loose. To make contact, the plug is twisted after being inserted, thus locking it in place.

twistor memory   A form of noncapacitive *read-only memory*, in which pieces of magnetizable metal (''twistors'') are embedded within a plastic sheet and *encoded* by orienting their poles one way or the other. The values of *bits* are read by sensing their fields. Twistor memory is *nonvolatile* (retains its contents in the absence of electrical power), and is used chiefly in telephone switching equipment.

two-dimensional array   An arrangement of data elements into a conceptualized grid having rows and columns. Individual elements are identified by specifying their row and column numbers (*subscripts*).

two-pass compiler   A common design of *language processors*. On the first pass through the program, the *compiler* checks the *syntax* of *statements* and builds a *table* of all symbols, indicating whether they are computational variables or *labels* that require the assignment of *memory addresses*. On the second pass, the compiler actually translates program statements into executable *machine language*, using the symbol table to form the instructions involving variables and addresses.

twos complement   A *binary complement*, in which a value is complemented by setting all its Øs to 1s and resetting all its 1s to Øs. In older computers, subtraction was often done by complementing the minuend and adding it to the subtrahend, then adding 1 to the result. This produced the same value as true subtraction while saving the expense of special circuitry. As costs of electronics have fallen, complementary subtraction using the twos complement method has become more troublesome and costly than the circuitry to do real subtraction, and consequently it is seldom used in modern machines.

TX Abbreviation for transmit and transmitter. Used only in writing.

TYPE In programming, a general classification of data to which a given element belongs, e.g., text, integer, *real*. The TYPE constrains the kinds of things that can be done to an element of data. For example, elements TYPEd as text cannot be mathematically added, as the result would be gibberish. The TYPE also determines the manner of treating an element of data within the computer system; *memory* assigned a real (floating-point) number is handled differently than that assigned to an integer, and that, in turn, differs from the way character data are treated. Some programming languages (notably Pascal and its derivatives) are extremely rigorous in enforcing TYPEs and are thus called "strongly typed languages," while others such as BASIC pay scant attention to TYPEs. *Assembly languages* have no concept of TYPE at all, making it entirely the programmer's responsibility to ensure that an integer is not added to a character. The purpose of TYPEs is to prevent programmers from making silly mistakes of this sort, which inevitably lead to bad results.

typeahead buffer A *buffer* in a keyboard or a microcomputer that holds information keyed before the *CPU* is ready to accept it.

U

UART (Pronounced "you art") Universal Asynchronous Receiver-Transmitter. An electronic circuit that reformats *bytes* of data between the parallel (*bits* side by side) representation within a device and the serial (bits in a row) method of transmitting them over a communications line. The same UART handles data moving in either direction (in or out of a machine).

UCSD University of California at San Diego. UCSD is the developer of *p-code* and the *p-system* for making *software* portable among a variety of computer types, and holds various copyright and trademark rights to this technology.

ULSI (Letters pronounced separately) Ultra-Large-Scale Integration. See *large-scale integration*.

ultra-large-scale integration See *large-scale integration*.

unambiguous name The name of a *file* specified exactly as it is known to a computer system; i.e., without the use of *wildcard* characters. See also *ambiguous name*.

unary A logical/mathematical operation with one *operand*, e.g., negation of a number. For another example of a unary operation, see *twos complement*. Synonymous with *monadic*.

unattended operation Functioning of a communicating machine capable of receiving and/or initiating calls without direct human intervention. See also *automatic call origination*.

unbundled　*Software* and *hardware* that, although related, are sold independently of each other. To unbundle a package means to extract certain parts of it and sell them separately.

uncatalog　To remove an entry from the *system catalog* so that the system no longer "knows" of the *file*'s existence.

unconditional branch　A *GOTO instruction* that, whenever encountered, causes execution to jump to a specified point in the program. A *RETURN* instruction is also an unconditional branch. No programmatic comparison or decision is made prior to executing an unconditional branch.

underfloor cabling　Cables and wiring strung under the raised flooring in a computer room.

underflow　(1) Generation of a numeric value smaller than the computer's *word size* is capable of containing. If the smallest possible value is .00001 and a program calculates a value of .000000002, underflow results.

(2) In a computer using *stack architecture*, an underflow occurs as a result of a program error that reads more values from the stack than there are. This causes the *stack pointer* to point to an area outside the stack, thereby retrieving false values, damaging data or program *instructions*, and wreaking other havoc.

unformatted file　Any data *file* that does not follow some consistent organization in terms of *record length*, order of data elements, etc. Text files are typically unformatted.

uninterruptible power supply　Abbreviated UPS; letters pronounced separately. A power conditioning unit placed between commercial power (*street power*) and the computer room. A UPS uses street power to charge a bank of batteries. *Room power* is then drawn from the batteries and converted into the appropriate *alternating current* by electronic circuitry. This isolates the computing machinery from power surges, brownouts, etc., and also furnishes a source of power during brief outages. A UPS typically stores enough power to keep the systems going for half an hour during an outage.

unit record device   Any data storage device that handles data in *blocks* and *records* that comprise units of information, e.g., *disk drives*.

universal asynchronous receiver-transmitter   See *UART*.

unlatch   See *latch*.

unlike device types   Data storage devices that differ in their operation or characteristics, e.g., *tape* and *disk drives*. When a *file* is *concatenated* across unlike device types, the *operating system* must adapt and reformat the data so that they can be treated consistently by the program.

unpacked data   Numeric data in which one *byte* represents each digit. Contrasts with *packed*.

unprotect   To remove constraints on access to a *file* so that any program may read and modify the data it contains.

unsigned integer   An integer value without a sign (+ or −), and therefore assumed to be positive.

unsigned real number   A *real (floating-point)* value without a sign (+ or −), and therefore assumed to be positive.

unsolicited message   A warning or error message issued by a program to indicate that something has gone wrong. Some *software* systems (especially those running on large computers) report their status in response to an operator query; an unsolicited message appears even when a status query has not been made.

unsolicited status   Same as *unsolicited message*.

up   A computer system is ''up'' when it is running, and ''down'' when it is not.

update service A subscription service offered by a vendor of *hardware* or *software* to its customers, guaranteeing that updates to products will be installed within a certain period of time after available, and that documentation will be updated to reflect these changes.

upper case Capital letters.

UPS See *uninterruptible power supply*.

up time The amount of time a computer system is operational, usually expressed as a percentage of the total number of hours it ought to be "up." If the system should be available 100 hours a week and it was actually operational 98 hours, up time is 98 percent.

user Any person who uses a computer system or some part of one. In data-processing parlance "users" are those outside the organization, i.e., not computer professionals, who are clients of the organization.

user-defined function In a computer program, a *subroutine* that calculates and returns a mathematical value according to *instructions* furnished by the programmer. Most *high-level programming languages* have *built-in functions* to compute such commonly used values as logarithms, square roots, tangents, etc. Few, however, include a built-in function to find the area of a circle, so if a programmer needs to compute this value, it is necessary to write the appropriate instructions in the form of a user-defined function.

user exit A "do-nothing" *instruction* built into a *software* product where a customer can install a *hook* to activate some custom feature. If the exit is not used, execution simply proceeds past it. To invoke the exit, the "do-nothing" instruction is changed to a *branch* that jumps into the custom feature. After the feature has completed, it returns control to the next instruction following the exit. Because large data-processing organizations frequently modify and enhance software products to tailor them to local needs, software vendors build many exits into their products and furnish documentation as to their locations and purposes.

user-friendly   A buzz word meaning easy to use and suitable for non-data-processing professionals.

user interface   (1) An organizational unit within a data-processing department, serving as a liaison between the computer operations unit and the users of the system.

(2) The portion of an interactive computer program that issues messages to and receives commands from a terminal user.

user relations   Same as *user interface*, definition 1.

user-written code   A program written by the person or organization who actually uses it, according to local needs. Contrasts with *software package*. User-written code can also be a modification to a package that is invoked by a *user exit*.

utility program   A general-purpose computer program that performs some activity not specific to any particular *application*. An example is a *sort* program, which takes any *file* or set of files and arranges the contents into a specified order.

UV PROM eraser   A device that erases the contents of *erasable programmable read-only memory* (EPROM) *chips* by exposing them to ultraviolet light. This conditions the chips so that other data can be "burned" into them.

V

validate To check data to make sure they are suitable for their intended purposes, e.g., all values are within certain ranges, all information is complete and present, etc.

validity check The portion of a program that *validates* data.

vanilla See *plain vanilla*.

variable A value that fluctuates depending on other values or on circumstances during the execution of a program. The term has the same meaning in programming as in mathematics. Variables are represented by symbolic names in programs, e.g., X, PAY_RATE, DATE, BALANCE. In most *programming languages* there is a correlation between symbolic variable name and the *memory address* where the current value of the variable is kept. Whenever the variable is changed, its new value is written into the memory location assigned to its symbol, and whenever the variable is used in computations, its value is read from that location. In general, the symbolic name given to a variable is of no significance as far as the computer itself is concerned; if a variable named TAXRATE is used to total the number of employees, the program still functions properly. However, it is difficult for a human to understand and maintain a program that does not follow some logical consistency in the naming of variables, and thus this facet of programming is given considerable attention. *High-*

level programming languages implement a concept known as *TYPE* in assigning memory to and manipulating variables, so that the management of integer data differs from that of character data and it is unlikely that the two will be mixed because of a programming error. In *BASIC* the TYPE of a variable is implicit in the way variables are named; variable names ending with a '$' are character data, all others are numeric. Some BASICs further break down integer and *real* data by requiring a '%' suffix for integer numbers. In other languages, such as Pascal (known as a "strongly TYPEd language"), the TYPE of each variable must be declared at the beginning of the program, and symbolic names have no TYPE-identifying suffixes.

variable-length record   A data *record* whose length is not fixed. Usually the length of each record in such a format is prefixed to the data itself so that *software* can determine how many *bytes* of data to expect.

vary   To turn on or turn off, or to activate or deactivate. To "vary a device on-line" is to enter a command that tells the *systems software* that the device is active; to "vary off-line" has the opposite effect.

VDT   Video Display Terminal.

VDU   Video Display Unit. A term used chiefly in Britain, seldom in the United States.

vector   A set of *pointers* grouped in a predetermined order, usually indicating the entry point *addresses* of various program segments. To find a certain *routine*, the *software* reads a value of so many *bytes* into the vector and transfers control to the address it has read. Also called a jump vector or a vector table.

vectored interrupt   An *interrupt* that includes in its signal a value that points to a *vector* entry. Assume an interrupt has occurred and the value 6 has been provided. The *software* that intercepts the interrupt adds 6 to the *base address* of the vector to calculate the appropriate entry in the vector. That entry is then read, and it contains the address of the *routine* that is to take control when the interrupt occurs.

vendor management A technique for evaluating and managing the effectiveness of a vendor in data processing. The performance of the vendor in terms of repair service, delivery of new equipment, accuracy of billing, reliability of *hardware*, etc., is measured and periodically reviewed with vendor representatives, who take corrective action as necessary to keep their customer happy.

verb An *instruction* causing action in a *programming language*, e.g., PRINT, READ, ASSIGN.

verify To check the accuracy of data, especially as keyed on a data preparation or data input device, such as a *keypunch*.

vertical pitch The number of lines per inch measured vertically on a printed page.

vertical redundency check See *parity*.

vertical tab A *control character* that causes a printer to skip from the current line to another preset line farther down the page, leaving the intervening lines blank.

very large-scale integration See *large-scale integration*.

video display terminal A machine used to conduct interactive dialogs between a human and a computer. Information sent by the computer is displayed on a screen similar to that of a television set. Information sent by the human is keyed on a typewriterlike keyboard. More often called a *CRT*, sometimes also tube, monitor, or display device.

video monitor The viewing screen of a video display terminal.

virtual Giving an appearance of being without actually being; an important concept in medium- to large-scale data-processing systems, in which virtual techniques "trick" the computer system or a program into "believing" that there are more resources available than there actually are. For further discussion, see *virtual machine, virtual storage*.

virtual machine A portion of a computer system, or a portion of that computer's time, that belongs to an *operating system* and functions as an entirely complete system even though it is not. Under the virtual machine concept, two or more wholly independent operating systems share a computer concurrently in much the same way that several programs execute concurrently under the concept of *multiprogramming*. For a time, one operating system has control, and it is then *swapped out* and another is given control. A *software* system called a virtual machine monitor referees this process, enabling two or more independent and fully functional operating systems to occupy the same *hardware* system without "knowing" of each other's existence. This is a useful means of migrating from one kind of operating system to another, since programs can be converted at a leisurely pace rather than all at once because of an arbitrarily imposed *cutover* date.

virtual storage A method for assigning a program a larger *address space* than is actually available. In virtual storage the *memory* of the machine is divided into units called *pages*, and the program *code* and its data work areas are broken into pages of the same size. Only the program pages that are actually in use need be in memory at any given time; the rest can be held on a fast *direct-access storage device* from which they are fetched as needed, and to which they are written as processing fills them with results. The *operating system* monitors the use of pages and makes sure that pages are brought into memory as required and written out as completed. Thus, even if a program needs a total of several million *bytes* of memory, only a few thousand bytes are required at any time.

When *paging* occurs in a virtual storage system, an available page frame might be anywhere in memory and not necessarily within the addressing range of the program (where it "thinks" the page is). The operating system thus performs a function called *dynamic address translation*, in which the actual address of an item is automatically calculated based on where the program thinks it is relative to the location of the page containing it. Pages of a program and its data can therefore be scattered all over the memory and disk storage, yet the program functions as though it owned a large monolithic area of memory.

In this way, and in concert with *multiprogramming* techniques, several dozen programs, each using 16 *megabytes* of memory, can all be in concurrent execution on a single computer that has only 4 megabytes of real memory.

VLSI   Very Large-Scale Integration. See *large-scale integration*.

voice-grade circuit   A telephone line designed to carry voice frequency signals in the range of 300 to 3000 *Hz*. Data signals may also be transmitted on such a line so long as they fall within this range. This is a normal phone line.

voiceprinting   Computerized analysis of human speech to detect certain characteristics unique to an individual's voice, so that the owner of the voice can later be identified by those characteristics in a manner similar to fingerprint identification.

voice recognition   Input of data or commands to a computer system by speech. In order to accomplish this, the computer must first be "taught" to recognize the speaker's voice by means of *voiceprinting*, and then it must be taught the patterns of words and their corresponding meanings with the cooperation of the speaker. Because of its tedium, complexities, and almost insuperable difficulties, voice recognition is a largely experimental notion that promises to have a long infancy.

voice response unit   See *audio response unit*.

voice synthesizer   A computer output device that simulates a human voice speaking. The voice synthesizer converts *bytes* of data into sounds, stringing these sounds together to form words. This is different than an *audio response unit*, in which prerecorded words are selected by bytes whose values indicate which words are to be "played" over the line, and in what order. The voice synthesizer creates spoken words by combining syllable and letter sounds.

volatile memory   *Memory* that loses its contents when power is removed.

VOLSER   (Pronounced "vol seer," with the emphasis on the last syllable) Volume/Serial. A complete unit of storage space, such as a reel of *tape* or a *disk drive*, that is identified to the computer system by a *volume/serial number*.

voltage spike   A sudden surge of electricity on a power line, usually of extremely short duration. Voltage spikes are often associated with lightning.

volume   A data storage device or *medium* treated as a complete unit, such as a reel of *magnetic tape* or a *disk pack*.

volume table of contents   See *VTOC*.

volume/serial number   See *VOLSER*.

VRC   Vertical Redundancy Check. See *parity*.

VT   Vertical Tab.

VTOC   (Pronounced "vee tock") Volume Table Of Contents. Same idea as the table of contents in a book. On a *disk pack*, a list of all the *files* it contains and where to find them on the device (track *addresses*). Also called a *directory*.

W

wafer A large, flat crystal of semiconductor material on which many *chips* are manufactured. After the circuitry has been applied, the wafer is sawed into pieces to make individual chips.

wait state A "hold" state (suspended animation) in which a computer system halts operation and awaits a signal to continue. When the signal is received, operation resumes at the point where it stopped. Wait states usually occur when the system has detected a failure that it cannot diagnose, so it stops for human intervention.

walkthrough An administrative process for reviewing the design and operation of a new program or *job*.

warm boot To reload or *reinitialize systems software* in such a way that programs currently in execution are unaffected.

warm start Same as *warm boot*.

warning A message issued by a program when it has encountered an error condition and continues to run (i.e., the error was not *fatal*).

water-chilled An electronic device cooled by a liquid that runs through small pipes gathering and carrying off heat.

WATS (Pronounced as a word) Wide Area Telecommunications Service. A quantity pricing arrangement for long-distance service; a company buys a WATS line for a monthly fee entitling it to place or receive an unlimited number of calls within a certain time period and geographic area. 800 numbers ("toll-free") are WATS lines.

wideband Same as *broadband*.

wild card A symbolic character taken to mean "any character" in a *search argument*. Suppose that the character "?" is a wild card, and that the argument used to search a list of names is SM?TH?. Names satisfying this argument might be SMITH, SMYTH, SMYTHE, SMETH, and SMITHE, since any character (including none) will satisfy the wild card.

Winchester disk A type of *disk drive* in which the *pack* (the rotating data storage *medium*) is contained within an airtight housing called an *HDA* that keeps out dust and contaminants. This dramatically increases the reliability and recording *density* of the disk.

window A period of time set aside for an expected event, such as a response to a signal. To "open the window" is to begin the waiting period (e.g., set a timer); to "close the window" is to end the waiting period.

window editor An interactive *editing* program that treats the viewing area of a *video display* as though it were a window with a view of the computer's *memory*. This conceptualized window may be "moved around" by commands to look at different areas of memory, while other commands effect changes in what is seen.

wiring harness A group of wires that are gathered and held together by straps.

word A fixed-length package of information handled as a unit within a computer system. A word is usually a multiple of some integral number of *bytes*, but its length is typically expressed in *bits*: an 8-bit word (one byte), a 32-bit word (four bytes), etc. The word length of a given computer is determined by the capacity of the *CPU registers*. All data move between the CPU and memory in units of words, and all manipulations in registers are done on words.

word boundary   A *memory address* that is evenly divisible by the *word length* of the computer. If the word length is 32 *bits* (four *bytes*) and the address is 14, it is not a word boundary, since 14 is not evenly divisible by 4; 16 is a word boundary. This is significant in that some computers will only move data from the *CPU* to a word boundary in memory, or back.

word length   The number of *bits* in a computer *word*.

word processing   The programmatic manipulation of text, in which English (and other language's) words are treated as units of data. Word processing is used to create, format, edit, and print documents such as memos, letters, and this book.

working set   In *virtual storage*, the pages of program *code* and data that must actually be in *memory* at a given instant for the program to work efficiently (i.e., to avoid excessive *paging*).

wrap mode   A method of display management on a *video* screen. The portion of a line exceeding the width of the screen "wraps around" to the start of the next line so that it can be seen.

write-protect   A method either in *hardware* or in *software* to protect certain storage *media* from being written on by a program. On 8" *floppy disks* this is done by uncovering a notch on one edge of the diskette; when the notch is uncovered, the disk drive will not honor a write request, thus protecting the diskette contents from being overlaid by other data. (On 5" disks the opposite is true.) Various software techniques are used to write-protect individual *files*.

writer   The output control portion of a *job entry system* that sends reports to the printer and controls the *spool*.

WTO   (Letters are pronounced separately) Write To Operator. A message issued by a program and displayed on the system *console* for information or status reporting purposes. A WTO is merely an advisory message.

WTOR   (Letters are pronounced separately) Write To Operator with Reply. A message issued by a program and routed to the system *console* for action by the operator. A WTOR might request a *tape mount*, or it might seek permission to read secured information from a *file*. Execution of the program is suspended until the operator replies to the message.

X

X.25 interface A specification establishing standards for connection of communicating devices to an *HDLC packet switching* network.

XOFF (Pronounced "x-off") Transmitter Off. A "shut up" signal sent by a receiving machine to a transmitter, telling it to stop sending if it is sending, or not to send if it is preparing to do so.

XON (Pronounced "x-on") Transmitter On. A "ready to receive" signal sent by a receiving machine to a transmitter, telling it to go ahead if it has anything to send.

XOR Exclusive OR. A *logic* operation in which two *bits* or electrical pulses are combined, producing one resulting bit according to the following rules:

$$0 \text{ XOR } 0 \longrightarrow 0$$
$$0 \text{ XOR } 1 \longrightarrow 1$$
$$1 \text{ XOR } 0 \longrightarrow 1$$
$$1 \text{ XOR } 1 \longrightarrow 0$$

This is similar to logical OR, except that OR returns a TRUE (1) value if both bits are 1.

XREF Abbreviation for cross reference.

XY address The intersection of *XY coordinates*.

XY coordinates The specification of a location (*address*) by the use of graphing. A plane is delineated into horizontal

312

units of measurement (the X axis) and vertical units (the Y axis). The location of any point can then be expressed by identifying its X and Y coordinates. In data processing, XY coordinates are often used as *cursor addresses* on a display screen (corresponding to column and row numbers), as *subscripts* of an *array* element, and for other such indexing.

Z

z-axis The "front-to-rear" axis in three dimensions (horizontal and vertical being X and Y, respectively).

Z80 A *microprocessor chip* manufactured by Zilog, Inc. The Z80 is an *8-bit CPU* frequently used in microcomputers.

zap (1) As a verb, to modify *machine language instructions* in a program while the program is in *memory* and either executing or preparing to execute.

(2) To apply a change to the executable copy of a program without re*compiling* the program.

(3) As a noun, a change applied as above.

zero fill To *pad* the unused portion of a numeric *field* with zeros. If a field is five digits long and is currently occupied by the number 78, after zero fill it reads ØØØ78.

zero flag A *bit* in the *CPU status byte* that is set to 1 to indicate that the *register* currently contains all zeros or that two compared values are equal, and reset to zero to show the opposite.

ZULU time Greenwich Meridian Time. The international point of reference for the time of day.

Numerics

8-bit   A *microprocessor* whose *word length* is one *byte*.

16-bit   A *microprocessor* whose *word length* is two *bytes*.

103-compatible   Refers to the de facto standard for low-speed *modems*, the Bell System 103 Data Set. Modems made by others that operate on the same principles and frequencies, and which can therefore communicate with the Bell 103, are said to be 103-compatible.

3270   An IBM *video display* terminal that serves as a *generic device type*.

3780   An IBM *remote job entry* terminal that serves as a *generic device type*.

6502   A *microprocessor chip* manufactured by Mostek, Inc. The 6502 is an *8-bit CPU* that supports color graphics. It is most widely used as the CPU in 8-bit machines produced by Apple Computer, Inc., and Commodore Business Machines, Inc.

80-80 listing   A standard printout format of 80 columns by 80 lines.

8080   A *microprocessor chip* manufactured by Intel, Inc. The 8080 is an *8-bit CPU* widely used in microcomputers.

8085   A *microprocessor chip* manufactured by Intel, Inc. The 8085 is a *16-bit CPU* developed especially for microcomputers.

68000   A *microprocessor chip* manufactured by Motorola, Inc. The 68000 is a *16-bit CPU* developed especially for microcomputers. It is sometimes referred to in speech as the "68K." Also called the M68000.

Technology Today and Tomorrow from MENTOR and SIGNET

MENTOR and SIGNET Books of Special Interest

MENTOR and SIGNET Books of Related Interest